# HORACE WALPOLE
## *A MEMOIR*

*Horace Walpole in his Library
at Strawberry Hill*

# HORACE WALPOLE

*A MEMOIR*

WITH AN APPENDIX OF
BOOKS PRINTED AT THE
STRAWBERRY HILL
PRESS

By *AUSTIN DOBSON*

FOURTH EDITION REVISED
AND ENLARGED
BY

PAGET TOYNBEE

BOOKS FOR LIBRARIES PRESS
FREEPORT, NEW YORK

First Published 1927
Reprinted 1971

INTERNATIONAL STANDARD BOOK NUMBER:
0-8369-5883-7


LIBRARY OF CONGRESS CATALOG CARD NUMBER:
77-164599


PRINTED IN THE UNITED STATES OF AMERICA

# EDITOR'S PREFACE TO THE FOURTH EDITION

THIS *Memoir* was originally published in 'a limited and costly edition' at New York in 1890. A second, revised, edition appeared in England in 1893. This was followed in 1910 by a third, further revised, with the quotations corrected in the light of Mrs. Paget Toynbee's edition of the *Letters of Horace Walpole*, which had been published in 1903–5. Since the issue of the third edition a large amount of new material has been brought to light, none of which was available to Austin Dobson. The originals of the letters of Madame du Deffand to Horace Walpole, more than 800 in number, selections from which had been published by Miss Berry in 1810, and which had since been lost sight of, were discovered and edited by Mrs. Paget Toynbee, and were published in 1912. A year or two later the present Editor had placed at his disposal an extensive collection of unpublished Walpole MSS. belonging to the late Sir Francis Waller, Bart., of Woodcote, Warwick. The Editor's work upon these and other material has resulted in the publication in the course of the last ten years of a series of volumes,[1] which have been utilized in the preparation of the present edition of the *Memoir*.

It remains to indicate the lines on which the revision has been carried out. Corrections in the body of the work have been made for the most part *sub silentio*, with as little disturbance as practicable of the original text. Additions by the Editor, both in text and notes, are distinguished by being enclosed in square brackets. The Author's Prefaces have been retained as explanatory of the extent of his revision in the successive editions. A new and fuller Index has been provided.

It is hoped that now it has been brought up to date the *Memoir*, which has come to be regarded as a classic in its own sphere, may acquire a new lease of life, and, in spite of the intrusion of an alien hand, may appeal with undiminished charm to an ever-widening circle of readers.

PAGET TOYNBEE.

FIVEWAYS, BURNHAM, BUCKS,
2 *July* 1926.

---

[1] A detailed list of these will be found on pp. ix–x.

# AUTHOR'S PREFATORY NOTE
## TO THE SECOND EDITION

THE following *Memoir* of Horace Walpole was written for, and at the suggestion of, Messrs. Dodd, Mead, and Company of New York. A limited and costly edition, printed at the De Vinne Press, was issued by them in 1890, and a small number of copies were published in this country. By the English critics into whose hands the book fell, it was kindly treated; and a wish was expressed that it should be re-issued in some simpler and less expensive form.

In the present reprint, it has been thought undesirable, considering the favour accorded to the first edition, to interfere seriously with the original text, and the most substantial additions have therefore been made in the form of further foot-notes. Both narrative and bibliography have, however, been minutely revised, and several minor rectifications have been inserted. Had it not been for the exigencies of printing in America, a portion of the notes now added would probably have been included in the earlier issue; the remainder are mainly the result of fresh contributions, made in the interval, to the ever-growing store of ' Walpoliana '.

AUSTIN DOBSON.

EALING, *April* 1893.

# AUTHOR'S PREFACE TO THE THIRD EDITION

SINCE the issue, in 1893, of the second edition of this *Memoir*, little has been written concerning Horace Walpole. To the biographical presentment of the subject there is consequently not much to add. But, during the interval, Walpole's correspondence has been newly edited by Mrs. Paget Toynbee, who, besides materially increasing the number of letters, must be fairly held to have surpassed all her predecessors by the extent and accuracy of her labours. In these circumstances, I have felt it my duty to bring my quotations into conformity with her text. Beyond this, coupled with some further examination of facts and dates, I have confined myself to re-casting a few notes, and correcting certain minute mistakes, for the discovery of which, in two instances, I was indebted to Mrs. Paget Toynbee's courtesy.

AUSTIN DOBSON.

EALING, *September* 1910.

## List of Editions of Works of Horace Walpole, or of Works relating to him, published since 1910 (date of the third Edition of the 'Memoir ').

*Lettres de la Marquise du Deffand à Horace Walpole* (1766–80). Première Édition Complète, Augmentée d'environ 500 Lettres Inédites, Publiées d'après les Originaux, avec une Introduction, des Notes, et une Table des Noms, par Mrs. Paget Toynbee.

*The Correspondence of Gray, Walpole, West, and Ashton* (1734–71), including more than one hundred Letters now first published, chronologically arranged and edited, with Introduction, Notes, and Index, by Paget Toynbee.

*Supplement to the Letters of Horace Walpole*, chronologically arranged and edited, with Notes and Indices, by Paget Toynbee.

*Journal of the Printing-Office at Strawberry Hill.* Now first printed from the MS. of Horace Walpole, with Notes and Index, by Paget Toynbee.

*Reminiscences written by Mr. Horace Walpole in 1788* : for the amusement of Miss Mary and Miss Agnes Berry ; with *Notes of Conversations with Lady Suffolk.* Now first printed in full from the original MSS., with Notes and Index, by Paget Toynbee.

*Satirical Poems published anonymously by William Mason, with Notes by Horace Walpole.* Now first printed from his MS. Edited, with an Exposé of the Mystification, Notes, and Index, by Paget Toynbee.

*Strawberry Hill Accounts.* Now first printed from the MS. of Horace Walpole. Edited, with Notes and Index, by Paget Toynbee.

It is a pleasure to record here a remarkable tribute to Horace Walpole on the part of a French writer, Dr. Paul Yvon, whose exhaustive work, *La Vie d'un Dilettante : Horace Walpole. Essai de Biographie psychologique et littéraire* deals with every aspect of Walpole's many-sided existence. The work is of great interest, and is pleasantly written, but its value as an authority is somewhat impaired by sundry small inaccuracies, which it is to be hoped will disappear in a future edition.

# CONTENTS

*Contents* xiii

## CHAPTER VII

## CHAPTER VIII

## CHAPTER IX

## CHAPTER X

# LIST OF ILLUSTRATIONS

# CHAPTER I

*The Walpoles of Houghton ; Horace Walpole born, 24 September 1717 (O.S.) ; Lady Louisa Stuart's story ; scattered facts of his boyhood ; minor anecdotes,—'la belle Jennings' the bugles ; interview with George I before his death; portrait at this time ; goes to Eton, 26 April 1727 ; his studies and schoolfellows ; the 'triumvirate', the 'quadruple alliance' ; entered at Lincoln's Inn, 27 May 1731 ; leaves Eton, 23 Sept. 1734 ; goes to King's College, Cambridge, 11 March 1735 ; his university studies ; letters from Cambridge ; verses in the* GRATULATIO ; *verses in memory of Henry VI ; death of Lady Walpole, 20 August 1737.*

# I

THE Walpoles of Houghton in Norfolk, ten
miles from King's Lynn, were an ancient
family tracing their pedigree to a certain Reginald
de Walpole who was living in the time of William
the Conqueror. Under Henry II, there was a
Sir Henry de Walpol of Houton and Walpol; and
thenceforward an orderly procession of Henrys
and Edwards and Johns (all 'of Houghton')
carried on the family name to the coronation of
Charles II, when, in return for his vote and
interest as a member of the Convention Parliament, one Edward Walpole was made a Knight
of the Bath. This Sir Edward was in due time
succeeded by his son, Robert, who married well,
sat for Castle Rising,[1] one of the two family
boroughs (the other being King's Lynn, for which
his father had been member), and reputably filled
the combined offices of county magnate and colonel
of militia. But his chief claim to distinction is
that his eldest son, also a Robert, afterwards became the famous statesman and Prime Minister

[1] Another member for Castle Rising was Samuel Pepys,
the Diarist.

to whose 'admirable prudence, fidelity, and success' England owes her prosperity under the first Hanoverians. It is not, however, with the life of 'that corrupter of parliaments, that dissolute tipsy cynic, that courageous lover of peace and liberty, that great citizen, patriot, and statesman '—to borrow a passage from one of Mr. Thackeray's graphic vignettes—that these pages are concerned. It is more material to their purpose to note that in the year 1700, and on the 30th day of July in that year (being the day of the death of the Duke of Gloucester, heir presumptive to the crown of England), Robert Walpole junior, then a young man of three-and-twenty, and late scholar of King's College, Cambridge, took to himself a wife. The lady chosen was Miss Catherine Shorter, eldest daughter of John Shorter, of Bybrook, an old Elizabethan red-brick house near Ashford in Kent. Her grandfather, Sir John Shorter, had been Lord Mayor of London under James II, and her father was a Norway timber merchant, having his wharf and counting-house on the Southwark side of the Thames, and his town residence in Norfolk Street, Strand, where, in all probability, his daughter met her future husband. They had a family of four sons and two daughters. One of the sons, William, died young. The fourth son, Horatio [1] or Horace, born, as he himself tells us, on the 24th September 1717, O.S., is the subject of this memoir.

With the birth of Horace Walpole is connected a scandal so industriously repeated by his later biographers, that (although it has received far more attention than it deserves) it can scarcely be left unnoticed here. He had, it is asserted, little in common, either in tastes or appearance, with his elder brothers Robert and Edward, and he was born eleven years after the rest of his father's children. This led to a suggestion which first found definite expression in the *Introductory Anecdotes* supplied by Lady Louisa Stuart to Lord Wharncliffe's edition of the works of her grandmother, Lady Mary Wortley Montagu.[2] It was to the effect that Horace was not the son of

---

[1] ' The name of *Horatio* I dislike. It is theatrical ; and not English. I have, ever since I was a youth, written and subscribed *Horace*, an English name for an Englishman. In all my books (and perhaps you will think of the *numerosus Horatius*) I so spell my name ' (Pinkerton's *Walpoliana*, 2nd ed., i. 63).

[2] It is also to be found asserted as a current story in the *Note Books* (unpublished) of the Duchess of Portland, the daughter of Edward Harley, 2nd Earl of Oxford, and the ' noble, lovely, little Peggy ' of her father's friend and *protégé*, Matthew Prior.

Sir Robert Walpole, but of one of his mother's admirers, Carr, Lord Hervey, elder brother of Pope's 'Sporus', the Hervey of the *Memoirs*. It is advanced in favour of this supposition that his likeness to the Herveys, both physically and mentally, was remarkable; that the whilom Catherine Shorter was flighty, indiscreet, and fond of admiration; and that Sir Robert's cynical disregard of his wife's vagaries, as well as his own gallantries (his second wife, Miss Skerret, had been his mistress), were matters of notoriety. On the other hand, there is no indication that any suspicion of his parentage ever crossed the mind of Horace Walpole himself. His devotion to his mother was one of the most consistent traits in a character made up of many contradictions; and although between the frail and fastidious virtuoso and the boisterous, fox-hunting Prime Minister there could have been but little sympathy, the son seems nevertheless to have sedulously maintained a filial reverence for his father, of whose enemies and detractors he remained, until his dying day, the implacable foe. Moreover, it must be remembered that, admirable as are Lady Louisa Stuart's recollections, in speaking of Horace Walpole she is speaking of one whose caustic pen and satiric tongue had never spared the reputation of the vivacious lady whose granddaughter she was.

With this reference to what can be, at best, but an insoluble question, we may return to the story of Walpole's earlier years. Of his childhood little is known beyond what he has himself told in the *Short Notes of my Life* which he drew up for the use of Mr. Berry, the nominal editor of his works.[1] His godfathers, he says, were the Duke of Grafton and his father's second brother, Horatio, who afterwards became Baron Walpole of Wolterton. His godmother was his aunt, the beautiful Dorothy Walpole, who, escaping the snares of Lord Wharton, as related by Lady Louisa Stuart, had become the second wife of Charles, second Viscount Townshend. In 1724, he was ' inoculated for the small-pox '; and in the following year was placed with his cousins, Lord Townshend's younger sons, at Bexley in Kent,[2] under the charge of one Weston, son to the Bishop of

[1] These, hereafter referred to as the *Short Notes*, are the chief authority for three parts of Walpole's not very eventful life. They were first published with the concluding series of his *Letters to Sir Horace Mann*, 2 vols., 1844.

[2] [His first two letters (to Lady Walpole) were written from here in 1725 ; they are printed in the *Supplement* (vol. i, pp. 1-2) to Mrs. Paget Toynbee's edition of the *Letters of Horace Walpole*.]

Exeter of that name. In 1726, the same course was pursued at Twickenham, and in the winter months he went to Lord Townshend's. Much of his boyhood, however, must have been spent in the house 'next the College' at Chelsea, of which his father became possessed in 1722. It still exists in part, with but little alteration, as the infirmary of the hospital, and Ward No. 7 is said to have been its dining-room.[1] With this, or with some other reception-chamber at Chelsea, is connected one of the scanty anecdotes of this time. Once, when Walpole was a boy, there came to see his mother one of those formerly famous beauties chronicled by Anthony Hamilton—'la belle Jennings', elder sister to the celebrated Duchess of Marlborough, and afterwards Duchess of Tyrconnell. At this date she was a needy Jacobite seeking Lady Walpole's interest in order to obtain a pension. She no longer possessed those radiant charms which under Charles had revealed her even through the disguise of an orange-girl; and now, says Walpole, annotating his own copy of the *Memoirs of Grammont*, 'her eyes being dim, and she full of flattery, she commended the beauty of the prospect; but unluckily the room

[1] Martin's *Old Chelsea*, 1889, p. 82 ; Beaver's *Memorials of Old Chelsea*, 1892, p. 291.

in which they sat looked only against the garden-wall '.[1]

Another of the few events of his boyhood which he records, illustrates the old proverb that ' One half of the world knows not how the other half lives ' rather than any particular phase of his biography. Going with his mother to buy some bugles (beads), at the time when the opposition to his father was at its highest, he notes that having made her purchase,—beads were then out of fashion, and the shop was in some obscure alley in the City where lingered unfashionable things, —Lady Walpole bade the shopman send it home. Being asked whither, she replied ' To Sir Robert Walpole's '. ' And who '—rejoined he coolly— ' is Sir Robert Walpole ? ' [2] But the most interesting incident of his youth was the visit he paid to the King which he has himself related in Chapter I of the *Reminiscences*. How it came about

[1] Cunningham, v. 36, and ix. 519. The Duchess of Tyrconnell's portrait, copied by Milbourn from the original at Lord Spencer's, was one of the prominent ornaments of the Great Bedchamber at Strawberry Hill. (See *Works of Lord Orford*, ii. 495-6.) There are some previously unpublished particulars respecting her as ' Mlle. Genins ' in M. Jusserand's extremely interesting *French Ambassador at the Court of Charles the Second*, 1892, pp. 153 *et seq.*, 170, 182.

[2] *Walpole to the Miss Berrys*, 5 Mar. 1791.

he does not know, but at ten years old an over-mastering desire seized him to inspect His Majesty. This childish caprice was so strong that his mother, who seldom thwarted him, solicited the Duchess of Kendal (the *maîtresse en titre*) to obtain for her son the honour of kissing King George's hand before he set out upon that visit to Hanover from which he was never to return. It was an unusual request, but being made by the Prime Minister's wife could scarcely be refused. To conciliate etiquette and avoid precedent, however, it was arranged that the audience should be in private and at night. 'Accordingly, the night but one before the King began his last journey [i.e., on 1 June 1727], my mother carried me at ten at night to the apartment of the Countess of Walsingham [Melusina von der Schulenberg, the Duchess's reputed niece], on the ground-floor towards the garden at St. James's, which opened into that of her aunt . . . apartments occupied by George II after his Queen's death, and by his successive mistresses, the Countesses of Suffolk [Mrs. Howard] and Yarmouth [Amelia von Walmoden]. Notice being given that the King was come down to supper, Lady Walsingham took me alone into the Duchess's anti-room, where we found alone the King and her. I knelt down, and kissed his

hand, he said a few words to me, and my con-
ductress led me back to my mother. The person
of the King is as perfect in my memory as if I saw
him but yesterday. It was that of an elderly man,
rather pale, and exactly like his pictures and coins ;
not tall, of an aspect rather good than august,
with a dark tye wig, a plain coat, waistcoat and
breeches of snuff-coloured cloth, with stockings
of the same colour, and a blue ribband over all.
So entirely was he my object, that I do not believe
I once looked at the Duchess ; but as I could not
avoid seeing her on entering the room, I remember
that just beyond His Majesty stood a very tall,
lean, ill-favoured old lady ; but I did not retain
the least idea of her features, nor know what the
colour of her dress was.' [1]    In the *Walpoliana*
(i. 25) [2] Walpole is made to say that his introducer
was his father, and that the King took him up in
his arms and kissed him. Walpole's own written

[1] [*Reminiscences written in* 1788 (ed. Toynbee, Oxford,
1924), pp. 11-12.]

[2] The book referred to is a ' little lounging miscellany '
of notes and anecdotes by John Pinkerton, and was printed
soon after Walpole's death, by Bensley, who lived in Johnson's old house, No. 8, Bolt Court. It requires to be used
with caution (see *Quarterly Review*, vol. lxxii, No. cxliv) ;
and must not be confused with Lord Hardwicke's privately
printed *Walpoliana*, which relate to Sir Robert Walpole.

account is the more probable one. His audience must have been one of the last the King granted, for, as already stated, it was almost on the eve of his departure; and ten days later, when his chariot clattered swiftly into the courtyard of his brother's palace at Osnabrück, he lay dead in his seat, and the reign of his successor had begun.

Although Walpole gives us a description of George I, he does not, of course, supply us with any portrait of himself. But in Mr. Peter Cunningham's edition of the *Correspondence*, there is a copy of an oil-painting by Hogarth belonging (1857) to Mrs. Bedford of Kensington, which, upon the faith of a Cupid who points with an arrow to the number ten upon a dial, may be accepted as representing him about the time of the above interview. It is a full length of a slight, effeminate-looking lad in a stiff-skirted coat, knee breeches, and open-breasted laced waistcoat, standing in a somewhat affected attitude at the side of the afore-mentioned sun-dial. He has dark, intelligent eyes, and a profusion of light hair curling abundantly about his ears and reaching to his neck. If the date given in the *Short Notes* be correct, he must have already become an Eton boy, since he says that he went to that school on the 26th April

1727, and he adds in the *Reminiscences* that he shed a flood of tears for the King's death when, ' with the other scholars at Eton College ', he walked in procession to the proclamation of his successor. Of the cause of this emotion he seems rather doubtful, leaving us to attribute it, partly to the King's condescension in gratifying his childish loyalty, partly to the feeling that, as the Prime Minister's son, it was incumbent on him to be more concerned than his school-fellows, while the spectators, it is hinted, placed it to the credit of a third and not less cogent cause—the probability of that Minister's downfall. Of this, however, as he says, he could not have had the slightest conception.[1] His tutor at Eton was Henry Bland, eldest son of the master of the school. ' I remember ',—says Walpole, writing later (29 June 1744) to his relative and school-fellow Conway,—' when I was at Eton, and Mr. Bland had set me an extraordinary task, I used sometimes to pique myself upon not getting it, because it was not immediately my school business. What ! learn more than I was absolutely forced to learn ! I felt the weight of learning that ; for I was a blockhead, and pushed up above my parts.' That, as the son of the great Minister,

[1] [*Reminiscences*, ed. cit., p. 13.]

he was pushed, is probably true ; but, despite his own disclaimer, it is clear that his abilities were by no means to be despised. Indeed, one of the *pièces justificatives* in the story of Lady Louisa Stuart, though advanced for another purpose, is distinctly in favour of something more than average talent. Supporting her theory as to his birth by the statement that in his boyhood he was left so entirely in the hands of his mother as to have little acquaintance with his father, she goes on to say that ' Sir Robert Walpole took scarcely any notice of him, till his proficiency at Eton School, when a lad of some standing, drew his attention, and proved that, whether he had, or had not, a right to the name he went by, he was likely to do it honour '.[1] Whatever this may be held to prove, it certainly proves that he was not the blockhead he declares himself to have been.

Among his schoolmates he made many friends. For his cousins, Henry (afterwards Marshal) Conway and Lord Hertford, Conway's elder brother, he formed an attachment which lasted through life, and many of his best letters were

---

[1] This is quoted by Mr. Hayward and others as if the last words were Sir Robert Walpole's. But Lady Louisa Stuart says nothing to indicate this (Lady Mary Wortley Montagu's *Letters*, etc., 1887, i, xciii).

written to these relatives. Other associates were
the later lyrist, Charles Hanbury Williams, and
the famous wit, George Augustus Selwyn, both
of whom, if the child be father to the man, must
be supposed to have had unusual attractions for
their equally witty schoolmate. Another contemporary at school, to whom, in after life, he
addressed many letters, was William Cole, subsequently to develop into a laborious antiquary,
and probably already exhibiting proclivities towards
' tall copies ' and black letter. But his chiefest
friends, no doubt, were grouped in the two bodies
christened respectively the ' triumvirate ' and the
' quadruple alliance '.

Of these the ' triumvirate ' was the less important. It consisted of Walpole and the two sons
of Brigadier-General Edward Montagu. George,
the elder, afterwards M.P. for Northampton, and
the recipient of some of the most genuine specimens
of his friend's correspondence, is described in
advanced age as ' a gentleman-like body of the
*vieille cour* ', usually attended by a younger brother,
who was still a midshipman at the mature age
of sixty, and whose chief occupation consisted in
carrying about his elder's snuff-box. Charles
Montagu, the remaining member of the ' triumvirate ', became a Lieut.-General and Knight of

the Bath.  But it was George, who had ' a fine sense of humour, and much curious information ', who was Walpole's favourite.  ' Dear George ' —he writes to him from Cambridge (6 May 1736)—' were not the playing fields at Eton food for all manner of flights ?  No old maid's gown, though it had been tormented into all the fashions from King James to King George, ever underwent so many transformations as those poor plains have in my idea.  At first I was contented with tending a visionary flock, and sighing some pastoral name to the echo of the cascade under the bridge. How happy should I have been to have had a kingdom only for the pleasure of being driven from it, and living disguised in an humble vale ! As I got further into Virgil and Clelia, I found myself transported from Arcadia to the garden of Italy ;  and saw Windsor Castle in no other view than the *Capitoli immobile saxum.*'    Farther on he makes an admission which need scarcely surprise us.  ' I can't say I am sorry I was never quite a schoolboy :  an expedition against bargemen, or a match at cricket, may be very pretty things to recollect ;  but, thank my stars, I can remember things that are very near as pretty.  The beginning of my Roman history was spent in the asylum, or conversing in Egeria's hallowed grove ;  not in thumping and pummelling King Amulius's herdsmen.' The description seems to indicate a schoolboy of a rather refined and effeminate type, who would probably fare ill with robuster spirits. But Walpole's social position doubtless preserved him from the persecution which that variety generally experiences at the hands—literally the hands—of the tyrants of the playground.

The same delicacy of organisation seems to have been a main connecting link in the second or 'quadruple alliance' already referred to—an alliance, it may be, less intrinsically intimate, but more obviously cultivated. The most important figure in this quartet was a boy as frail and delicate as Walpole himself, 'with a broad, pale brow, sharp nose and chin, large eyes, and a pert expression', who was afterwards to become famous as the author of one of the most popular poems in the language, the *Elegy written in a Country Church Yard.* Thomas Gray was at this time about thirteen, and consequently somewhat older than his schoolmate. Another member of the association was Richard West, also slightly older, a grandson of the Bishop Burnet who wrote the *History of My Own Time,* and son of the Lord Chancellor of Ireland. West, a slim, thoughtful lad, was the most precocious genius of the party,

c

already making verses in Latin and English, and making them even in his sleep. The fourth member was Thomas Ashton, afterwards Fellow of Eton College and Rector of St. Botolph, Bishopsgate. Such was the group which may be pictured sauntering arm in arm through the Eton meadows, or threading the avenue which is still known as the 'Poet's Walk'. Each of the four had his nickname, either conferred by himself or by his schoolmates. Ashton, for example, was Almanzor; Gray was Orosmades; West was Favonius (or Zephyrus); and Walpole himself, Celadon.[1]

On 27 May 1731, Walpole was entered at Lincoln's Inn, his father intending him for the law. 'But'—he says in the *Short Notes*—'I never went thither, not caring for the profession.' On 23 September 1734, he left Eton for good, and no further particulars of his school-days remain.[2] That they were not without their pleasant memories may, however, be inferred from the letters already quoted, and especially from one to George Montagu written some time afterwards

[1] [See *Correspondence of Gray, Walpole, West, and Ashton* ed. Toynbee, Oxford, 1915), vol. i, pp. xvii–xx.]

[2] [Two letters written to Lady Walpole from Eton in Sept. 1733 are printed in *Supplement* (vol. i, pp. 3–4) to *Letters of Horace Walpole* (ed. Toynbee).]

upon the occasion of a visit to the once familiar scenes. It is dated from the Christopher Inn, a famous old hostelry, well known to Eton boys : —' The Christopher—Lord ! how great I used to think anybody just landed at the Christopher ! But here are no boys for me to send for ! Here I am, like Noah, just returned into his old world again, with all sorts of queer feels about me.—By the way, the clock strikes the old cracked sound —I recollect so much, and remember so little, and want to play about, and am so afraid of my playfellows, and am ready to *shirk* Ashton, and can't help *making fun* of myself, and envy a *dame* over the way, that has just locked in her boarders, and is going to sit down in a little hot parlour to a very bad supper, so comfortably ! and I could be so *jolly* a dog if I did not *fat*, which, by the way, is the first time the word was ever applicable to me. In short, I should be *out* of all *bounds* if I was to tell you half I feel, how young again I am one minute, and how old the next.—But do come and feel with me, when you will, to-morrow . . adieu ! If I don't compose myself a little more before Sunday morning, when Ashton is to preach,[1] I shall certainly *be in a bill for laughing at church ;*

---

[1] [He had been ordained in 1740, and elected a Fellow of Eton in 1745.]

but how to help it, to see him in the pulpit, when the last time I saw him here, was standing up *funking* over against a conduct [1] to be catechised.' [2]

In March 1735, after an interval of residence in London, Walpole took up his residence at Cambridge in his father's college of King's. By this time the ' quadruple alliance ' had been broken up by the defection of West, who, much against his will, had gone to Christ Church, Oxford. Ashton and Gray had, however, been a year at Cambridge, the latter as a pensioner (i. e. commoner) of Peterhouse, the former at Walpole's own college, King's. Cole and the Conways were also at Cambridge, so that much of the old intercourse must have been continued. Walpole's record of his university studies is of the most scanty kind. He does little more than give us the names of his tutors, public and private. In civil law he attended the lectures of Dr. Dickens of Trinity Hall ; in anatomy, those of Dr. Battie. French, he says, he had learnt at Eton. His Italian master at Cambridge was Signor Piazza (who had at least

[1] Eton term for chaplain.

[2] [This letter, of which the date is not given, but which Cunningham places after Mar. 1737, was almost certainly written in Aug. 1746 (see Mrs. Toynbee's note in *Notes and Queries*, Sept. 23, 1899 ; and Tovey, *Gray and his Friends*, p. 3, n.).]

an Italian name !), and his instructor in drawing was the miniaturist Bernard Lens,[1] the teacher of the Duke of Cumberland and the Princesses Mary and Louisa. Lens was the author of a *New and Complete Drawing Book for curious young Gentlemen and Ladies that study and practice the noble and commendable Art of Drawing, Colouring,* etc., and is kindly referred to in the later *Anecdotes of Painting.* In mathematics, which Walpole seems to have hated as cordially as Swift and Goldsmith and Gray did, he sat at the feet of the blind Professor Nicholas Saunderson, author of the *Elements of Algebra.*[2] Years afterwards (*à propos* of a misguided enthusiast who had put the forty-seventh proposition of Euclid into Latin verse) he tells one of his correspondents the result of these ministrations : ' I . . . was always so

[1] [A reproduction of a drawing of Horace Walpole by Lens (who died in 1740), the original of which is at Chewton Priory, forms the frontispiece to vol. i. of Mrs. Toynbee's edition of the *Letters.*]

[2] Saunderson had lost both his eyes in infancy from smallpox. This, however, did not prevent him from lecturing on Newton's *Optics,* and becoming Lucasian Professor of Mathematics at Cambridge. Another undergraduate who attended his lectures was Chesterfield. (See Letter to Jouneau, 12 Oct. 1712.) There is an interesting account of Saunderson by a former pupil, together with an excellent portrait, in the *Gentleman's Magazine* for Sept. 1754.

incapable of learning mathematics, that I could not even get by heart the multiplication table, as blind Professor Saunderson honestly told me, above threescore years ago, when I went to his lectures at Cambridge.    After the first fortnight he said to me, " Young man, it would be cheating you to take your money ;  for you can never learn what I am trying to teach you."  I was exceedingly mortified, and cried ;  for, being a Prime Minister's son, I had firmly believed all the flattery with which I had been assured that my parts were capable of anything.    I paid a private instructor for a year ;  but, at the year's end, was forced to own Saunderson had been in the right.' [1]   This private instructor was in all probability Mr. Trevigar, who, Walpole says, read lectures to him in mathematics and philosophy.   From other expressions in his letters, it must be inferred that his progress in the dead languages, if respectable, was not brilliant.   He confesses, on one occasion, his inability to help Cole in a Latin epitaph, and he tells Pinkerton that he never was a good Greek scholar.

His correspondence at this period, chiefly addressed to West and George Montagu, is not extensive.   But it is already characteristic.   In

[1] *Walpole to Miss Berry,* 16 Aug. 1796.

one of his letters to Montagu he encloses a
translation of a little French dialogue between
a turtle-dove and a passer-by. The verses are of
no particular merit, but in the comment one
recognizes a cast of style soon to be familiar.
'You will excuse this gentle nothing, I mean
mine, when I tell you, I translated it out of pure
good-nature for the use of a disconsolate wood-
pigeon in our grove, that was made a widow by
the barbarity of a gun. She coos and calls me so
movingly, 'twould touch your heart to hear her.
I protest to you it grieves me to pity her. She is
so allicholly¹ as any thing. I'll warrant you now
she's as sorry as one of us would be. Well, good
man, he's gone, and he died like a lamb. She's an
unfortunate woman, but she must have patience.'²
In another letter to West, after expressing his
astonishment that Gray should be at Burnham
in Buckinghamshire, and yet be too indolent to
revisit the old Eton haunts in his vicinity, he goes
on to gird at the university curriculum. At Cambridge, he says, they are supposed to betake themselves 'to some trade, as logic, philosophy, or
mathematics'. But he has been used to the

---

¹ 'Indeed, she is given too much to allicholly and
musing' (*Merry Wives of Windsor*, act I, sc. iv).
² *Walpole to Montagu*, 30 May 1736.

delicate food of Parnassus, and can never condescend to the grosser studies of Alma Mater. ' Sober cloth of syllogism colour suits me ill : or, what's worse, I hate clothes that one must prove to be of no colour at all. If the Muses *cœlique vias et sidera monstrent*, and *quâ vi maria alta tumescant ;* why *accipiant :* but 'tis thrashing, to study philosophy in the abstruse authors. I am not against cultivating these studies, as they are certainly useful ; but then they quite neglect all polite literature, all knowledge of this world. Indeed, such people have not much occasion for this latter ; for they shut themselves up from it, and study till they know less than any one. Great mathematicians have been of great use ; but the generality of them are quite unconversible : they frequent the stars, *sub pedibusque vident nubes*, but they can't see through them. I tell you what I see ; that by living amongst them, I write of nothing else : my letters are all parallelograms, two sides equal to two sides ; and every paragraph an axiom, that tells you nothing but what every mortal almost knows.' [1]    In an earlier note he has been on a tour to Oxford, and, with a premonition of the future connoisseur of Strawberry Hill, criticises the gentlemen's seats on the road.    Coming

[1] *Walpole to West*, 17 Aug. 1736.

back, we saw Easton Neston [in Northampton-
shire], a seat of Lord Pomfret's, where in an old
greenhouse is a wonderful fine statue of Tully,
haranguing a numerous assemblage of decayed
emperors, vestal virgins with new noses, Colossus's,
Venus's, headless carcases and carcaseless heads,
pieces of tombs, and hieroglyphics.' [1]  A little
later he has been to his father's seat at Houghton :
' I am return'd again to Cambridge, and can tell
you what I never expected, that I like Norfolk.
Not any of the ingredients, as Hunting or Country
Gentlemen, for I had nothing to do with them,
but the county; which a little from Houghton
is woody, and full of delightful prospects.  I went
to see Norwich and Yarmouth, both which I like
exceedingly.  I spent my time at Houghton for
the first week almost alone ; We have a charming
Garden all Wilderness;  much adapted to my
Romantick inclinations.' [2]  In after life the liking
for Norfolk here indicated does not seem to have
continued, especially when his father's death had
withdrawn a part of its attractions.  He ' hated
Norfolk '—says Mr. Cunningham.  ' He did not
care for Norfolk ale, Norfolk turnips, Norfolk

---

[1]  *Walpole to Montagu,* 20 May 1736.
[2]  [*Walpole to Charles Lyttelton,* 27 July 1736 (in *Letters*
ed. Toynbee, vol. i, pp. 19–20).]

dumplings, or Norfolk turkeys. Its flat, sandy, aguish scenery was not to his taste.' He preferred ' the rich blue prospects ' of his mother's county, Kent.

Of literary effort while at Cambridge Walpole's record is not great. In 1736, he was one of the group of university poets—Gray and West being also of the number—who addressed congratulatory verses to Frederick, Prince of Wales, upon his marriage with the Princess Augusta of Saxe-Gotha; and he wrote a poem [1] to the memory of the founder of King's College, Henry VI. This is dated 2 February 1738. In the interim Lady Walpole died. Her son's references to his loss display the most genuine regret. In a letter to Charles Lyttelton [2] (afterwards the well-known Dean of Exeter, and Bishop of Carlisle), dated 18 September 1737, he dwells with much feeling on ' the surprizing calmness and courage which my dear Mother show'd before her death. I believe few women wou'd behave so well, & I am certain no man cou'd behave better. For three or four days before she dyed, she spoke of it with less indifference than one speaks of a cold ; and while she was sensible, which she was

[1] [Printed in *Works of Lord Orford* (1798), vol. i, pp. 1–3.]
[2] [In *Letters*, ed. Toynbee, vol. i, pp. 24–5.]

within her two last hours, she discovered no manner of apprehension.' That his warm affection for her was well known to his friends may be inferred from a passage in one of Gray's letters to West:—'While I write to you, I hear the bad news of Lady Walpole's death on Saturday night last.[1] Forgive me if the thought of what my poor Horace must feel on that account, obliges me to have done.'[2] Lady Walpole was buried at Houghton. On her monument in Henry VIIth's Chapel in Westminster Abbey, may be read the piously eulogistic inscription which her youngest son composed to her memory—an inscription not easy to reconcile in all its terms with the current estimate of her character. But in August 1737, she was considerably over fifty, and had probably long outlived the scandals of which she had been the subject in the days when Kneller and Eckardt painted her as a young and beautiful woman.

[1] 20 Aug. 1737.

[2] [Dated 22 Aug. 1737 (see *Correspondence of Gray, Walpole, West, and Ashton*, vol. i, p. 154; in which is also printed (pp. 155–6) a touching letter from Gray to Walpole himself on the occasion).]

# CHAPTER II

*Patent places under Government ; starts with Gray on the Grand Tour, March, 1739 ; from Dover to Paris ; life at Paris ; Versailles ; the Convent of the Chartreux ; life at Rheims ; a fête galante ; the Grande Chartreuse ; starts for Italy ; the tragedy of Tory ; Turin, Genoa, academical exercises at Bologna ; life at Florence ; Rome, Naples, Herculaneum ; the pen of Radicofani ; English at Florence ; Lady Mary Wortley Montagu ; preparing for home ; quarrel with Gray ; Walpole's apologia ; his illness, and return to England.*

THAT, in those piping days of patronage when even very young ladies of quality drew pay as cornets of horse, the son of the Prime Minister of England should be left unprovided for, was not to be expected. While he was still resident at Cambridge, lucrative sinecures came to Horace Walpole. Soon after his mother's death, his father appointed him Inspector of Imports and Exports in the Custom House, a post which he resigned in January 1738, on succeeding Colonel William Townshend as Usher of the Exchequer. When, later in the year, he came of age (24 September), he 'took possession of two other little patent-places in the Exchequer, called Comptroller of the Pipe, and Clerk of the Estreats', which had been held for him by a substitute. In 1782, when he still filled them, the two last-mentioned offices produced together about £300 per annum, while the Ushership of the Exchequer, at the date of his obtaining it, was reckoned to be worth £900 a year. 'From that time (he says) I lived on my own income, and travelled at my own expence; nor did I during my father's life receive from him but £250 at different times; which I say not in derogation of his extreme tenderness and goodness to me, but

to show that I was content with what he had given
to me, and that from the age of twenty I was no
charge to my family.' [1]

He continued at King's College for some time
after he had attained his majority, only quitting
it formally at the beginning of 1739, not without
regretful memories of which his future correspondence was to bear the traces. If he had neglected
mathematics, and only moderately courted the
classics, he had learnt something of the polite
arts and of modern continental letters—studies
which would naturally lead his inclination in the
direction of the inevitable ' Grand Tour '. Two
years earlier he had very unwillingly declined an
invitation from George Montagu and Lord Conway to join them in a visit to Italy.[2] Since that
date his desire for foreign travel, fostered no doubt
by long conversations with Gray, had grown
stronger, and he resolved to see ' the palms and
temples of the south ' after the orthodox eighteenth-
century fashion. To think of Gray in this connection was but natural, and he accordingly invited

[1] *Account of my Conduct*, etc., in *Works of Lord Orford*
(1798), ii. 364. [By 1780 he was in receipt of £4,200 a
year, but he puts the average for twelve years at no more
than £1,800 (*op. cit.* p. 368).]
[2] [See his letter to Montagu of 20 Mar. 1737.]

his friend (who had now quitted Cambridge, and was vegetating rather disconsolately in his father's house on Cornhill) to be his travelling companion. Walpole was to act as paymaster; but Gray was to be independent. Furthermore, Walpole made a will under which, if he died abroad, Gray was to be his sole legatee.[1] Dispositions so advantageous and considerate scarcely admitted of refusal, even if Gray had been backward, which he was not. The two friends accordingly set out for Paris. Walpole makes the date of departure 10 March 1739; Gray says they left Dover at twelve on the 29th, N.S.

The first records of the journey come from Amiens in a letter written by Gray to his mother. After a rough passage across the Straits, they reached Calais at five. Next afternoon (Easter Monday) they started for Boulogne in the then new-fangled invention, a post-chaise—a vehicle which Gray describes 'as of much greater use than beauty, resembling an ill-shaped chariot, only with the door opening before instead of [at] the side'. Of Boulogne they see little, and of Montreuil (where later Sterne engaged La Fleur) Gray's only record, besides the indifferent fare,

[1] [See Walpole's first letter to Mason of 2 March 1773 *Letters*, ed. Toynbee, viii. 247). It is not likely that Gray was made aware of this.]

D

is that ' Madame the hostess made her appearance
in long lappets of bone lace, and a sack of linsey-
woolsey '.  From Montreuil they go by Abbeville
to Amiens, where they visit the cathedral, and the
chapels of the Jesuits and Ursuline Nuns.  But
the best part of this first letter is the little picture
with which it (or rather as much of it as Mason
published) concludes.  ' The country we have
passed through hitherto has been flat, open, but
agreeably diversified with villages, fields well-
cultivated, and little rivers.  On every hillock is
a wind-mill, a crucifix, or a Virgin Mary dressed
in flowers, and a sarcenet robe ;  one sees not
many people or carriages on the road ;  now and
then indeed you meet a strolling friar, a country-
man with his great muff, or a woman riding
astride on a little ass, with short petticoats, and a
great head-dress of blue wool.' [1]

The foregoing letter is dated the 1st April,
N.S., and it speaks of reaching Paris on the 3rd.
But it was only on the evening of Saturday the
4th that they rolled into the French capital,
' driving through the streets a long while before
they knew where they were '.[2]  Walpole had
wisely resolved not to hurry, and they had besides

[1] *Gray to Mrs. Gray,* 1 Apr. 1739.
[2] [*Gray to West,* 12 Apr. 1739.]

broken down at Luzarches, and lingered at St. Denis over the curiosities of the abbey, particularly a vase of oriental onyx carved with Bacchus and the nymphs, of which they had dreamed ever since. At Paris, they found a warm welcome among the English residents—notably from Mason's patron, Lord Holdernesse, and Walpole's cousins, the Conways. They seem to have plunged at once into the pleasures of the place, pleasures in which, according to Walpole, cards and eating played far too absorbing a part. At Lord Holdernesse's they met at supper the famous author of *Manon Lescaut*, M. l'Abbé Antoine-François Prévost d'Exiles, who had just put forth the final volume of his tedious and scandalous *Histoire de M. Cleveland, fils naturel de Cromwell.* They went to the spectacle of *Pandore* at the Salle des Machines of the Tuileries ; and they went to the opera, where they saw the successful *Ballet de la Paix*, a curious hotchpot, from Gray's description, of cracked voices and incongruous mythology. With the Comédie Française they were better pleased, although Walpole, strange to say, unlike Goldsmith ten years later, was not able to commend the performance of Molière's *L'Avare.* They saw Mademoiselle Gaussin (as yet unrivalled by the unrisen Mademoiselle Clairon) in La Noue's tragedy of *Mahomet Second*, then recently produced, with Dufresne in the leading male part; and they also saw the prince of *petits-maîtres*, Grandval, acting with Dufresne's sister, Mademoiselle Jeanne-Françoise Quinault (an actress 'somewhat in Mrs. Clive's way', says Gray),[1] in the *Philosophe Marié* of Philippe Néricault Destouches, a charming comedy already transferred to the English stage in the version by John Kelly of *The Universal Spectator*.

Theatres, however, are not the only amusements which the two travellers chronicle to the home-keeping West. A great part of their time is spent in seeing churches and palaces full of pictures. Then there is the inevitable visit to Versailles, which, in sum, they concur in condemning. 'The great front', says Walpole, 'is a lumber of littleness, composed of black brick, stuck full of bad old busts, and fringed with gold rails.' Gray (he says) likes it; but Gray is scarcely more complimentary,—at all events is quite as hard upon the *façade*, using almost the same phrases of depreciation. It is 'a huge heap of littleness', in hue 'black, dirty red, and yellow; the first proceeding from stone changed by age; the second, from a mixture of brick; and the last,

[1] *Gray to West*, 12 Apr. 1739.

from a profusion of tarnished gilding.  You cannot see a more disagreeable *tout ensemble* ; and, to finish the matter, it is all stuck over in many places with small busts of a tawny hue between every two windows.'  The garden, however, pleases him better ; nothing could be vaster and more magnificent than the *coup d'œil* with its fountains and statues and grand canal.  But the ' general taste of the place ' is petty and artificial —' all is forced, all is constrained about you ; statues and vases sowed everywhere without distinction ;  sugar loaves and minced pies of yew ;  scrawl work of box, and little squirting *jets d'eau,* besides a great sameness in the walks, cannot help striking one at first sight, not to mention the silliest of labyrinths, and all Æsop's fables in water '.[1]  ' The garden is littered with statues and fountains, each of which has its tutelary deity.  In particular, the elementary god of fire solaces himself in one.  In another, Enceladus, in lieu of a mountain, is overwhelmed with many waters.  There are avenues of water-pots, who disport themselves much in squirting up *cascadelins.* In short, 'tis a garden for a great child.' [2]  The day following, being Whitsunday, they witness a

[1]  *Gray to West,* 22 May 1739.
[2]  *Walpole to West,* no date, 1739.

grand ceremonial—the installation of nine Knights of the Saint-Esprit—' high mass celebrated with music, great crowd, much incense, King, Queen, Dauphin, Mesdames, Cardinals, and Court: Knights arrayed by His Majesty; reverences before the altar, not bows but curtsies; stiff hams : much tittering among the ladies; trumpets, kettle-drums, and fifes '.[1]

It is Gray who thus summarises the show. But we must go to Walpole for the account of another expedition, the visit to the Convent of the Chartreux, the uncouth horror of which, with its gloomy chapel and narrow cloisters, seems to have fascinated the Gothic soul of the future author of the *Castle of Otranto*. Here, in one of the cells, they make the acquaintance of a fresh initiate into the order—the account of whose environment suggests retirement rather than solitude. ' He was extremely civil, and called himself Dom Victor. We have promised to visit him often. Their habit is all white : but besides this he was infinitely clean in his person ; and his apartment and garden, which he keeps and cultivates without any assistance, was neat to a degree. He has four little rooms, furnished in the prettiest manner, and hung with good prints. One of them is a

[1] *Gray to West*, 22 May 1739.

library, and another a gallery.   He has several
canary-birds disposed in a pretty manner in breeding cages.   In his garden was a bed of good tulips
in bloom, flowers and fruit-trees, and all neatly
kept.   They are permitted at certain hours to
talk to strangers, but never to one another, or to
go out of their convent.'   In the same institution
they saw Le Sueur's history (in pictures) of St.
Bruno, the founder of the Chartreux.   Walpole
had not yet studied Raphael at Rome, but these
pictures, he considered, excelled everything he had
seen in England and Paris.[1]

   ' From Paris,' say Walpole's *Short Notes*,
' after a stay of about two months, we went
with my cousin Henry Conway, to Rheims, in
Champagne, [and] staid there three months.'
One of their chief objects was to improve themselves in French.   ' You must not wonder ', he
tells West, ' if all my letters resemble dictionaries,
with French on one side and English on t' other ;
I deal in nothing else at present, and talk a couple
of words of each language alternately from morning till night.' [2]   But he does not seem to have yet
developed his later passion for letter-writing, and
the ' account of our situation and proceedings ' is

[1] *Walpole to West*, no date, 1739.
[2] *Walpole to West*, 18 June 1739.

still delegated to Gray, some of whose despatches
at this time are not preserved.  There is, however,
one from Rheims to Gray's mother which gives a
vivid idea of the ancient French Cathedral city,
slumbering in its vast vine-clad plain, with its
picturesque old houses and lonely streets, its long
walks under the ramparts, and its monotonous
frog-haunted moat.  They have no want of
society, for Henry Conway procured them introductions everywhere ; but the Rhemois are more
constrained, less familiar, less hospitable than the
Parisians.  Quadrille is the almost invariable
amusement, interrupted by one entertainment
(for the Rémois as a rule give neither dinners
nor suppers), to wit, a five o'clock *goûter*, which
is 'a service of wine, fruits, cream, sweetmeats,
crawfish, and cheese ', after which they sit down
to cards again.  Occasionally, however, the demon
of impromptu flutters these ' set, gray lives ', and
(like Dr. Johnson) even Rheims must ' have a
frisk '.  ' For instance,' says Gray, ' the other
evening we happened to be got together in a
company of eighteen people, men and women of
the best fashion here, at a garden in the town to
walk ; when one of the ladies bethought herself
of asking, Why should we not sup here ?  Immediately the cloth was laid by the side of a fountain

under the trees, and a very elegant supper served
up ; after which another said, Come, let us sing ;
and directly began herself.  From singing we
insensibly fell to dancing, and singing in a round ;
when somebody mentioned the violins and immediately a company of them was ordered.  Minuets
were begun in the open air, and then came country
dances, which held till four o'clock next morning ;
at which hour the gayest lady there proposed, that
such as were weary should get into their coaches,
and the rest of them should dance before them
with the music in the van ;  and in this manner
we paraded through all the principal streets of
the city, and waked everybody in it.'  Walpole,
adds Gray, would have made this entertainment
chronic.  But ' the women did not come into it ',
and shrank back decorously ' to their dull cards,
and usual formalities '.[1]

At Rheims the travellers lingered on in the
hope of being joined by Selwyn and George
Montagu.[2]  In September they left Rheims for
Dijon, the superior attractions of which town
made them rather regret their comparative rusti-
cation of the last three months.  From Dijon they
passed southward to Lyons, whence Gray sent to

[1] [*Gray to Mrs. Gray,* 21 June 1739.]
[2] [*Walpole to West,* 20 July 1739.]

West (then drinking the Tunbridge waters) a daintily elaborated conceit touching the junction of the Rhone and the Saône.[1]   While at Lyons they made an excursion to Geneva to escort Henry Conway, who had up to this time been their companion, on his way to that place.  They took a roundabout route in order to visit the Convent of the Grande Chartreuse, and on the 28th Walpole writes to West from 'a Hamlet among the mountains of Savoy'.[2]   He is to undergo many transmigrations, he says, before he ends his letter.   'Yesterday I was a shepherd of Dauphiné; to-day an Alpine savage; to-morrow a Carthusian monk; and Friday a Swiss Calvinist.' When he next takes up his pen, he has passed through his third stage, and visited the Chartreuse. With the convent itself neither Gray nor his companions seem to have been much impressed, probably because their expectations had been indefinite.   For the approach and the situation they had only enthusiasm.   Gray is the accredited landscape-painter of the party, but here even Walpole breaks out : 'The road, West, the road ! winding round a prodigious mountain, and surrounded with others, all shagged with hanging woods, obscured with pines, or lost in clouds !

[1] [*Gray to West*, 18 Sept. 1739.]        [2] Échelles.

Below, a torrent breaking through cliffs, and tumbling through fragments of rocks ! Sheets of cascades forcing their silver speed down channelled precipices, and hasting into the roughened river at the bottom ! Now and then an old foot-bridge, with a broken rail, a leaning cross, a cottage, or the ruin of an hermitage ! This sounds too bombast and too romantic to one that has not seen it, too cold for one that has. If I could send you my letter post between two lovely tempests that echoed each other's wrath, you might have some idea of this noble roaring scene, as you were reading it. Almost on the summit, upon a fine verdure, but without any prospect, stands the Chartreuse.' [1]

The foregoing passage is dated Aix-in-Savoy, 30 September. Two days later, passing by Annecy, they came to Geneva. Here they stayed a week to see Conway settled, and made a ' solitary journey ' back to Lyons, but by a different road, through the spurs of the Jura and across the plains of La Bresse. At Lyons they found letters awaiting them from Sir Robert Walpole, desiring his son to go to Italy, a proposal with which Gray, only too glad to exchange the over-commercial city of Lyons for ' the place in the world that best deserves seeing ', was highly delighted. Accord-

[1] *Walpole to West*, Sept. 28–2 Oct. 1739.

ingly we speedily find them duly equipped with
' beaver bonnets, beaver gloves, beaver stockings,
muffs, and bear-skins ' *en route* for the Alps.   At
the foot of Mont Cenis their chaise was taken to
pieces and loaded on mules, and they themselves
were transferred to low matted legless chairs
carried on poles—a not unperilous mode of
progression, when, as in this case, quarrels took
place among the bearers.   But the tragedy of the
journey happened before they had quitted the
chaise.   Walpole had a fat little black spaniel of
King Charles's breed, named Tory, and he had
let the little creature out of the carriage for the
air.   While it was waddling along contentedly at
the horses' heads, a gaunt wolf rushed out of a fir
wood, and exit poor Tory before any one had time
to snap a pistol.[1]   In later years, Gray would
perhaps have celebrated this mishap as elegantly
as he sang the death of his friend's favourite cat,
but in these pre-poetic days he restricts himself to
calling it an ' odd accident enough '.[2]

[1] [*Walpole to West*, 11 Nov. 1739.]

[2] [*Gray to Mrs. Gray*, 7 Nov. 1739.]   Tory, however, was
not *illachrymabilis*.   He found his *vates sacer* in one
Edward Burnaby Greene, once of Bennet College ; and
in referring to this, thirty-five years later, Walpole explains
how Tory got his name.   ' His godmother was the widow
of Alderman Parsons [Humphrey Parsons of Goldsmith's

' After eight days' journey through Greenland,'
—as Gray puts it to West,—they reached Turin,[1]
where among other English they found Pope's
friend, Joseph Spence, Professor of Poetry at
Oxford.   Beyond Walpole's going to Court, and
their visiting an extraordinary play called *La
Rappresentazione dell' Anima Dannata* (for the
benefit of an Hospital), a full and particular
account of which is contained in one of Spence's
letters to his mother,[2] nothing remarkable seems
to have happened to them in the Piedmontese
capital.   From Turin they went on to Genoa,
—' the happy country where huge lemons grow '
(as Gray quotes,[3] not textually, from Waller),—
whose blue sea and vine-trellises they quit reluc-
tantly for Bologna, by way of Tortona, Piacenza,
Parma (where they inspect the Correggios in the
Duomo), Reggio, and Modena.   At Bologna, in
the absence of introductions, picture-seeing is
their main occupation.   ' Except pictures and
statues', writes Walpole, ' we are not very fond
of sights.' . . . ' Now and then we drop in at a

" black champagne "], who gave him at Paris to Lord
Conway, and he to me ' (*Walpole to Cole*, 10 Dec. 1775).
    [1] [*Gray to West*, 16 Nov. 1739.]
    [2] Spence's *Anecdotes*, ed. Singer (1820), pp. 397–400.
    [3] [*Gray to West*, 21 Nov. 1739.]

procession, or a high-mass, hear the music, enjoy a strange attire, and hate the foul monkhood. Last week was the feast of the Immaculate Conception.  On the eve we went to the Franciscans' church to hear the academical exercises.  There were *moult* and *moult* clergy, about two dozen dames, that treated one another with *illustrissima* and brown kisses, the vice-legate, the gonfalonier, and some senate.  The vice-legate . . . is a young personable person, of about twenty, and had on a mighty pretty cardinal-kind of habit; 'twou'd make a delightful masquerade dress.  We asked his name: Spinola.  What, a nephew of the cardinal-legate ?  *Signor, no : ma credo che gli sia qualche cosa.*  He sat on the right-hand with the gonfalonier in two purple fauteuils.  Opposite was a throne of crimson damask, with the device of the Academy, the Gelati; [1]  and trimmings of

[1] ' Jarchius has taken the trouble to give us a list of those clubs, or academies [i.e. *the academies of Italy*], which amount to five hundred and fifty, each distinguished by somewhat whimsical in the name.  The academicians of Bologna, for instance, are divided into the Abbandonati, the Ansiosi, the Ociosi, Arcadi, Confusi, Dubbiosi, etc. There are few of these who have not published their transactions, and scarce a member who is not looked upon as the most famous man in the world, at home ' (Goldsmith, in *The Bee*, No. vi, for 10 Nov. 1759).

gold.  Here sat at a table, in black, the head
of the Academy, between the orator and the first
poet.  At two semicircular tables on either hand
sat three poets and three;  silent among many
candles.  The chief made a little introduction,
the orator a long Italian vile harangue.  Then
the chief, the poet, the poets,—who were a Fran-
ciscan, an Olivetan, an old abbé, and three lay,—
read their compositions;  and to-day they are
pasted up in all parts of the town.  As we came
out of the church, we found all the convent and
neighbouring houses lighted all over with lanthorns
of red and yellow paper, and two bonfires.' [1]

In the Christmas of 1739, the friends crossed
the Apennines, and entered Florence.  If they
had wanted introductions at Bologna, there was
no lack of them in Tuscany, and they were to
find one friend who afterwards figured largely in
Walpole's correspondence.  This was Mr. (afterwards Sir Horace) Mann, British Minister
Plenipotentiary at the Court of Florence.  ' He
is the best and most obliging person in the world,'
says Gray,[2] and his house, with a brief interval,
was their residence for fifteen months.  Their
letters from Florence are less interesting than

[1] *Walpole to West,* no date, 1739.
[2] [*Gray to Mrs. Gray,* 19 Dec. 1739.]

those from which quotations have already been made, while their amusements seem to have been more independent of each other than before. Gray occupied himself in the galleries taking the notes of pictures and statuary afterwards published (in part) by Mr. Tovey,[1] and in forming a collection of MS. music : Walpole, on the other hand, had slightly cooled in his eagerness for the antique, which now ' pleases him calmly '. ' I recollect '—he says—' the joy I used to propose if I could but see the Great Duke's gallery; I walk into it now with as little emotion as I should into St. Paul's. The statues are a congregation of good sort of people, that I have a great deal of unruffled regard for.'[2]  The fact was, no doubt, that society had now superior attractions.    As the son of the English Prime Minister, and with Mann, who was a relation,[3] at his elbow, all doors were open to him   A correct record of his time would probably show an unvaried succession

[1] [In *Gray and his Friends*, pp. 216–22 ; the originals of the notes printed by Tovey are in the John Morris Collection in Eton College Library.  Copious other notes (as yet unprinted) are in possession of Sir John Murray.]

[2] [*Walpole to West*, 24 Jan. 1740.]

[3] Dr. Doran (' *Mann* ' *and Manners at the Court of Florence*, 1876, i. 2) describes this connection as ' a distant cousinship '.

of suppers, balls, and masquerades. In the carnival week, when he snatches 'a little unmasqued moment' to write to West, he says he has done nothing lately 'but slip out of his domino into bed, and out of bed into his domino. The end of the Carnival is frantic, bacchanalian; all the morn one makes parties in masque to the shops and coffee-houses, and all the evening to the operas and balls.' [1] If Gray was of these junketings, his letters do not betray it. He was probably engaged in writing uncomplimentary notes on the Venus de' Medici, or transcribing a score of Pergolesi.

The first interruption to these diversions came in March, when they quitted Florence for Rome in order to witness the coronation of the successor of Clement XII, who had died in the preceding month. On their road from Siena they were passed by a shrill-voiced figure in a red cloak with a white handkerchief on its head which they took for a fat old woman, but which afterwards turned out to be Farinelli's rival, Senesino. [2] Rome disappointed them—especially in its inhabitants and general desolation. 'I am very glad'—writes Walpole —'that I see it while it yet exists'; [3] and he

---

[1] [*Walpole to West*, 27 Feb. 1740.]
[2] [*Walpole to West*, 22–3 Mar. 1740.]
[3] [*Walpole to West*, 16 Apr. 1740.]

goes on to prophesy that before a great number
of years it will cease to exist. ' I am persuaded ',
he says again, ' that in an hundred years Rome
will not be worth seeing ; 'tis less so now than
one would believe.   All the public pictures are
decayed or decaying ;  the few ruins cannot last
long ;  and the statues and private collections must
be sold, from the great poverty of the families.' ¹
Perhaps this last consideration, coupled with the
depressing character of Roman hospitality ('Roman
conversations   are   dreadful   things ! '—he   tells
Conway), revived his virtuoso tastes.   ' I am far
gone in medals, lamps, idols, prints, etc., and all
the small commodities to the purchase of which
I can attain ;  I would buy the Coliseum if I
could.' ²   Meanwhile, as the cardinals are quarrel-
ling, the coronation is still deferred ;  and they
visit Naples, whence they explore Herculaneum,
then but recently exposed and identified.³   But
neither Gray nor Walpole waxes very eloquent
upon this theme, probably because at this time
the excavations were only partial, while Pompeii
was, of course, as yet under ground.   Walpole's

---

¹ [*Walpole to West*, 7 May 1740.]
² [*Walpole to Conway*, 23 Apr. 1740.]
³ [*Walpole to West*, 14 June 1740 ;  *Gray to Mrs. Gray*,
17 June 1740.]

next letter is written from Radicofani—'a vile
little town at the foot of an old citadel '—which
again is at ' the top of a black barren mountain '
—the whole reminding the writer of ' Hamilton's
Bawn ' in Swift's verses.   In this place, although
the traditional residence of one of the Three Kings
of Cologne, there is but one pen, the property of
the Governor, who when Walpole borrows it,
sends it to him under ' conduct of a sergeant and
two Swiss ' with special injunctions as to its
restoration, a precaution which in Walpole's view
renders it worthy to be ranked with the other
precious relics of the poor Capuchins of the place,
concerning which he presently makes rather un-
kindly fun.[1]   A few days later they were once
more in the Casa Ambrosio, Mann's pleasant
house at Florence, with the river running so close
to them that they could fish out of the windows.[2]
' I have a terreno [ground-floor] all to myself,'
—says Walpole,—' with an open gallery on the
Arno where I am now writing to you [*i.e.*, Con-
way].   Over against me is the famous Gallery ;
and, on either hand, two fair bridges.   Is not this
charming and cool ? ' [3]   Add to which, on the

[1] [*Walpole to Conway*, 5 July 1740.]
[2] [*Gray to Philip Gray*, 16 July 1740.]
[3] [*Walpole to Conway*, 9 July 1740.]

bridges aforesaid, in the serene Italian air, one may linger all night in a dressing-gown, eating iced fruits to the notes of a guitar.[1]    But (what was even better than music and moonlight) there is the society that was the writer's ' fitting environment '.    Lady Pomfret, with her daughters, Lady Charlotte, afterwards governess to the children of George III, and the beauty Lady Sophia, held a ' charming conversation ' once a week ; while the Princess de Craon has ' a constant pharaoh and supper every night, where one is quite at one's ease '.[2]    Another lady-resident, scarcely so congenial to Walpole, was his sister-in-law, the wife of his eldest brother, Robert, who, with Lady Pomfret, made certain (in Walpole's eyes) wholly preposterous pretensions to the yet uninvented status of blue-stocking.    To Lady Walpole and Lady Pomfret was speedily added another ' she-meteor ' in the person of the celebrated Lady Mary Wortley Montagu.[3]

When Lady Mary arrived in Florence in the summer of 1740, she was a woman of more than fifty, and was just entering upon that unexplained exile from her country and husband which was

[1]  [*Gray to Philip Gray*, 16 July 1740.]
[2]  [*Walpole to Conway*, 9 July 1740.]
[3]  [*Walpole to West*, 31 July 1740.]

prolonged for two and twenty years. Her brilliant
abilities were unimpaired ; but it is probable that
the personal eccentricities which had exposed her
to the satire of Pope, had not decreased with years.
That these would be extenuated under Walpole's
malicious pen was not to be expected ; still less,
perhaps, that they would be treated justly. Although, as already intimated, he was not aware of
the scandal respecting himself which her descen-
dants were to revive, he had ample ground for
antipathy. Her husband was the bitter foe of
Sir Robert Walpole ; and she herself had been
the firm friend and protectress of his mother's
rival and successor, Miss Skerret.[1] Accordingly,
even before her advent, he makes merry over the
anticipated issue of this portentous ' triple alliance '
of mysticism and nonsense, and later he writes to
Conway,—' Did I tell you Lady Mary Wortley
is here ? She laughs at my Lady Walpole, scolds
my Lady Pomfret, and is laughed at by the whole
town. Her dress, her avarice, and her impudence
must amaze any one that never heard her name.
She wears a foul mob, that does not cover her

[1] Shortly after Lady Walpole's death, Sir Robert Walpole married his mistress, Maria Skerret, who died 4 June,
1738, leaving a daughter, Horace Walpole's half-sister,
subsequently Lady Mary Churchill.

greasy black locks, that hang loose, never combed or curled; an old mazarine blue wrapper, that gapes open and discovers a canvas petticoat. . . . In three words I will give you her picture as we drew it in the *Sortes Virgilianæ,—Insanam vatem aspicies.* I give you my honour we did not choose it; but Gray, Mr. Coke, Sir Francis Dashwood, and I, with several others, drew it fairly amongst a thousand for different people.' [1]    In justice to Lady Mary it is only fair to say that she seems to have been quite unconscious that she was an object of ridicule, and was perfectly satisfied with her reception at Florence. 'Lord and Lady Pomfret'—she tells Mr. Wortley—'take pains to make the place agreeable to me, and I have been visited by the greatest part of the people of quality.' [2]    But although Walpole's portrait is obviously malicious (some of its details are suppressed in the above quotation), it is plain that even unprejudiced spectators could not deny her peculiarities. 'Lady Mary'—said Spence—'is one of the most shining characters in the world, but shines like a comet; she is all irregularity, and always wandering; the most wise, the most

[1] *Walpole to Conway,* 25 Sept. 1740.
[2] *Letters and Works* of Lady Mary Wortley Montagu, ii. 325.

imprudent; loveliest, most disagreeable; best-natured, cruellest woman in the world: "all things by turns but nothing long." ' [1]

By this time the new pope, Benedict XIV, had been elected. But although the friends were within four days' journey of Rome, the fear of heat and malaria forced them to forgo the spectacle of the coronation. They continued to reside with Mann at Florence until May in the following year. Upon Gray the 'violent delights' of the Tuscan capital had already begun to pall. It is —he says—' an excellent place to employ all one's animal sensations in, but utterly contrary to one's rational powers '. [2] Walpole, on the other hand, is in his element. ' I am so well within and without,' he says in the same letter which sketches Lady Mary, ' that you would scarce know me: I am younger than ever, think of nothing but diverting myself, and live in a round of pleasures. We have operas, concerts, and balls, mornings and evenings. I dare not tell you all of one's idlenesses: you would look so grave and sena-torial, at hearing that one rises at eleven in the morning, goes to the opera at nine at night, to supper at one, and to bed at three! But literally

[1] Spence's *Anecdotes*, ed. Singer [1820], p. xviii.
[2] [*Gray to West*, 31 July 1740.]

here the evenings and nights are so charming and so warm, one can't avoid 'em.' [1]    In a later letter he says he has lost all curiosity, and 'except the towns in the straight road to Great Britain, shall scarce see a jot more of a foreign land '.[2]    Indeed, save a sally concerning the humours of ' Moll Worthless ' (Lady Mary) and Lady Walpole, and the record of the purchase of a few pictures, medals, and busts [2]—one of the last of which, a Vespasian in basalt, was subsequently among the glories of the Twickenham Gallery—his remaining letters from Florence contain little of interest.    Early in 1741, the homeward journey was mapped out.    They were to go to Bologna to hear the Viscontina sing ; they were to visit the Fair at Reggio, and so by Venice homewards.[3]

But whether the Viscontina was in voice or not, there is, as far as our travellers are concerned, absence of evidence.    No further letter of Gray from Florence has been preserved, nor is there any mention of him in Walpole's next despatch to West from Reggio.    At that place a misunderstanding seems to have arisen, and they parted, Gray going forward to Venice with two

[1] [*Walpole to Conway,* 25 Sept. 1740.]
[2] [*Walpole to West,* 2 Oct. 1740.]
[3] [*Gray to West,* 21 Apr. 1741.]

other travelling companions, Mr. John Chute
and Mr. Whithed.   In the rather barren record
of Walpole's story, this misunderstanding naturally
assumes an exaggerated importance.   But it was
really a very trifling and a very intelligible affair.
They had been too long together; and the first
fascination of travel, which formed at the outset
so close a bond, had gradually faded with time.
As this alteration took place, their natural dispositions began to assert themselves, and Walpole's
normal love of pleasure and Gray's retired studi-
ousness became more and more apparent.   It is
probable too, that, in all the Florentine gaieties,
Gray, who was not a great man's son, fell a little
into the background.[1]   At all events the separation
was imminent, and it needed but a nothing to bring
it about.[2]   Whatever the proximate cause, both
were silent on the subject, although, years after
the quarrel had been made up, and Gray was dead,

[1] [The detailed notes of the objects of interest at Florence
in Gray's MS. *Journals* (now in possession of Sir John
Murray) point plainly to his having spent a great part of
his time alone.]

[2] The alleged opening by Walpole of a letter of Gray
rests upon the authority of a shadowy Mr. Roberts of the
Pell-office, who told it to Isaac Reed in 1799, more than
half a century after the event.   [(See *Correspondence of
Gray, Walpole, West, and Ashton*, vol. i, pp. xxiv–xxix).]

Walpole took the entire blame upon himself. When Mason was preparing Gray's *Memoirs* in 1773, he authorized him to insert a note by which, in general terms, he admitted himself to have been in fault, assigning as his reason for not being more explicit, that while he was living it would not be pleasant to read his private affairs discussed in magazines and newspapers. But to Mason personally he was at the same time thoroughly candid, as well as considerate to his departed friend :—' I am conscious', he says, ' that in the beginning of the differences between Gray and me, the fault was mine. I was too young, too fond of my own diversions, nay, I do not doubt, too much intoxicated by indulgence, vanity, and the insolence of my situation, as a Prime Minister's son, not to have been inattentive and insensible to the feelings of one I thought below me ; of one, I blush to say it, that I knew was obliged to me ; of one whom presumption and folly perhaps made me deem not my superior *then* in parts, though I have since felt my infinite inferiority to him. I treated him insolently : he loved me and I did not think he did. I reproached him with the difference between us, when he acted from conviction of knowing he was my superior; I often disregarded his wishes of seeing places, which I would not quit other amusements to visit, though I offered to send him to them without me. Forgive me, if I say that his temper was not conciliating. At the same time that I will confess to you that he acted a more friendly part, had I had the sense to take advantage of it; he freely told me of my faults. I declared I did not desire to hear them, nor would correct them. You will not wonder that with the dignity of his spirit, and the obstinate carelessness of mine, the breach must have grown wider till we became incompatible.' [1]

'Sir, you have said more than was necessary' —was Johnson's reply to a peace-making speech from Topham Beauclerk. It is needless to comment further upon this incident, except to add that Walpole's generous words show that the disagreement was rather the outcome of a sequence of long-strained circumstances than the result of

[1] *Walpole to Mason*, 2 Mar. 1773. The letters to Mason were first printed in 1851 by Mitford. But Pinkerton, in the *Walpoliana* (2nd ed.), i. 97–8, had reported much the same thing. 'The quarrel between Gray and me [Walpole] arose from his being too serious a companion. I had just broke loose from the restraints of the university, with as much money as I could spend, and I was willing to indulge myself. Gray was for antiquities, &c., while I was for perpetual balls and plays. The fault was mine.'

momentary petulance. For a time reconciliation was deferred, but eventually it was effected by a lady, and the intimacy thus renewed continued for the remainder of Gray's life.

Shortly after Gray's departure in May, Walpole fell ill of a quinsy. He did not, at first, recognize the gravity of his ailment, and doctored himself. By a fortunate chance, Joseph Spence, then travelling as governor to the Earl of Lincoln, was in the neighbourhood, and responding to a message from Walpole, 'found him scarce able to speak'.[1] Spence immediately sent for medical aid, and summoned from Florence one Antonio Cocchi, a physician and author of some eminence. Under Cocchi's advice, Walpole speedily showed signs of improvement, though, in his own words in the *Short Notes*, he ' was given over for five hours, escaping with great difficulty '. The sequel may be told from the same source. ' I went to Venice with Henry Clinton, Earl of Lincoln, and Mr. Joseph Spence, Professor of Poetry,[2] and after a month's stay there, returned with them by sea from Genoa, landing at Antibes, and by the way of Toulon, Marseilles, Aix, and through Languedoc to Montpellier, Toulouse, and Orleans, arrived at Paris, where

[1] [See Spence's *Anecdotes*, ed. Singer (1820), p. xxix.]
[2] [At Oxford.]

I left the Earl and Mr. Spence, and landed at
Dover, September 12th, 1741, O.S., having been
chosen Member of Parliament for Kellington,[1]
in Cornwall, at the preceding General Election,[2]
which Parliament put a period to my father's
administration, which had continued above twenty
years.'

[1] [Callington, which he represented till 1754, when he
was elected for Castle-Rising, in Norfolk.]

[2] [Of May.]

# CHAPTER III

# III

ALTHOUGH, during his stay in Italy, Walpole had neglected to accumulate the store of erudition which his friend Gray had been so industriously hiving for home consumption, he can scarcely be said to have learned nothing, especially at an age when much is learned unconsciously. His epistolary style, which, with its peculiar graces and pseudo-graces, had been already formed before he left England, had now acquired a fresh vivacity from his increased familiarity with the French and Italian languages; and he had carried on, however discursively, something more than a mere flirtation with antiquities. Dr. Conyers Middleton, whose once famous *Life of Cicero* was published early in 1741, and who was himself an antiquary of distinction, thought highly of Walpole's attainments in this way,[1] and indeed more than one passage in a poem

[1] [Walpole not only brought back to England a valuable collection of his own, but in 1744 he bought Middleton's collection (see his letter to Mann of 18 June 1744).] In the Preface to his *Germana quaedam Antiquitatis eruditae Monumenta* (1745) Middleton wrote : ' Ex his autem agri Romani divitiis, neminem profecto de peregrinatoribus

F

written by Walpole to Ashton at this time could
scarcely have been penned by any one not fairly
familiar with (for example) the science of those
' medals ' upon which Mr. Joseph Addison had
discoursed so learnedly after his Italian tour :—

> ' What scanty precepts ! studies how confin'd !
> Too mean to fill your comprehensive mind ;
> Unsatisfy'd with knowing when or where
> Some Roman bigot rais'd a fane to FEAR ;
> On what green medal VIRTUE stands express'd,
> How CONCORD's pictur'd, LIBERTY how dress'd ;
> Or with wise ken judiciously define,
> When Pius marks the honorary coin
> Of CARACALLA, or of ANTONINE.' [1]

The poem from which these lines are taken—
*An Epistle from Florence.*[2]    *To Thomas Ashton*,

nostris, thesaurum inde deportasse credo, et rerum delectu
et pretio magis aestimabilem, ac quem amicus meus nobilis
Horatius Walpole in Angliam nuper advexit ; juvenis
non tam generis nobilitate, ac paterni nominis gloria, quam
ingenio, doctrina, et virtute propria illustris.  Ille vero haud
citiùs fere in patriam reversus est, quam de studiis meis, ut
consuerat, familiariter per literas quaerens, mihi ultro de
copia sua, quicquid ad argumenti mei rationem, aut libelli
ornamentum pertineret, pro arbitrio meo utendum obtulit.'
(pp. viii–ix).        [1] *Works of Lord Orford* (1798), i. 6.

    [2] [This poem was suggested by Middleton's *Letter from
Rome* (1729).  See *Walpole to Middleton*, 22 Nov. 1741, in
*Supplement* (vol. i, pp. 44–5) to *Letters of Horace Walpole*
(ed. Toynbee).]

*Esq. Tutor to the Earl of Plimouth*—extends to some four hundred lines, and exhibits another side of Walpole's activity in Italy. 'You have seen' —says Gray to West in July, 1740—'an Epistle to Mr. Ashton, that seems to me full of spirit and thought, and a good deal of poetic fire.' Writing to Walpole eight years later, Gray seems still to have retained his first impression. 'Satire'—he says—'will be heard, for all the audience are by nature her friends; especially when she appears in the spirit of Dryden, with his strength, and often with his versification, such as you have caught in those lines on the Royal Unction, on the Papal dominion, and Convents of both Sexes; on Henry VIII and Charles II, for these are to me the shining parts of your Epistle. There are many lines I could wish corrected, and some blotted out, but beauties enough to atone for a thousand worse faults than these.' [1] Walpole has never been ranked among the poets; [2] but Gray's

[1] [See *Correspondence of Gray, Walpole, West, and Ashton,* vol. ii, pp. 92–3.]

[2] [Yet he wrote two of the most delightful poems for children; viz. the Patent for appointing Countess Temple poet laureate to the fairies (see *Walpole to Montagu,* 11 Jan. 1764), and the verses to Lady Anne Fitzpatrick, when about five years old, with a present of shells (in *Works of Lord Orford,* iv. 387). These are included in D. Nichol Smith's

praise, in which Middleton and others concurred,
justifies a further quotation.  This is the passage
on the Royal Unction and the Papal Dominion:—

> ' When at the altar a new monarch kneels,
> What conjur'd awe upon the people steals !
> The chosen HE adores the precious oil,
> Meekly receives the solemn charm, and while
> The priest some blessed nothings mutters o'er,
> Sucks in the sacred grease at every pore :
> He seems at once to shed his mortal skin,
> And feels divinity transfus'd within.
> The trembling vulgar dread the royal nod,
> And worship God's anointed more than God.
>
> ' Such sanction gives the prelate to such kings !
> So mischief from those hallow'd fountains springs.
> But bend your eye to yonder harass'd plains,
> Where king and priest in one united reigns ;
> See fair Italia mourn her holy state,
> And droop oppress'd beneath a papal weight :
> Where fat celibacy usurps the soil,
> And sacred sloth consumes the peasant's toil :
> The holy drones monopolize the sky,
> And plunder by a vow of poverty.
> The Christian cause their lewd profession taints,
> Unlearn'd, unchaste, uncharitable saints.' [1]

That the refined and fastidious Horace Walpole of later years should have begun as a passable

*Oxford Book of Eighteenth Century Verse*.  See also *Horace
Walpole as a Poet*, by Paul Yvon.]

[1] *Works of Lord Orford* (1798), vol. i, pp. 8–9.

imitator of Dryden is sufficiently piquant. But that the son of the great courtier Prime Minister should have distinguished himself by the vigour of his denunciations of kings and priests, especially when, as his biographers have not failed to remark, he was writing to one about to take orders, is more noticeable still. Written at the same time as this poem (which was published in 1748 in Dodsley's *Collection of Miscellaneous Poems*),[1] and character- ized by the same anti-monarchical spirit, was his *Inscription for the Neglected Column in the Place of St. Mark at Florence.*[2]

His letters to Mann, his chief correspondent at this date, are greatly occupied, during the next few months, with the climax of the catastrophe recorded at the end of the preceding chapter— the resignation of Sir Robert Walpole. The first[3] of the long series was written on his way home

---

[1] [See *Short Notes of my Life*, under 1748.]

[2] [Printed in *Works of Lord Orford* (1798), i. 7–18.]

[3] [The first, that is, that Walpole thought worth tran- scribing and preserving with the series ; fourteen earlier letters to Mann, some in a very fragmentary state, written between Apr. 16, 1740 and Aug. 1741 (nine from Rome, the others from Reggio, Venice, Genoa, and Paris), are printed in *Supplement* (vol. i, pp. 12–44) to *Letters of Horace Walpole* (ed. Toynbee). The complete series to Mann consists of 837 letters.]

in September, 1741, when he had for his fellow-passengers the Viscontina, Amorevoli, and other Italian singers, then engaged in invading England. He appears to have at once taken up his residence with his father in Downing Street.   Into the net-work of circumstances which had conspired to array against the great peace Minister the for-midable opposition of disaffected Whigs, Jacobites, Tories, and adherents of the Prince of Wales, it would here be impossible to enter.   But there were already signs that Sir Robert was nodding to his fall; and that, although the old courage was as high as ever, the old buoyancy was begin-ning to flag.   Failing health added its weight to the scale.   In October Walpole tells his corre-spondent that he had ' been very near sealing this letter with black wax ', for his father had been in danger of his life, but was recovering, though he is no longer the Sir Robert that Mann once knew. He who formerly would snore before they had drawn his curtains, now never slept above an hour without waking; and ' he who at dinner always forgot that he was Minister ', now sat silent with eyes fixed for an hour together.[1]  At the opening of Parliament, however, there was an ostensible majority of forty for the Court, and Walpole

[1] [*Walpole to Mann*, 8, 19 Oct. 1741.]

seems to have regarded this as encouraging. But
one of the first motions was for an enquiry into
the state of the nation, and this was followed by
a division upon a Cornish petition which reduced
the majority to seven,—a variation which sets the
writer nervously jesting about apartments in the
Tower. Seven days later the opposition obtained
a majority of four, and although Sir Robert, still
sanguine in the remembrance of past successes,
seemed less anxious than his family, matters were
growing grave, and his youngest son was reconcil-
ing himself to the coming blow. It came practically on the 21st January 1742, when Pulteney
moved for a secret committee, which (in reality)
was to be a committee of accusation against the
Prime Minister. Walpole defeated this manœuvre
with his characteristic courage and address, but
only by a narrow majority of three. So inconsiderable a victory upon so crucial a question was
perilously close to a reverse, and when in the succeeding case of the disputed Chippenham Election,
the Government were defeated by one, he yielded
to the counsels of his advisers, and decided to resign.
He was thereupon raised to the peerage as Earl of
Orford, with a pension of £4,000 a year,[1] while

[1] He gave this up at first, but afterwards, when his affairs became involved, reclaimed it (*Walpole to Mann*, 18 June 1744).

his daughter (born before marriage) by his second wife, Miss Skerret, was created [1] an Earl's daughter. His fall was mourned by no one more sincerely than by the master he had served so staunchly for so long; and when he went to kiss hands at St. James's upon taking leave, the old King fell upon his neck, embraced him, and broke into tears. [2]

The new Earl himself seems to have taken his reverses with his customary equanimity, and, like the shrewd 'old Parliamentary hand' that he was, to have at once devoted himself to the difficult task of breaking the force of the attack which he foresaw would be made upon himself by those in power.    He contrived adroitly to foster dissension and disunion among the heterogeneous body of his opponents; he secured that the new Ministry should be mainly composed of his old party, the Whigs; and he managed to discredit his most formidable adversary, Pulteney. One of the first results of these precautionary measures was that a motion by Lord Limerick for a committee to examine into the conduct of the last twenty years was thrown out by a small

[1] [The phrase is Walpole's own—'the poor girl . . . must be *created* an earl's daughter, as her birth would deprive her of the rank ' (*to Mann*, 4 Feb. 1742).]

[2] [*Walpole to Mann*, 4 Feb. 1742.]

majority. A fortnight later the motion was renewed in a fresh form, the scope of the examination being limited to the last ten years. Upon this occasion Horace Walpole made his maiden speech,[1] a graceful and modest, if not very forcible, effort on his father's side. In this instance, however, the Government were successful, and the Committee was appointed. Yet, despite the efforts to excite the public mind respecting Lord Orford, the case against him seems to have faded away in the hands of his accusers. The first report of the Committee, issued in May, contained nothing to criminate the person against whom the enquiry had been directly levelled; and despite the strenuous and even shameless efforts of the Government to obtain evidence inculpating the late Minister, the Committee were obliged to issue a second report in June of which—so far as the chief object was concerned—the gross result was nil. By the middle of July, Walpole was able to tell Mann that the ' long session was over, and the Secret Committee already forgotten ' —as much forgotten, he says in a later letter, ' as if it had happened in the last reign '.[2]

[1] [Walpole, who tells Mann that it ' was very favourably heard ', transcribes the speech in his letter to him of 24 Mar. 1742.]          [2 *Walpole to Mann*, 20 Aug. 1742.]

When Sir Robert Walpole had resigned, he had quitted his official residence in Downing Street (which ever since he first occupied it in 1735 has been the official residence of the First Lord of the Treasury), and moved to No. 5, Arlington Street, opposite to, but smaller than, the No. 17 in which his youngest son had been born, and upon the site of which William Kent built a larger house for Mr. Pelham.   No. 5 is now distinguished by a tablet erected by the Society of Arts proclaiming it to have been the house of the ex-Minister. From Arlington Street, or from the other home at Chelsea already mentioned, most of Walpole's letters were dated during the months which succeeded the crisis.   But in August, when the House had risen, he migrated with the rest of the family to Houghton—the great mansion in Norfolk which had now taken the place of the ancient seat of the Walpoles, where during the summer months his father had been accustomed in his free-handed manner to keep open house to all the county.   Fond of hospitality, fond of field-sports, fond of gardening and all out-door occupations, Lord Orford was at home among the flat expanses and Norfolk turnips.   But the family seat had no such attractions to his son, fresh from the multi-coloured continental life, and still bearing about him, in a certain frailty of physique and enervation of spirit, the tokens of a sickly child-hood. ' Next post '—he says despairingly to Mann—' I shall not be able to write to you; and when I am there [at Houghton], shall scarce find materials to furnish a letter above every other post. I beg, however, that you will write con-stantly to me; it will be my only entertainment; for I neither hunt, brew, drink, nor reap.' [1] ' Consider '—he says again—' I am in the barren land of Norfolk, where news grows as slow as anything green; and besides, I am in the house of a fallen minister !' [2] Writing letters (in com-pany with the little white dog ' Patapan ' [3] which he had brought from Rome as a successor to the defunct Tory), walking, and playing comet with his sister Lady Mary,[4] seem to have been his chief

[1] [*Walpole to Mann*, 29 July 1742.]
[2] [*Walpole to Mann*, Aug. 1742.]
[3] Patapan's portrait was painted in 1743 (see *Walpole to Mann*, 25 Apr. 1743) by John Wootton, who illustrated Gay's *Fables* in 1727 with Kent. It hung in Walpole's bed-room at Strawberry, and belonged in 1892 to Lord Lifford. In 1743 Walpole wrote a Fable in imitation of La Fontaine, to which he gave the title of *Patapan; or, the Little White Dog*. [The MS., which has never been printed, is in possession of Earl Waldegrave at Chewton Priory.]                    [4] [*Walpole to Mann*, 28 Aug. 1742.]

resources.   A year later he pays a second visit to
Houghton, and he is still unreconciled to his
environment.   'Only imagine that I here every
day see men, who are mountains of roast beef,
and only just seem roughly hewn out into the
outlines of human form, like the giant-rock at
Pratolino !   I shudder when I see them brandish
their knives in act to carve, and look on them as
savages that devour one another.'   Then there are
the enforced civilities to entirely uninteresting
people—the intolerable female relative, who is
curious about her cousins to the fortieth remove.
' I have an Aunt here, a family piece of goods,
an old remnant of inquisitive hospitality and
economy, who, to all intents and purposes, is as
beefy as her neighbours.   She wore me so down
yesterday with interrogatories, that I dreamt all
night she was at my ear with " who 's " and
" why 's ", and " when 's " and " where 's ", till
at last in my very sleep I cried out " for heaven's
sake, Madam, ask me no more questions ".'   And
then, in his impatience of bores in general, he goes
on to write a little essay upon that ' growth of
English root ', that ' awful yawn, which sleep
cannot abate ', as Byron calls it,—Ennui.   ' I am
so far from growing used to mankind [he means
" uncongenial mankind "] by living amongst them,

that my natural ferocity and wildness does but
every day grow worse. They tire me, they fatigue
me ; I don't know what to do with them ; I don't
know what to say to them ; I fling open the windows, and fancy I want air ; and when I get by
myself, I undress myself, and seem to have had
people in my pockets, in my plaits, and on my
shoulders ! I indeed find this fatigue worse in the
country than in town, because one can avoid it
there, and has more resources ; but it is there too.
I fear 'tis growing old ; but I literally seem to
have murdered a man whose name was Ennui,
for his ghost is ever before me. They say there
is no English word for *ennui ;* I think you may
translate it most literally by what is called " entertaining people " and " doing the honours " : that
is, you sit an hour with somebody you don't know
and don't care for, talk about the wind and the
weather, and ask a thousand foolish questions,
which all begin with, " I think you live a good
deal in the country," or " I think you don't love
this thing or that ". Oh ! 'tis dreadful ! ' [1]

[1] *Walpole to Chute,* 20 Aug. 1743. Mr. John Chute was
a friend whom Walpole had made at Florence, and with
whom, as already stated in Chapter II, Gray had travelled
when they parted company. Until, by the death of a
brother, he succeeded to the estate called The Vyne in
Hampshire, he lived principally abroad. His portrait by

But even Houghton, with its endless ' doing
the honours ', must have had its compensations.
There was a library, and—what must have had
even stronger attractions for Horace Walpole—
that magnificent and almost unique collection of
pictures which under a later member of the family,
the third Earl of Orford, passed to Catherine of
Russia.  For years Lord Orford, with unwearied
diligence and exceptional opportunities, had been
accumulating these treasures.  Mann in Florence,
Vertue in England, and a host of industrious
foragers had helped to bring together the price-
less canvases which crowded the rooms of the
Minister's house next the Treasury at Whitehall.
And if he was inexperienced as a critic, he was
far too acute a man to be deceived by the shiploads
of ' Holy Families, Madonnas, and other dismal
dark subjects, neither entertaining nor orna-
mental ', against which the one great native
artist of his time, the painter of the ' Rake's
Progress ', so persistently inveighed.  There was
no doubt about the pedigrees of the Wouvermans
and Teniers, the Guidos and Rubens, the Van-

Müntz after Pompeio Battoni hung over the door in Walpole's bedchamber at Strawberry Hill.  An exhaustive
*History of The Vyne* was published in 1888 by the late Mr.
Chaloner W. Chute, at that time its possessor.—[Müntz's
portrait of Chute is now (1926) at The Vyne].

dykes and Murillos, which decorated the rooms
at Downing Street and Chelsea and Richmond.
From the few records which remain of prices,
it would seem that, in addition to the merit of
authenticity, many of the pictures must have had
the attraction of being ' bargains '. In days when
£4,000 or £5,000 is no extravagant price to be
given for an old master, it is instructive to read
that £750 was the largest sum ever given by Lord
Orford for any one picture, and Walpole himself
quotes this amount as £630. For four great
Snyders, which Vertue bought for him, he only
paid £428, and for a portrait of Clement IX by
Carlo Maratti [1] no more than £200. Many of the
other pictures in his gallery cost him still less, being
donations—no doubt sometimes in gratitude for
favours to come—from his friends and adherents.
The Earl of Pembroke, Lord Waldegrave, the
Duke of Montagu, Lord Tyrawley, were among
these. But, upon the whole, the collection was
gathered mainly from galleries like the Zambec-
cari at Bologna, the Arnaldi Palace at Florence,
the Pallavicini at Rome, and from the stores of
noble collectors in England. [2]

[1] [From the Arnaldi Palace at Florence.]
[2] [The whole collection cost Sir Robert Walpole £40,000
(*Walpole to Cole*, 12 July 1779).]

In 1743, the majority of these had apparently been concentrated at Houghton, where there was special accommodation for them. ' My Lord ', says Horace, groaning over a fresh visit to Norfolk, ' has pressed me so much, that I could not with decency refuse : he is going to furnish and hang his picture-gallery, and wants me.' [1]  But it is impossible to believe that he really objected to a duty so congenial to his tastes.  In fact, he was really greatly interested in it.  His letters contain frequent references to a new Domenichino, a Virgin and Child, which Mann is sending from Florence, and he comes up to London to meet this and other pictures, and is not seriously inconsolable to find that owing to the quarantine for the plague on the continent, he is detained for some days in town.  One of the best evidences of his solicitude in connection with the arrangements of the Houghton collection is, however, the discourse which he wrote in the summer of 1742 under the title of a *Sermon on Painting*, and which he himself tells us [2] was actually preached by the Earl's chaplain in the gallery, and afterwards repeated at Stanno,[3] his elder brother's

---

[1] [*Walpole to Mann*, 25 Apr. 1743.]
[2] [In *Short Notes of my Life*, under 1742.]
[3] [Stanhoe Hall, about four miles from Houghton,

house.  The text was taken from Psalm CXV.
—' They have Mouths, but they speak not :
Eyes have they, but they see not : neither is
there any Breath in their Nostrils,' and the writer,
illustrating his theme by reference to the pictures
around his audience in the gallery, or dispersed
through the building, manages to eulogize the
painter's art with considerable skill.  He touches
upon the pernicious effect which the closely
realized representation of popish miracles must
have upon the illiterate spectator, and points out
how much more commendable and serviceable is
the portraiture of benignity, piety, and chastity
—how much more instructive the incidents of the
Passion, where every ' touch of the pencil is a
lesson of contrition, each figure an apostle to call
you to repentance '.  He lays stress, as Lessing
and other writers have done, on the universal
language of the brush, and indicates its abuse when
restricted to the reproduction of inquisitors, vision-
aries, imaginary hermits, ' consecrated gluttons ',
or ' noted concubines ', after which (as becomes
his father's son) he does not fail to disclose its
more fitting vocation, to perpetuate the likeness
of William the Deliverer, and the benign, the

where Sir Robert's eldest son lived with his mistress (*Walpole
to Mann*, 10 June 1743).]

honest house of Hanover. *The Dives and Lazarus*
of Veronese and the *Prodigal Son* of Salvator
Rosa, both on the walls, are pressed into his service, and the famous *Usurers* of Quentin Matsys
also prompt their parable.   Then, after adroitly
dwelling upon the pictorial honours lavished upon
mere asceticism to the prejudice of real heroes,
taking Poussin's picture of Moses Striking the
Rock for his text, he winds at the conclusion into
what was probably the ultimate purpose of his
discourse, a neatly veiled panegyric of Sir Robert
Walpole under guise of the great lawgiver of the
Israelites, which may be cited as a favourable
sample of this curious oration :—

'But it is not necessary to dive into profane history for examples of unregarded merit: the Scrip-
tures themselves contain instances of the greatest
patriots, who lie neglected, while new-fashioned
bigots or noisy incendiaries are the reigning
objects of public veneration.   See the great Moses
himself!   the lawgiver, the defender, the pre-
server of Israel!   Peevish orators are more run
after, and artful Jesuits more popular.   Examine
but the life of that slighted patriot: how boldly
in his youth he undertook the cause of liberty!
Unknown, without interest, he stood against the
face of Pharaoh!   He saved his countrymen from

the hand of tyranny, and from the dominion of an idolatrous king : how patiently did he bear for a series of years the clamours and cabals of a factious people, wandering after strange lusts, and exasperated by ambitious ringleaders ! How oft did he intercede for their pardon, when injured himself ! How tenderly deny them specious favours, which he knew must turn to their own destruction ! See him lead them through opposition, through plots, through enemies, to the enjoyment of peace, and to the possession of *a land flowing with milk and honey !* Or with more surprize see him in the barren desert, where sands and wilds overspread the dreary scene, where no hopes of moisture, no prospect of undiscovered springs could flatter their parching thirst ; see how with a miraculous hand

" He struck the rock, and strait the waters flow'd."

Whoever denies his praise to such evidence of merit, or with jealous look can scowl on such benefits, is like the senseless idol, that *has a mouth that speaks not, and eyes that cannot see.'*

If, in accordance with some perverse fashion of the day, the foregoing production had not been disguised as a sermon, and actually preached with the orthodox accompaniment of bands and doxology, there is no reason why it should not have been regarded as a harmless and not unaccomplished essay on Art.   But the objectionable spirit of parody upon the ritual, engendered by the strife between ' High ' and ' Low ' (Walpole himself wrote some *Lessons for the Day*, 1742,[1] which are to be found in the works of Sir Charles Hanbury Williams), seems to have dictated the title of what in other respects is a serious *Spectator*, and needed no spice of irreverence to render it palatable.   The *Sermon* had, however, one valuable result, namely, that it suggested to its author the expediency of preparing some record of the pictorial riches of Houghton upon the model of the famous *Aedes Barbarinae* and *Giustinianae*.   The dedication of the *Aedes Walpolianae* is dated 24 August 1743, but it was not actually published until 1747, and then only in an edition of 200 copies to give away. Another enlarged and more accurate edition was issued in 1752,[2] and it was finally reprinted in the second volume of the *Works of Lord Orford* (1798), pp. 221–78, where it is followed by the *Sermon on Painting*.   Professing to be more a catalogue of the pictures than a description of them, it nevertheless gives a good idea of a collec-

[1] [See *Walpole to Mann*, 14 July 1742 ; and *Supplement* (vol. ii, pp. 78–80) to *Letters of Walpole* (ed. Toynbee).]
[2] [See *Short Notes of my Life*, under 1747.]

tion which (as its historian says) both in its extent
and the condition of its treasures excelled most of
the existing collections of Italy.  In an ' Introduction ', the characteristics of the various artists are
distinguished with much discrimination, although
it is naturally more sympathetic than critical.
Perhaps one of its happiest pages is the following
excursus upon a poem of Prior :—' I cannot
conclude this topic of the ancient painters without
taking notice of an extreme pretty instance of
Prior's taste, and which may make an example
on that frequent subject the resemblance between
poetry and painting, and prove that taste in the
one will influence in the other.  Everybody has
read his tale of Protogenes and Apelles.  If they
have read the story in Pliny they will recollect,
that by the latter's account it seemed to have been
a trial between two Dutch performers.  The
Roman author tells you, that when Apelles was
to write his name on a board, to let Protogenes
know who had been to enquire for him, he drew
an exactly strait and slender line.  Protogenes
returned, and with his pencil, and another colour,
divided his competitor's.  Apelles, on seeing the
ingenious minuteness of the Rhodian master, took
a third colour, and laid on a still finer and indi-
visible line.—But the English poet, who could

distinguish the emulation of genius from nice experiments about splitting hairs, took the story into his own hands, and in a less number of trials, and with bolder execution, comprehended the whole force of painting, and flung drawing, colouring, and the doctrine of light and shade into the noble contention of those two absolute masters. In Prior, the first wrote his name in a perfect design, and

> ' ——with one judicious stroke
> On the plain ground Apelles drew
> A circle regularly true.'

Protogenes knew the hand, and showed Apelles that his own knowledge of colouring was as great as the other's skill in drawing.

> ' Upon the happy line he laid
> Such obvious light and easy shade,
> That Paris' apple stood confest,
> Or Leda's egg, or Chloe's breast.' [1]

Apelles acknowledged his rival's merit, without

[1] ' Mr. Vertue the engraver made a very ingenious conjecture on this story ; he supposes that Apelles did not draw a strait line, but the outline of a human figure, which not being correct, Protogenes drew a more correct figure within his ; but that still not being perfect, Apelles drew a smaller and exactly proportioned one within both the former.' (*Walpole.*)

jealously persisting to refine on the masterly reply :
" Pugnavere pares, succubuere pares." ' [1]

Among the other efforts of his pen at this time
were some squibs in ridicule of the new Ministry.
One was a parody of a scene in *Macbeth* ; the
other of a scene in Corneille's *Cinna*. He also
wrote a paper against Lord Bath in the *Old
England Journal.* [2]

In the not very perplexed web of Horace
Walpole's life, the next occurrence of importance
is his father's death. When, as Sir Robert Walpole, he had ceased to be Prime Minister he was
sixty-five years of age, and though his equanimity
and wonderful constitution still seemed to befriend
him, he had personally little desire, even if the
ways had been open, to recover his ancient power.
' I believe nothing could prevail on him to return
to the Treasury '—writes his son to Mann in
1743. ' He says he will keep the 12th of February,
—the day he resigned,—with his family as long as
he lives.' [3] He continued, nevertheless, to assist
his old master with his counsel, and more than one
step of importance by which the King startled his

---

[1] *Works of Lord Orford* (1798), ii. 229–30. The final
quotation is from Martial.
[2] [See *Short Notes of my Life*, under 1743, 1744.]
[3] [*Walpole to Mann*, 13 Jan. 1743.]

new Ministry owed its origin to a confidential con-
sultation with Lord Orford.   When, in January,
1744, the old question of discontinuing the Hanoverian troops was revived with more than ordinary
insistence, it was through Lord Orford's timely
exertions, and his personal credit with his friends,
that the motion was defeated by an overwhelming
majority.   On the other hand, a further attempt
to harass him by another Committee of Secret
Enquiry was wholly unsuccessful, and signs were
not wanting that his old prestige had by no means
departed.   Towards the close of 1744, however,
his son begins to chronicle a definite decline in his
health.   He is evidently suffering seriously from
stone, and is forbidden to take the least exercise [1]
by the King's serjeant-surgeon, that famous Mr.
Ranby who was the friend of Hogarth and Fielding.[2]   In January of the next year, he is trying a
famous specific for his complaint, Mrs. Stephens's
medicine.[3]  Six weeks later, he has been alarmingly
ill for about a month ;  and although reckoned out
of absolute danger, is hardly ever conscious more
than four hours out of the four-and-twenty, from

[1] [*Walpole to Mann*, 26 Nov. 1744.]
[2] Ranby wrote a *Narrative of the last Illness of the Earl
of Orford*, 1745, which provoked much controversy.
[3] [*Walpole to Mann*, 24 Dec. 1744 ;  14 Jan. 1745.]

the powerful opiates he takes in order to deaden pain.[1]  A fortnight later, on the 18th March, 1745, he died at Arlington Street in his sixty-ninth year.  At first his son dares scarcely speak of his loss,[2] but a week or two afterwards he writes more fully.  After showing that the state of his circumstances proved how little truth there had been in the charges of self-enrichment made against him, Walpole goes on to say:—' It is certain, he is dead very poor : his debts, with his legacies, which are trifling, amount to fifty thousand pounds.  His estate, a nominal eight thousand a year, much mortgaged.  In short, his fondness for Houghton has endangered Houghton.  If he had not so overdone it, he might have left such an estate to his family as might have secured the glory of the place for many years : another such debt must expose it to sale.  If he had lived, his unbounded generosity and contempt of money would have run him into vast difficulties.  However irreparable his personal loss may be to his friends, he certainly died critically well for himself : he had lived to stand the rudest trials with honour, to see his character universally cleared, his enemies brought to infamy for their

[1] [*Walpole to Mann*, 4 Mar. 1745.]
[2] [*Walpole to Mann*, 29 Mar. 1745.]

ignorance or villainy, and the world allowing him to be the only man in England fit to be what he had been; and he died at a time when his age and infirmities prevented his again undertaking the support of a government which engrossed his whole care, and which he foresaw was falling into the last confusion.  In this I hope his judgment failed!  His fortune attended him to the last; for he died of the most painful of all distempers, with little or no pain.' [1]

From the *Short Notes* we learn further:—
' He [my father] left me the house in Arlington Street in which he died, 5000*l*. in money, and 1000*l*. a year from the Collector's place in the Custom House, and the surplus to be divided between my brother Edward and me.'

[1] *Walpole to Mann*, 15 Apr. 1745.

# CHAPTER IV

DURING the period between Walpole's return to England and the death of Lord
Orford, his letters, addressed almost exclusively
to Mann, are largely occupied with the occurrences which accompanied and succeeded his
father's downfall. To Lord Orford's *protégé*
and relative these particulars were naturally of
the first importance, and Walpole's function of
' General Intelligencer ' fell proportionately into
the background. Still there are occasional references to current events of a merely social character.
After the Secret Committee, he is interested (probably because his friend Conway was pecuniarily
interested) in the Opera, and the reception by the
British public of the Viscontina, Amorevoli, and
the other Italian singers whom he had known
abroad.[1] Of the stage he says comparatively little,
dismissing poor Mrs. Woffington, who had then
just made her appearance at Covent Garden, as
' a bad actress ' who nevertheless ' has life '[2]—
an opinion in which he is supported by Conway,
who calls her ' an impudent Irish-faced girl '. In

[1] [*Walpole to Mann*, 5 Nov. 1741.]
[2] [*Walpole to Mann*, 22 Oct. 1741.]

the acting of Garrick, after whom all the town is
(as Gray writes [1]) 'horn-mad' in May, 1742, he
sees nothing wonderful, although he admits that
it is heresy to say so, since that infallible stage
critic, the Duke of Argyll, has declared him
superior to Betterton.    But he praises 'a little
simple farce' at Drury Lane, *Miss Lucy in Town*,
by Henry Fielding, in which his future friend,
Mrs. Clive, and Beard mimic Amorevoli and the
Muscovita.    The same letter contains a reference
to another famous stage-queen, now nearing eighty,
Anne Bracegirdle, who should have had the money
that Congreve left to Henrietta, Duchess of Marlborough.    'Tell Mr. Chute (he says) that his
friend Bracegirdle breakfasted with me this morning.    As she went out, and wanted her clogs, she
turned to me, and said, " I remember at the play-
house, they used to call, Mrs. Oldfield's chair !
Mrs. Barry's clogs ! and Mrs. Bracegirdle's pat-
tens ! " ' [2]    One pictures a handsome old lady, a
little bent, and leaning on a crutch stick as she
delivers this parting utterance at the door.[3]

[1] [*Gray to Chute*, 24 May N.S. 1742.]

[2] *Walpole to Mann*, 26 May 1742.

[3] According to Pinkerton, another anecdote connects
Mrs. Bracegirdle with the Walpoles.    'Mr. Shorter, my
mother's father [he makes Horace say], was walking down
Norfolk Street in the Strand, to his house there, just before

Among the occurrences of 1742 which find fitting record in the correspondence, is the opening of that formidable rival to Vauxhall, Ranelagh Gardens.   All through the spring the great Rotunda, with its encircling tiers of galleries and supper-boxes—the *coup d'œil* of which Johnson thought was the finest thing he had ever seen,—had been rising slowly at the side of Chelsea Hospital.   In April it was practically completed and almost ready for visitors.   Walpole of course breakfasts there like the rest of the *beau monde*.   'The building is not finished (he says), but they get great sums by people going to see it and breakfasting in the house :   there were yesterday no less than three hundred and eighty persons, at eighteenpence a-piece.   You see how poor we are, when, with a tax of four shillings in the pound, we are laying out such sums for cakes and ale.' [1]   A week or two later comes the formal inauguration.

poor Mountfort the player was killed in that street, by assassins hired by Lord Mohun. This nobleman, lying in wait for his prey, came up and embraced Mr. Shorter by mistake, saying ' Dear Mountfort ' ! It was fortunate that he was instantly undeceived, for Mr. Shorter had hardly reached his house before the murder took place ! (*Walpoliana*, 2nd ed. ii. 97). Mountfort, it will be remembered, owed his death to Mrs. Bracegirdle's liking for him.

[1] *Walpole to Mann*, 22 Apr. 1742.

'Two nights ago [1] Ranelagh Gardens were
opened at Chelsea; the Prince, Princess, Duke,
much nobility, and much mob besides, were there.
There is a vast amphitheatre, finely gilt, painted,
and illuminated, into which everybody that loves
eating, drinking, staring, or crowding, is admitted
for twelvepence. The building and disposition of
the gardens cost sixteen thousand pounds. Twice
a week there are to be ridottos, at guinea tickets,
for which you are to have a supper and music.
I was there last night—the writer adds—but did
not find the joy of it,' [2] and, at present, he prefers
Vauxhall because of the approach by water, that
'*trajet du fleuve fatal*'—as it is styled in the
*Vauxhall de Londres* which a French poet dedicated in 1769 to M. de Fontenelle. He seems,
however, to have taken Lord Orford to Ranelagh,
and he records in July that they walked with a
train at their heels like two chairmen going to
fight—from which he argues a return of his
father's popularity.[3] Two years later Fashion
has declared itself on the side of the new garden,
and Walpole has gone over to the side of Fashion.
'Every night constantly (he tells Conway) I go
to Ranelagh; which has totally beat Vauxhall.

[1] 24 May.    [2] *Walpole to Mann*, 26 May 1742.
[3] [*Walpole to Mann*, 29 July 1742.]

Nobody goes anywhere else—everybody goes there. My Lord Chesterfield is so fond of it, that he says he has ordered all his letters to be directed thither. If you had never seen it, I would make you a most pompous description of it, and tell you how the floor is all of beaten princes —that you can't set your foot without treading on a Prince of Wales or Duke of Cumberland. The company is universal : there is from his Grace of Grafton down to children out of the Foundling Hospital,—from my Lady Towns-hend to the Kitten [1]—from my Lord Sandys to your humble cousin and sincere friend.' [2]

After Lord Orford's death, the next landmark in Horace Walpole's life is his removal to the house at Twickenham, subsequently known as Strawberry Hill. To a description of this historical mansion the next chapter will be in part devoted. In the meantime, we may linger for a moment upon the record which these letters contain of the famous '45. No better opportunity will probably occur of exhibiting Walpole as the reporter of history in the process of making.

[1] [Dick Edgcumbe's mistress—see *Supplement* (vol. iii, pp. 119, 374, 382) to *Letters of Horace Walpole* (ed. Toyn-bee).]

[2] *Walpole to Conway*, 29 June 1744.

Much that he tells Mann and Montagu is no
doubt little more than the skimming of the last
*Gazette,* but he had always access to trustworthy
information, and is seldom a dull reporter even of
newspaper news.  Almost the next letter to that in
which he dwells at length upon the loss of his father,
records the disaster of Tournay or Fontenoy,[1] in
which, he tells Mann, Mr. Conway has highly
distinguished himself, magnificently engaging—
as appears from a subsequent communication [2]—
no fewer than two French grenadiers at once.
His account of the battle is bare enough ;  but
what apparently interests him most is the patriotic
conduct of the Prince of Wales, who made a
*chanson* on the occasion after the fashion of the
Regent Orleans :—

> ' VENEZ, mes chères Déesses,
> Venez calmer mon chagrin ;
> Aidez, mes belles Princesses,
> À le noyer dans le vin.
> Poussons cette douce Ivresse
> Jusqu'au milieu de la nuit,
> Et n'écoutons que la tendresse
> D'un charmant vis-à-vis.
>
> \*    \*    \*
>
> ' Que m'importe, que l'Europe

[1] [*Walpole to Mann,* 11 May 1745.]

[2] [See Walpole's note to his letter to Conway of 1 July
1745.]

Ait un, ou plusieurs tyrans ?
Prions seulement Calliope,
Qu'elle inspire nos vers, nos chants.
Laissons Mars et toute la gloire ;
Livrons-nous tous à l'amour ;
Que Bacchus nous donne à boire ;
A ces deux faisons la cour.'

The goddesses addressed were Lady Catherine Hanmer, Lady Fauconberg, and Lady Middlesex, who played Congreve's *Judgment of Paris* at Leicester House, with His Royal Highness as Paris, and Prince Lobkowitz for Mercury. Walpole says of the song that it ' miscarried in nothing but the language, the thoughts, and the poetry '. Yet he copies the whole five verses, of which the above are two, for Mann's delectation.

A more logical sequence to Fontenoy than the lyric of Leicester House, is the descent of Charles Edward upon Scotland. In August Walpole reports to Mann that there is a proclamation out ' for apprehending the Pretender's son ',[1] who had landed in July ; in September he is marching on Edinburgh.[2] Ten days later the writer is speculating half ruefully upon the possibilities of being turned out of his comfortable sinecures

[1] [*Walpole to Mann*, 7 Aug. 1745.]
[2] [*Walpole to Mann*, 6 Sept. 1745 ; and *to Sir C. H. Williams*, 21 Sept. 1745 (in *Supplement*, vol. iii, p. 387).]

H 2

in favour of some forlorn Irish Peer. ' I shall
wonderfully dislike being a loyal sufferer in a
thread-bare coat, and shivering in an ante-chamber at Hanover, or reduced to teach Latin and
English to the young princes at Copenhagen.
The Dowager Strafford has already written cards
for my Lady Nithisdale, my Lady Tullibardine,
the Duchess of Perth and Berwick, and twenty
more revived peeresses, to invite them to play at
whisk, Monday three months : for your part,
you will divert yourself with their old taffeties,
and tarnished slippers, and their awkwardness,
the first day they go to Court in shifts and clean
linen.  Will you ever write to me in my garret
at Herenhausen ? ' [1]  Then upon this come the
contradictions of rumour, the ' general supine-
ness ', the raising of regiments, and the disaster of
Preston Pans, with its inevitable condemnation of
Cope.  ' I pity poor him, who with no shining
abilities, and no experience, and no force, was
sent to fight for a crown !  He never saw a battle
but that of Dettingen, where he got his red ribbon :
Churchill, whose led-captain he was, and my Lord
Harrington, had pushed him up to this misfortune. [2]

[1] *Walpole to Montagu*, 17 Sept. 1745.

[2] Walpole later in a note to this letter revised this verdict :—' General Cope was tried afterwards for his beha-

We have lost all our artillery, five hundred men taken—and *three* killed, and several officers, as you will see in the papers. This defeat has frightened everybody but those it rejoices, and those it should frighten most; but my Lord Granville still buoys up the King's spirits, and persuades him it is nothing.' [1]

Nothing, indeed, it proved in the issue. But Walpole was wiser in his immediate apprehensions than King George's advisers, who were not wise. In his subsequent letters we get scattered glimpses of the miserable story that ended in Culloden. Towards the end of October he is auguring hopefully from the protracted neglect of the rebels to act upon their success.[2] In November they are in England.[3] But the backwardness of the Jacobites to join them is already evident, and he writes ' in the greatest confidence of our getting over this ugly business '.[4] Early in December they have reached Derby, only to be soon gone

viour in this action, and it appeared very clearly, that the Ministry, his inferior officers, and his troops, were greatly to blame ; and that he did all he could, so ill-directed, so ill-supplied, and so ill-obeyed.'

[1] *Walpole to Mann,* 27 Sept. 1745.
[2] [*Walpole to Mann,* 21 Oct. 1745.]
[3] [*Walpole to Mann,* 15 Nov. 1745.]
[4] [*Walpole to Mann,* 29 Nov. 1745.]

again, miserably harassed, and leaving their sick and cannon behind.[1]   With the new year come tidings to Mann that the rebellion is dying down in England, and that General Hawley has marched northward to put it quite out.[2]   Once more, on the 17th January, it flares fitfully at Falkirk,[3] and then fades as suddenly.   The battle that Walpole hourly expects, not without some trepidation, for Conway is one of the Duke of Cumberland's aides-de-camp, is still deferred, and it is April before the two armies face each other on Culloden Moor.   Then he writes jubilantly to his Florentine correspondent :—' On the 16th, the Duke, by forced marches, came up with the rebels, a little on this side Inverness—by the way, the battle is not christened yet ;   I only know that neither Preston Pans nor Falkirk are to be godfathers.   The rebels, who had fled from him after their victory,[4] and durst not attack him, when so much exposed to them at his passage of the Spey, now stood him, they seven thousand, he ten. They broke through Barril's regiment and killed Lord Robert Kerr, a handsome young gentleman, who was cut to pieces with about thirty wounds ;

[1] [*Walpole to Mann*, 9 Dec. 1745.]
[2] [*Walpole to Mann*, 3 Jan. 1746.]
[3] [*Walpole to Mann*, 28 Jan. 1746.]        [4] At Falkirk.

but they were soon repulsed, and fled; the whole engagement not lasting above a quarter of an hour. The young Pretender escaped; Mr. Conway says, he hears, wounded: he certainly was in the rear. They have lost above a thousand men in the engagement and pursuit; and six hundred were already taken; among which latter are their French Ambassador and Earl Kilmarnock. The Duke of Perth and Lord Ogilvie are said to be slain. . . . Except Lord Robert Kerr, we lost nobody of note: Sir Robert Rich's eldest son has lost his hand, and about a hundred and thirty private men fell. The defeat is reckoned total, and the dispersion general; and all their artillery is taken. It is a brave young Duke! The town is all blazing round me,[1] as I write, with fire works and illuminations: I have some inclination to lap up half a dozen skyrockets, to make you drink the Duke's health. Mr. Dodington,[2] on the first report, came out with a very pretty illumination; so pretty, that I believe he had it by him, ready for *any* occasion.' [3]

Walpole's account of these occurrences is, of course, hearsay, although, as regards Culloden, he probably derived the details from Conway,

[1] In Arlington Street.     [2] In Pall Mall.
[3] *Walpole to Mann*, 25 Apr. 1746.

who was present. But in some of the events which ensued, he is either actually a spectator himself, or fresh from direct communication with those who have been spectators. One of the most graphic passages in his entire correspondence is his description of the trial of the rebel lords, at which he assisted; and another is his narrative of the executions of Kilmarnock and Balmerino, written down from the relation of eye-witnesses. It is hardly possible to get much nearer to history.

' I am this moment come from the conclusion of the greatest and most melancholy scene I ever yet saw ! You will easily guess it was the trials of the rebel Lords. As it was the most interesting sight, it was the most solemn and fine : a coronation is a puppet-show, and all the splendour of it idle ; but this sight at once feasted one's eyes and engaged all one's passions. It began last Monday ; three parts of Westminster Hall were inclosed with galleries, and hung with scarlet; and the whole ceremony was conducted with the most awful solemnity and decency, except in the one point of leaving the prisoners at the bar, amidst the idle curiosity of some crowd, and even with the witnesses who had sworn against them, while the Lords adjourned to their own House to consult. No part of the royal family was there, which was a proper regard to the unhappy men, who were become their victims. . . . I had armed myself with all the resolution I could, with the thought of their crimes and of the danger past, and was assisted by the sight of the Marquis of Lothian in weepers for his son [1] who fell at Culloden—but the first appearance of the prisoners shocked me! their behaviour melted me!' After going on to speak of Lord Kilmarnock and Lord Cromartie (afterwards reprieved) he continues :—

'For Lord Balmerino, he is the most natural brave old fellow I ever saw : the highest intrepidity, even to indifference. At the bar he behaved like a soldier and a man ; in the intervals of form, with carelessness and humour. He pressed extremely to have his wife, his pretty Peggy,[2] with him in the Tower. . . . Lady Cromartie only sees her husband through the grate, not choosing to be shut up with him, as she thinks she can serve him better by her intercession without : she is big with child and very handsome : so are their daughters. When they were to be brought from the Tower in separate coaches, there was some dispute in which the axe must go—old Balmerino cried, "Come, come, put it with me." At the bar he plays with his fingers upon the axe, while he

[1] Lord Robert Kerr.    [2] Margaret Chalmers.

talks to the gentleman-gaoler; and one day somebody coming up to listen, he took the blade and
held it like a fan between their faces. During the
trial, a little boy was near him, but not tall enough
to see; he made room for the child and placed him
near himself.' [1]

Balmerino's gallant demeanour evidently fascinated Walpole. In his next letter [2] he relates
how on his way back to the Tower the sturdy old
dragoon had stopped the coach at Charing Cross
to buy some 'honey-blobs' (gooseberries); and
when afterwards he comes to write his account
of the execution, although he tells the story of
Kilmarnock's death with feeling, the best passage
is given to his companion in misfortune. He
describes how, on the fatal 15th August, before
he left the Tower, Balmerino drank a bumper to
King James; how he wore his rebellious regi-
mentals (blue and red) over a flannel waistcoat
and his shroud; how embracing Lord Kilmarnock he said, ' My Lord, I wish I could suffer
for both ! ' Then followed the beheading of
Kilmarnock, and the narrator goes on :—' The
scaffold was immediately new-strewed with saw-
dust, the block new-covered, the executioner

[1] *Walpole to Mann*, 1 Aug. 1746.
[2] [*Walpole to Montagu*, 2 Aug. 1746.]

new-dressed, and a new axe brought. Then came old Balmerino, treading with the air of a general. As soon as he mounted the scaffold, he read the inscription on his coffin, as he did again afterwards : he then surveyed the spectators, who were in amazing numbers, even upon masts upon ships in the river ; and pulling out his spectacles read a treasonable speech, which he delivered to the Sheriff, and said, the young Pretender was so sweet a Prince, that flesh and blood could not resist following him ; and lying down to try the block, he said, " If I had a thousand lives, I would lay them all down here in the same cause." He said if he had not taken the sacrament the day before, he would have knocked down Williamson, the Lieutenant of the Tower, for his ill-usage of him. He took the axe and felt it, and asked the headsman how many blows he had given Lord Kilmarnock ; and gave him three guineas. Two clergymen, who attended him, coming up, he said, " No, gentlemen, I believe you have already done me all the service you can." Then he went to the corner of the scaffold, and called very loud for the warder, to give him his perriwig, which he took off, and put on a night-cap of Scotch plaid, and then pulled off his coat and waistcoat and lay down ; but being told he was on the wrong side, vaulted round, and immediately gave the sign by tossing up his arm, as if he were giving the signal for battle.   He received three blows, but the first certainly took away all sensation.   He was not a quarter of an hour on the scaffold ; Lord Kilmarnock above half a one.   Balmerino certainly died with the intrepidity of a hero, but with the insensibility of one too.   As he walked from his prison to execution, seeing every window and top of house filled with spectators, he cried out, " Look, look, how they are all piled up like rotten oranges ! " ' [1]

In the old print of the execution, the scaffold on Tower Hill is shown surrounded by a wide square of dragoons, beyond which the crowd— ' the immense display of human countenances which surrounded it like a sea ', as Scott has it —are visible on every side.   No. 14 Tower Hill

---

[1] *Walpole to Mann*, 21 Aug. 1746.   Gray, who was at the trial, also mentions Balmerino, not so enthusiastically. ' He is an old soldier-like man, of a vulgar manner and aspect, speaks the broadest Scotch, and shews an intrepidity, that some ascribe to real courage, and some to brandy ' (*Letter to Wharton*, Aug.).   ' Old Balmerino, when he had read his paper to the people, pulled off his spectacles, spit upon his handkerchief, and wiped them clean for the use of his posterity ; and that is the last page of his history ' (*Letter to Wharton*, 11 Sept. 1746).

is said to have been the house from which the two lords were led to the block, and a trail of blood along the hall and up the first flight of stairs was long shown as indicating the route by which the mutilated bodies were borne to await interment in St. Peter's Chapel. A few months later Walpole records the execution in the same place of Simon Fraser, Lord Lovat, the cunning old Jacobite whose characteristic attitude and 'pawky' expression live for ever in the admirable sketch which Hogarth made of him at St. Albans. He died (says Walpole) 'extremely well, without passion, affectation, buffoonery, or timidity'.[1] But he is not so distinguished as either Kilmarnock or Balmerino, and, however Roman his taking-off, the chief memorable thing about it is, that it was happily the last of these sanguinary scenes in this country. The only other incident which it is here needful to chronicle in connection with the 'Forty Five' is Walpole's verses on the Suppression of the late Rebellion. On the 4th and 5th November, the anniversaries of King William's birth and landing, it was the custom to play Rowe's *Tamerlane*, and on the 4th this year (1746) the epilogue spoken by Mrs. Pritchard 'in the Character of the Comic Muse' was from

[1] [*Walpole to Mann*, 10 Apr. 1747.]

Walpole's pen.   According to the writer special
terrors had threatened the stage from the advent
of ' Rome's young missionary spark ', the Chevalier, and the Tragic Muse, raising, ' to eyes well-
tutor'd in the trade of grief,' ' a small and well-
lac'd handkerchief,' is represented by her lighter
sister as bewailing the prospect to her ' buskined
progeny ' after this fashion :—

> ' Ah ! sons, our dawn is over-cast, and all
> Theatric glories nodding to their fall.
> From foreign realms a bloody chief is come,
> Big with the work of slav'ry and of Rome.
> A general ruin on his sword he wears,
> Fatal alike to audience and to play'rs.
> For ah ! my sons, what freedom for the stage,
> When bigotry with sense shall battle wage ?
> When monkish laureats only wear the bays,
> Inquisitors lord chamberlains of plays ?
> Plays shall be damn'd that 'scap'd the critic's rage,
> For priests are still worse tyrants to the stage.
> Cato, receiv'd by audiences so gracious,
> Shall find ten Caesars in one St. Ignatius :
> And godlike Brutus here shall meet again
> His evil genius in a capuchin.
> For heresy the fav'rites of the pit
> Must burn, and excommunicated wit ;
> And at one stake we shall behold expire
> My Anna Bullen, and the Spanish Fryar.' [1]

After this the epilogue digresses into a com-

[1] *Works of Lord Orford* (1798), i. 25–7.

parison of the Duke of Cumberland with King William. Virgil, Juvenal, Addison, Dryden, and Pope, upon one of whose lines on Cibber Walpole bases his reference to the Lord Chamberlain, are all laid under contribution in this performance. It 'succeeded to flatter me '—he tells Mann, to whom he sent a copy of it a few days later,[1]—a Gallicism from which we must infer an enthusiastic reception.

Walpole's personal and domestic history does not present much interest at this period. His sister Mary (Catherine Shorter's daughter), who had married the Hon. George Cholmondeley,[2] had died long before her mother. In February, 1746, his half-sister, Lady Mary, his playmate at comet in the Houghton days, married Mr. Churchill— ' a foolish match ', in Horace's opinion, with which he has nothing to do.[3] With his second brother, Sir Edward Walpole, he seems to have had but little intercourse, and that scarcely of a fraternal character. In 1857, Cunningham published for the first time a very angry letter from Edward to his junior, in which the latter was

---

[1] [*Walpole to Mann*, 12 Nov. 1746.]
[2] [Subsequently (in 1733, two years after his wife's death) third Earl of Cholmondeley.]
[3] [*Walpole to Mann*, 6 Sept. 1745.]

bitterly reproached for his interference in disposing of the family borough of Castle Rising, and (incidentally) for his assumption of superiority, mental and otherwise.  To this communication Walpole prepared a most caustic and categorical answer, which, however, he never sent.[1]  For his nieces, Edward Walpole's natural daughters, of whom it will be more convenient to speak later, Horace seems always to have felt a sincere regard.  But although his brother had tastes which must have been akin to his own, for Edward Walpole was in his way an art patron (Roubiliac the sculptor, for instance, was much indebted to him) and a respectable musician, no real cordiality ever existed between them.  'There is nothing in the world'—he tells Montagu (25 May 1745)—'the Baron of Englefield [2] has such an aversion for as for his brother.' [3]

For his eldest brother's wife, the Lady Walpole who had formed one of the learned trio at Florence, he entertained no kind of respect, and his letters

[1] [It is printed in *Letters* (ed. Toynbee), vol. ii, pp. 91–6 ; the reply, very brief, actually sent, is dated 17 May 1745.]

[2] Englefield, i.e. Englefield Green, in Berkshire, on the summit of Cooper's Hill, near Windsor, where Edward Walpole lived.

[3] [In later life they were on friendly terms—see the letters exchanged between them in *Supplement* (vols. i and iii) to *Letters of Horace Walpole* (ed. Toynbee).]

are full of flouts at her Ladyship's manners and
morality. Indeed, between *préciosité* and ' Platonic
love ', her life does not appear to have been a particularly worshipful one, and her long sojourn
under Italian skies had not improved her. At
present she was Lady Orford, her husband, who
is seldom mentioned, and from whom she had
been living apart, having succeeded to the title
at his father's death. From Walpole's letters to
Mann, it seems that in April 1745, she was, much
to the dismay of her relatives, already preening
her wings for England. In September, she has
arrived, and Walpole is maliciously delighted at
the cold welcome she obtains from the Court
and from society in general, with the exception
of her old colleague, Lady Pomfret, and, that
in one sense congenial spirit, Lady Townshend.[1]
Later on, a definite separation from her husband
appears to have been agreed upon, which Walpole
fondly hopes may have the effect of bringing about
her departure for Italy. ' The Ladies O[rford]
and T[ownshend] '—he says—' have exhausted
scandal both in their persons and conversations.' [2]
However much this may be exaggerated (and
Walpole never spares his antipathies), the last we

[1] [*Walpole to Mann*, 6, 20, 27 Sept. 1745.]
[2] [*Walpole to Mann*, 17 Jan., 7 Feb., 6, 21 Mar. 1746.]

I

hear of Lady Orford is certainly on his side—for she has retired from town to a villa near Richmond with a lover for whom she has postponed that southward flight which her family so ardently desired.[1]   This fortunate Endymion, the Hon. Sewallis Shirley, son of Robert, first Earl Ferrers, had already been one of the most favoured lovers of the notorious ' lady of quality ' whose memoirs were afterwards foisted into *Peregrine Pickle*. To Lady Vane now succeeded Lady Orford, as eminent for wealth—says sarcastic Lady Mary Wortley Montagu—as her predecessor had been for beauty, and equal in her ' heroic contempt for shame '. This new connection was destined to endure.   It was in September 1746, that Walpole chronicled his sister-in-law's latest frailty, and on May 25th 1751, only a few weeks after her husband's death,[2] she married Shirley at the Rev. Alexander Keith's convenient ' little chapel in May Fair '.

In 1744, died Alexander Pope, to be followed a year later by the great Dean of St. Patrick's. Neither of these events leaves any lasting mark in Walpole's correspondence, indeed of Swift's death there is no mention at all.   A nearer bereave-

---

[1] [*Walpole to Mann*, 15 Sept. 1746.]
[2] Robert Walpole, second Earl of Orford, Horace Walpole's eldest brother, died 31 Mar. 1751.

ment was the premature loss of West, which had taken place two years before,[1] closing sorrowfully with faint accomplishment a life of promise. *Vale, et vive paullisper cum vivis*—he had written a few days earlier to Gray—his friend to the last.[2] With Gray, Walpole's friendship, as will be seen presently had been resumed. His own literary essays still lie chiefly in the domain of squib and *jeu d'esprit*. In April 1746, over the appropriate signature of ' Descartes ', he printed in No. II of *The Museum* a ' Scheme for Raising a Large Sum of Money for the Use of the Government, by laying a tax on Message-Cards and Notes ', and in No. V a pretended Advertisement and Table of Contents for a *History of Good Breeding, from the Creation of the World,* by the Author of the Whole Duty of Man. The wit of this is a little laboured, and scarcely goes beyond the announcement that ' The Eight last Volumes, which relate to *Germany,* may be had separate ', nor does that of the other exceed a mild reflection of Fielding's manner in some of his minor pieces. Among other things, we gather that it was the

---

[1] [1 June 1742.]
[2] [For West's friendship with Walpole and Gray, see *Correspondence of Gray, Walpole, West, and Ashton* (ed. Toynbee).]

custom of the fine ladies of the day to send open
messages on blank playing-cards, and it is stated as a
fact or a fancy that 'after the fatal day of Fontenoy',
persons of quality 'all wrote their notes on Indian
paper, which being red, when inscribed with Japan
ink, made a melancholy military kind of elegy on
the brave youths who occasioned the fashion, and
were often the honourable subject of the epistle '.[1]
The only remaining effort of any importance at
this time is the little poem of *The Beauties*, somewhat recalling Gay's Prologue to the *Shepherd's
Week*, and written in July 1746, to Eckardt the
painter.    Here is a specimen :—

> ' In smiling CAPEL's bounteous look
> Rich autumn's goddess is mistook.
> With poppies and with spiky corn,
> Eckardt, her nut-brown curls adorn ;
> And by her side, in decent line,
> Place charming BERKELEY, Proserpine.
> Mild as a summer sea, serene,
> In dimpled beauty next be seen
> AYLESB'RY, like hoary Neptune's queen.
>     With her the light-dispensing fair,
> Whose beauty gilds the morning air,
> And bright as her attendant sun,
> The new Aurora, LYTTELTON.
> Such Guido's pencil beauty-tip'd,
> And in ethereal colours dip'd,

[1] [These two pieces are printed in *Works of Lord Orford*
(1798), i. 132–9, 141–5.]

In measur'd dance to tuneful song
Drew the sweet goddess, as along
Heaven's azure 'neath their light feet spread,
The buxom hours the fairest led.' [1]

' Charming Berkeley,' here mentioned, afterwards became the third wife of Goldsmith's friend, Earl Nugent, and the mother of the little girl who played tricks upon the author of *She Stoops to Conquer* at her father's country seat of Gosfield ; ' Aylesb'ry, like hoary Neptune's queen,' married Walpole's friend, Conway, and ' the new Aurora, Lyttelton,' was that engaging Lucy Fortescue upon whose death in 1747 her husband wrote the monody so pitilessly parodied by Smollett.[2] Lady Almeria Carpenter, Lady Emily Lenox, Miss Chudleigh (afterwards the notorious Duchess of Kingston), and many other well-known names, *quos nunc perscribere longum est*, are also celebrated.

On the 12th of August 1746 Walpole an-

[1] *Works of Lord Orford* (1798), i. 21–2.
[2] Writing to Walpole 3 Mar. 1751, Gray says—' In the last volume [of *Peregrine Pickle*] is a character of Mr. Lyttelton, under the name of " Gosling Scrag ", and a parody of part of his Monody, under the notion of a pastoral on the death of his grandmother '.—[See *Correspondence of Gray, Walpole, West, and Ashton*, vol. ii, pp. 108–9. It was absurdly stated in Shenstone's *Letters* that Gray's ode on the death of Walpole's cat was also written in ridicule of Lyttelton's *Monody* (see *Walpole to Cole*, 14 June 1769).]

nounces to Mann that he has taken 'a pretty house at Windsor', to which he is going for the remainder of the summer; [1] and he dates from there to him on August 21st.    In September Gray writes to Wharton from Stoke that he sees Walpole 'usually once a week'.[2]    All is mighty free, and even friendly more than one could expect' [3]—and one of the first things posted off to Conway is Gray's *Ode on a Distant Prospect of Eton College*, which the sender desires he 'will please to like excessively'.[4]    He is drawn from his retreat by the arrival of a young Florentine acquaintance, the Marquis Rinuncini, to whom he has to do the London honours.    'I stayed literally an entire week with him, carried him to see palaces and Richmond Gardens and Park, and Chenevix's shop, and talked a great deal to him *alle conversazioni*.' [5]    'Chenevix's shop' suggests the main subject of the next chapter— the purchase and occupation of Strawberry Hill.

[1] [See also *to Montagu*, 11 Aug.    In his *Short Notes* Walpole says the house was 'within the precincts of the Castle'.]          [2] [*Gray to Wharton*, 11 Sept. 1746.]

[3] [*Gray to Wharton*, 13 Aug. 1746.]

[4] [*Walpole to Conway*, 3 Oct. 1746.]

[5] *Walpole to Mann*, 15 Sept. 1746.

# CHAPTER V

# V

ON the 5th of June 1747 Walpole announces to Mann that he has taken a little new farm, just out of Twickenham. 'The house is so small, that I can send it to you in a letter to look at: the prospect is as delightful as possible, commanding the river, the town,[1] and Richmond Park; and being situated on a hill descends to the Thames through two or three little meadows, where I have some Turkish sheep and two cows, all studied in their colours for becoming the view. This little rural *bijou* was Mrs. Chenevix's, the toy-woman *à la mode*,[2] who in every dry season is to furnish me with the best rain-water from Paris, and now

[1] Twickenham.

[2] She was the sister of Pope's Mrs. Bertrand, an equally fashionable toy-woman at Bath. Her shop, according to an advertisement in the *Daily Journal* for May 24, 1733, was then 'against Suffolk Street, Charing Cross'. It is mentioned in Fielding's *Amelia*. When, in Bk. viii, ch. i, Mr. Bondum the bailiff contrives to capture Captain Booth, it is by a false report that his Lady has been 'taken violently ill, and carried into Mrs. *Chenevix's* Toy-shop'. It is also mentioned in the Hon. Mrs. Osborne's *Letters*, 1891, p. 73; and again by Walpole himself in the *World* for 19 Dec. 1754.

and then with some Dresden china cows, who are to figure like wooden classics in a library : so I shall grow as much a shepherd as any swain in the *Astraea.*'    Three days later, further details are added in a letter to Conway, then in Flanders with the Duke of Cumberland :—' You perceive by my date [1] that I am got into a new camp, and have left my tub at Windsor.    It is a little play-thing-house that I got out of Mrs. Chenevix's shop, and is the prettiest bauble you ever saw. It is set in enamelled meadows, with filagree hedges :

> " A small Euphrates through the piece is roll'd,
> And little finches wave their wings in gold." [2]

' Two delightful roads, that you would call dusty, supply me continually with coaches and chaises : barges as solemn as Barons of the Exchequer move under my window ; Richmond Hill and Ham Walks bound my prospect ; . . . Dowagers as plenty as flounders inhabit all around, and Pope's ghost is just now skimming under my window by a most poetical moonlight.    I have about land enough to keep such a farm as Noah's,

[1] Twickenham, June 8.

[2] This is slightly varied from ll. 29–30 of Pope's fifth *Moral Essay* (' To Mr. Addison : Occasioned by his Dialogues on Medals ').

when he set up in the ark with a pair of each kind; but my cottage is rather cleaner than I believe his was after they had been cooped up together forty days. The Chenevixes had tricked it out for themselves: up two pair of stairs is what they call Mr. Chenevix's library, furnished with three maps, one shelf, a bust of Sir Isaac Newton, and a lame telescope without any glasses. Lord John Sackville *predecessed* me here, and instituted certain games called *cricketalia*, which have been celebrated this very evening in honour of him in a neighbouring meadow.' [1]

The house thus whimsically described, which grew into the Gothic structure afterwards so closely associated with its owner's name, was not, even at this date, without its history. It stood on the left bank of the Thames, at the corner of the Upper Road to Teddington, not very far from Twickenham itself. It had been built about 1698 as a ' country box ' by a retired coachman of the Earl of Bradford, and, from the fact that he was supposed to have acquired his means by starving his master's horses, was known popularly as Chopped-Straw Hall. Its earliest possessor not long afterwards let it out as a lodging-house, and finally, after several improvements, sub-let it

[1] *Walpole to Conway*, 8 June 1747.

altogether.   One of its first tenants was Colley
Cibber, who found it convenient when he was in
attendance for acting at Hampton Court ; and he
is said to have written in it the comedy called *The
Refusal ; or, the Ladies' Philosophy*, produced at
Drury Lane in 1721.   Then, for eight years, it
was rented by the Bishop of Durham, Dr. Talbot,
who was reported to have kept in it a better table
than the extent of its kitchen seemed, in Walpole's
judgment, to justify.   After the Bishop came a
Marquis, Henry Brydges, son of the Duke of
Chandos ;   after the Marquis, Mrs. Chenevix,
the toy-woman who, upon her husband's death, let
it for two years to the nobleman who *predecessed*
Walpole, Lord John Philip Sackville.   Before
this Mrs. Chenevix had taken lodgers, one of
whom was the celebrated theologian, Père Le
Courayer.   In May 1747, at the expiration of
Lord John Sackville's tenancy, Walpole took the
remainder of Mrs. Chenevix's lease ; and in 1749
had grown to like the situation so much that he
obtained a special act to purchase the fee simple
from the existing possessors, three minors of
the name of Mortimer.[1]   The price he paid was

[1] [For the above details, see Walpole's *Description of
Strawberry Hill*, printed in *Works of Lord Orford* (1798),
ii. 393–516.]

£1356 10s.[1]   Nothing was then wanting but the name, and in looking over some old deeds this was supplied.   He found that the ground on which it stood had been known originally as ' Strawberry-Hill-Shot '.   ' You shall hear from me ', he tells Mann in June 1748, ' from *Strawberry Hill*, which I have found out in my lease is the old name of my house;  so pray, never call it Twickenham again.'

The transformation of the toy-woman's ' villa-kin ' into a Gothic residence was not, however, the operation of a day.   Indeed, at first, the idea of re-building does not seem to have entered its new owner's mind.   But he speedily set about extending his boundaries, for by 26 December 1748, as he tells Mann, he has added nine acres to his original five, making fourteen in all—a ' territory prodigious in a situation where land is so scarce '.[2]   Among the

---

[1] [This sum, as appears from the Act of Parliament (for which Walpole paid £100), was the price paid, not for Strawberry Hill alone, but for the whole of the Mortimer estate, which included various parcels of land, etc. in Willesden.   In Walpole's private accounts the sum paid (in Sept. 1749) for the Strawberry Hill estate is entered as £776 10s. 0d. the balance (£580) of the purchase money was no doubt in respect of the Willesden portion of the estate. (See *Strawberry Hill Accounts*, ed. Paget Toynbee, pp. 47–8).]

[2] [Walpole continued to make further purchases of land, as opportunities offered, during the next forty years, so that

tenants of some of the buildings which he acquired
in making these additions was Richard Francklin,
the printer of the *Craftsman,* who, during Sir Robert
Walpole's administration, had been taken up for
printing that paper.    He occupied a small house in
what was afterwards known as the Flower Garden,
and Walpole permitted him to retain it during his
lifetime.    Walpole's letters towards the close of
1748 contain numerous references to his assiduity
in planting.    ' My present and sole occupation ',
he says in August, ' is planting, in which I have
made great progress, and talk very learnedly with
the nurserymen, except that now and then a
lettuce run to seed overturns all my botany, as
I have more than once taken it for a curious West
Indian flowering shrub.  Then the deliberation
with which trees grow, is extremely inconvenient
to my natural impatience.' [1]   Two months later
he is ' all plantation, and sprouts away like any
chaste   nymph   in   the   *Metamorphosis* '.[2]    In

at the time of his death in 1797 his estate comprised close on
forty-seven acres, which cost him first and last not far short
of £4000.  (See *Strawberry Hill Accounts,* pp. 48–50).  His
total expenditure on Strawberry Hill, including land, building, and furnishing, down to the end of 1795, according to
the *Accounts,* amounted to well over £20,000 (*op. cit.,* p. 21).]

[1] [*Walpole to Conway,* 29 Aug. 1748.]
[2] [*Walpole to Montagu,* 20 Oct. 1748.]

December, we begin to hear of that famous lawn so well known in the later history of the house. He is 'making a terrace the whole breadth of his garden on the brow of a natural hill, with meadows at the foot, and commanding the river, the village,[1] Richmond Hill, and the Park, and part of Kingston '.[2] A year after this, while he is still ' digging and planting till it is dark ',[3] come the first hints of the future building.[4] At Cheneys, in Buckinghamshire, he has seen some old stained glass, in the windows of an ancient house which had been degraded into a farm, and he thinks he will beg it of the Duke of Bedford (to whom the farm belongs), as it would be ' magnificent for Strawberry-castle '. Evidently he has discussed this (as yet) *château en Espagne* with Montagu. ' Did I tell you (he says) that I have found a text in Deuteronomy to authorise my future battlements ? " When thou buildest a new house, then shalt thou make a battlement for thy roof, that thou bring not blood upon thy house, if any man fall from thence." ' [3] In January, the new build-

1 Twickenham. 2 [*Walpole to Mann*, 26 Dec. 1748.]

3 [*Walpole to Montagu*, 28 Sept. 1749.]

4 [As early as Aug. 1748 he had built a new kitchen (eventually converted into the Waiting Room), and had started on a new room (afterwards known as the Breakfast Room). (See *Strawberry Hill Accounts*, pp. 1, 34.)]

ing is an established fact, as far as purpose is concerned.   In a postscript to Mann he writes :—
' I must trouble you with a commission, which I
don't know whether you can execute.   I am going
to build a little gothic castle at Strawberry Hill.
If you can pick me up any fragments of old painted
glass, arms, or anything, I shall be excessively
obliged to you.   I can't say I remember any
such things in Italy ;  but out of old chateaus, I
imagine, one might get it cheap, if there is any.' [1]

From a subsequent letter it would seem that
Mann, as a resident in Italy, had rather expostu-
lated against the style of architecture which his
friend was about to adopt, and had suggested the
Grecian.   But Walpole, rightly or wrongly, knew
what he intended.   ' The Grecian ', he said, was
' only proper for magnificent and public buildings.   Columns and all their beautiful ornaments
look ridiculous when crowded into a closet or a
cheesecake-house.   The variety is little, and
admits no charming irregularities.   I am almost
as fond of the *Sharawaggi*, or Chinese want of
symmetry, in buildings, as in grounds or gardens.
I am sure, whenever you come to England, you
will be pleased with the liberty of taste into which
we are struck, and of which you can have no

[1] [*Walpole to Mann,* 10 Jan. 1750.]

idea.' [1]  The passage shows that he himself anticipated some of the ridicule which was levelled by
unsympathetic people at the ' oyster-grotto-like
profanation ' which he gradually erected by the
Thames.  In the meantime it went on progress-
ing slowly, as its progress was entirely dependent
on his savings out of income, and the references
to it in his letters, perhaps because Mann was
doubtful, are not abundant.  ' The library, and
refectory or great parlour', he says in his *Description*, ' were entirely new built in 1753; the gallery,
round tower, great cloister, and cabinet, in 1760
and 1761 ; and the great north bed-chamber in
1770.' [2]  To speak of these later alterations would
be to anticipate too much, and the further description of Strawberry Hill will be best deferred until
his own account of the house and contents was
printed in 1774, four years after the last addition
above recorded.  But even before he made the
earliest of them, he must have done much to alter
and improve the aspect of the place, for Gray,
more admiring than Mann, praises what has been
done.  ' I am glad ', he tells Wharton, ' that you
enter into the spirit of Strawberry-castle.  It has
a purity and propriety of Gothicism in it (with

[1] [*Walpole to Mann,* 25 Feb. 1750.]
[2] [*Works of Lord Orford,* ii. 400.]

**K**

very few exceptions) that I have not seen elsewhere'; [1] and in an earlier letter [2] he implies
that its 'extreme littleness' is its chief defect.
But here, before for the moment leaving the
subject, it is only fair to give the proprietor's
own description of Strawberry Hill at this date,
i.e., in June 1753. After telling Mann that it
is 'so monastic' that he has 'a little hall decked
with long saints in lean arched windows and with
taper columns, which we call the Paraclete, in
memory of Eloisa's cloister', [3] he sends him a
sketch of it, and goes on :—'The enclosed en-
chanted little landscape, then, is Strawberry Hill.
. . . This view of the castle [4] is what I have just
finished, and is the only side that will be at all
regular. Directly before it is an open grove,
through which you see a field, which is bounded
by a serpentine wood of all kind of trees, and
flowering shrubs, and flowers. The lawn before

---

[1] [18 Sept. 1754.]          [2] [13 Aug. 1754.]

[3] [*Walpole to Mann*, 27 Apr. 1753.] In the Tribune (see
chap. viii) was a drawing by Mr. Bentley, representing two
lovers in a church looking at the tombs of Abelard and
Eloisa, and illustrating Pope's lines :—

'If ever chance two wand'ring lovers brings
To Paraclete's white walls and silver springs,' etc.

[4] Walpole notes, 'It was a view of the South Side towards
the north-east'.

the house is situated on the top of a small hill, from whence to the left you see the town and church of Twickenham encircling a turn of the river, that looks exactly like a seaport in miniature. The opposite shore is a most delicious meadow, bounded by Richmond Hill, which loses itself in the noble woods of the Park to the end of the prospect on the right, where is another turn of the river, and the suburbs of Kingston as luckily placed as Twickenham is on the left : and a natural terrace on the brow of my hill, with meadows of my own down to the river, commands both extremities. Is not this a tolerable prospect ? You must figure that all this is perpetually enlivened by a navigation of boats and barges, and by a road below my terrace, with coaches, post-chaises, waggons, and horsemen constantly in motion, and the fields speckled with cows, horses, and sheep. Now you shall walk into the house. The bow-window below leads into a little parlour hung with a stone-colour Gothic paper and Jackson's Venetian prints,[1] which I could never endure while they pretended, infamous as they are, to be

[1] The chiaroscuros of John Baptist Jackson, published at Venice in 1742. At this date he had returned to England, and was working in a paper-hanging manufactory at Battersea.

after Titian, &c., but when I gave them this air of barbarous bas-reliefs, they succeeded to a miracle : it is impossible at first sight not to conclude that they contain the history of Attila or Tottila done about the very aera.    From hence, under two gloomy arches, you come to the hall and stair-case, which it is impossible to describe to you, as it is the most particular and chief beauty of the castle.    Imagine the walls covered with (I call it paper, but it is really paper painted in perspective to represent) Gothic fretwork : the lightest Gothic balustrade to the staircase, adorned with antelopes (our supporters) bearing shields ;    lean windows fattened with rich saints in painted glass, and a vestibule open with three arches on the landing-place, and niches full of trophies of old coats of mail, Indian shields made of rhinoceros's hides, broadswords, quivers, long bows, arrows, and spears—all *supposed* to be taken by Sir Terry Robsart [1] in the holy wars.    But as none of this regards the enclosed drawing, I will pass to that. The room on the ground-floor nearest to you is a bedchamber, hung with yellow paper and prints, framed in a new manner, invented by Lord Cardigan ;    that is, with black and white borders printed.    Over this is Mr. Chute's bed-

[1] An ancestor of Sir Robert Walpole.

chamber, hung with red in the same manner. The bow-window room one pair of stairs is not yet finished; but in the tower beyond it is the charming closet where I am now writing to you. It is hung with green paper and water-colour pictures; has two windows; the one in the drawing looks to the garden, the other to the beautiful prospect; and the top of each glutted with the richest painted glass of the arms of England, crimson roses, and twenty other pieces of green, purple, and historic bits. I must tell you, by the way, that the castle, when finished, will have two-and-thirty windows enriched with painted glass. In this closet, which is Mr. Chute's College of Arms, are two presses of books of heraldry and antiquities, Madame Sévigné's Letters, and any French books that relate to her and her acquaintance. Out of this closet is the room where we always live, hung with a blue and white paper in stripes adorned with festoons, and a thousand plump chairs, couches, and luxurious settees covered with linen of the same pattern, and with a bow-window commanding the prospect, and gloomed with limes that shade half each window, already darkened with painted glass in chiaroscuro, set in deep blue glass. Under this room is a cool little hall, where we generally dine, hung with paper to imitate Dutch tiles.

' I have described so much that you will begin to think that all the accounts I used to give you of the diminutiveness of our habitation were fabulous; but it is really incredible how small most of the rooms are. The only two good chambers I shall have are not yet built: they will be an eating-room and a library, each twenty by thirty, and the latter fifteen feet high. For the rest of the house, I could send it to you in this letter as easily as the drawing, only that I should have no where to live until the return of the post. The Chinese summer-house, which you may distinguish in the distant landscape, belongs to my Lord Radnor.[1] We pique ourselves upon nothing but simplicity, and have no carvings, gildings, paintings, inlayings, or tawdry businesses.' [2]

From this it will appear that in June 1753, the library and refectory were not yet built, so that when he says in the printed *Descrip-*

[1] Lord Radnor's fantastic house on the river, which Walpole nicknamed Mabland, came between Strawberry Hill and Pope's Villa, and is a conspicuous object in old views of Twickenham, notably in that, dated 1757, by Müntz, a Swiss artist, for some time domiciled at Strawberry Hill (see below, p. 154). It was in the garden of Radnor House that Pope first met Warburton.

[2] *Walpole to Mann*, 12 June 1753.

*tion* [1] that they were new built in 1753, he must mean no more than that they had been begun. In a later letter [2] (of May 18, 1754) they were still unfinished. Meanwhile the house is gradually attracting more and more attention. George Montagu comes and is ' in raptures and screams, and hoops, and hollas, and dances, and crosses himself a thousand times over '.[3] The next visitor is ' Nolkejumskoi '—otherwise the Duke of Cumberland, whom Walpole likens to a gracious Gulliver surveying a castle in Lilliput.[4] Afterwards, attracted by the reports of Lady Hervey and Mr. Bristow (brother of the Countess of Buckingham), arrives my Lord Bath, who is stirred into celebrating it to the tune of a song of Bubb Dodington on Mrs. Strawbridge. His Lordship does not seem to have got further than two stanzas ; but Walpole, not to leave so complimentary a tribute in the depressed condition of a fragment, discreetly revised and completed it himself. The lines may fairly find a place here as an example of his lighter muse. The first and third verses are Lord Bath's, the rest being obviously

---

[1] [See above, p. 129.]
[2] [To Richard Bentley.]
[3] [*Walpole to Bentley*, 2 Mar. 1754.]
[4] [*Walpole to Bentley*, 17 July 1755.]

written in order to bring in ' Nolkejumskoi ' and
some personal friends :—

> ' Some cry up Gunnersbury,
>     For Sion some declare ;
> And some say that with Chiswick-house
>     No villa can compare :
> But ask the beaux of Middlesex,
>     Who know the county well,
> If Strawb'ry-hill, if Strawb'ry-hill
>     Don't bear away the bell ?
>
> ' Some love to roll down Greenwich-hill
>     For this thing and for that ;
> And some prefer sweet Marble-hill,
>     Tho' sure 'tis somewhat flat :
> Yet Marble-hill and Greenwich-hill,
>     If Kitty Clive can tell,
> From Strawb'ry-hill, from Strawb'ry-hill
>     Will never bear the bell.
>
> ' Tho' Surrey boasts its Oatlands,
>     And Clermont kept so jim,
> And some prefer sweet Southcote's,
>     'Tis but a dainty whim :
> For ask the gallant Bristow,
>     Who does in taste excell,
> If Strawb'ry-hill, if Strawb'ry-hill
>     Don't bear away the bell ?
>
> ' Since Denham sung of Cooper's,
>     There's scarce a hill around,
> But what in song or ditty
>     Is turn'd to fairy-ground—

Ah, peace be with their memories !
   I wish them wond'rous well ;
But Strawb'ry-hill, but Strawb'ry-hill
   Must bear away the bell.

' Great William dwells at Windsor,
   As Edward did of old,
And many a Gaul and many a Scot
   Have found him full as bold.
On lofty hills like Windsor
   Such heroes ought to dwell,
Yet little folks like Strawb'ry-hill,
   Like Strawb'ry-hill as well.' [1]

Cumberland Lodge, where, say the old guide-books, the hero of Culloden ' reposed after victory ', still stands on the hill at the end of the Long Walk at Windsor ; and at ' Gunnersbury ' lived the Princess Amelia. Some of the other houses referred to still exist. ' Sweet Marble-hill,' which, like Strawberry, was but recently put up for sale, had at this date for mistress the Countess Dowager of Suffolk (Mrs. Howard), for whom it had been built by her royal lover, George II ; and Chiswick-house (now the Marquis of Bute's), that famous structure of Kent which Lord Hervey said was ' too small

[1] The version here followed is that given in Walpole's *Description of Strawberry Hill*, in *Works of Lord Orford* (1798), ii. 513–14.

to inhabit, and too large to hang to one's watch ',
was the residence of Richard, Earl of Burlington.
Claremont ' kept so jim ',[1] was the seat of the
Duke of Newcastle at Esher; Oatlands, near
Weybridge, was another seat of the Duke of
Newcastle, which subsequently was bought by
the Duke of York;[2] and Sion House, near
Isleworth, on the Thames, belonged to Sir Hugh
Smithson, Earl, afterwards (1766) Duke of North-
umberland. Walpole and his friends, it will be
perceived, did not shrink from comparing small
things with great. But perhaps the most notable
circumstance about this glorification of Strawberry is that it should have originated with its
reputed author. ' Can there be ', says Walpole,
' an odder revolution of things, than that the
printer of the *Craftsman* should live in a house
of mine, and that the author of the *Craftsman*
should write a panegyric on a house of mine ? '[3]
The printer was Richard Francklin, already mentioned as his tenant; and Lord Bath, if not the
actual, was at least the putative, writer of most of
the *Craftsman's* attacks upon Sir Robert Walpole.

[1] [Smart, neat,—more usually *gim*.]

[2] [He paid £43,000 for it in 1788 (see *Walpole to Thomas
Walpole the Younger*, 21 July 1788).]

[3] [*Walpole to Bentley*, 17 July 1755.]

It is possible, however, that, as with the poem, part only of this honour really belonged to him.

Strawberry Hill and its improvements have, however, carried us far from the date at which this chapter begins, and we must return to 1747. Happily the life of Walpole, though voluminously chronicled in his correspondence, is not so crowded with personal incident as to make a space of six years a serious matter to recover, especially when tested by the brief but still very detailed record in the *Short Notes* of what he held to be its conspicuous occurrences. In 1747–49 his zeal for his father's memory involved him in a good deal of party pamphleteering, and in 1748, he had what he styles ' a remarkable quarrel ' with the Speaker, of which one may say that, in these days, it would scarcely deserve its qualifying epithet, although it produced more paper war. ' These things (he says himself), were only excusable by the lengths to which party had been carried against my father ; or rather, were not excusable even then.' For this reason it is needless to dwell upon them here, as well as upon certain other papers in *The Remembrancer* for 1749, and a tract called *Delenda est Oxonia,* prompted by a heinous scheme, which was meditated by the Ministry, of attacking the liberties of that University by vesting in the Crown the nomination of the Chancellor. 'This piece (he says), which I think one of my best, was seized at the printer's and suppressed.' [1] Then in November, 1749, comes something like a really 'moving incident',—he is robbed in Hyde Park. He was returning by moonlight to Arlington Street from Holland House,[2] Kensington, when his coach was stopped by two of the most notorious of 'Diana's foresters', Plunket and James Maclean, and the adventure had all but a tragic termination. Maclean's pistol went off by accident, sending a bullet so nearly through Walpole's head that it grazed the skin under his eye, stunned him and passed through the roof of the chariot.[3] His correspondence contains no more than a passing reference to this narrow escape, probably because it was amply reported (and expanded) in the public prints. But in a paper which he contributed to the *World* some years later, under guise of relating what had happened to one of his acquaintance, he reverts to this experience. 'The whole affair

[1] [A copy of this pamphlet in Walpole's handwriting is in the possession of Earl Waldegrave at Chewton Priory. It was printed in the *English Historical Review* for January, 1927.]

[2] [The residence of Henry Fox, afterwards Lord Holland. The incident occurred on Wednesday, Nov. 8.]

[3] [*Short Notes* for 1749.]

(he says) was conducted with the greatest good-breeding on both sides. The robber, who had only taken a purse *this way*, because he had that morning been disappointed of marrying a great fortune, no sooner returned to his lodgings, than he sent the gentleman [i.e., Walpole himself] two letters of excuses, which, with less wit than the epistles of Voiture, had ten times more natural and easy politeness in the turn of their expression. In the postscript, he appointed a meeting at Tyburn at twelve at night, where the gentleman might *purchase again* any trifles he had lost ; and my friend has been blamed for not accepting the rendezvous, as it seemed liable to be construed by ill-natured people into a doubt of the *honour* of a man, who had given him all the satĭsfaction in his power, for having *unluckily* been near shooting him through the head.' [1]

The 'fashionable highwayman' [2] (as Mr.

---

[1] *World,* 19 Dec. 1754 (printed in *Works of Lord Orford,* i. 177–8).—[Walpole did actually receive a letter from the highwaymen, signed A: B: & C: D:, offering to restore the stolen articles for the sum of forty guineas, to be paid at a given hour, at a preconcerted signal, at Tyburn. This letter, the original of which (on gilt-edged paper) was formerly in the Waller Collection, is printed in *Supplement* (vol. iii, pp. 132–5) to *Letters of Horace Walpole* (ed. Toynbee).]    [2] [*Walpole to Mann,* 2 Aug. 1750.]

Maclean was called) was taken soon afterwards and hanged. ' I am honourably mentioned in a Grub-street ballad (says Walpole) for not having contributed to his sentence,' and he goes on to say that there are as many prints and pamphlets about him as about that other sensation of 1750, the earthquake.[1]   Maclean seems nevertheless to have been rather a pinchbeck Macheath ; but for the moment, in default of larger lions, he was the rage.   After his condemnation, several thousand people visited him in his cell at Newgate, where he is stated to have fainted twice from the heat and pressure of the crowd.[2]   And his visitors were not all men.   In a note to *The Modern Fine Lady,* Soame Jenyns says that some of the brightest eyes were in tears for him ; and Walpole himself tells us that he excited the warmest commiseration in two distinguished beauties of the day, Lady Caroline Petersham and Miss Ashe.[3]

[1] [*Walpole to Mann,* 20 Sept. 1750.]
[2] [*Walpole to Mann,* 18 Oct. 1750.]
[3] [*Walpole to Mann,* 2 Aug. 1750.]   Another instance of Maclean's momentary vogue is supplied by a couplet in Gray's *Long Story,* which (if Gray's own note is correct) was written shortly after the execution :—

> ' A sudden fit of ague shook him,
>     He stood as mute as poor *Macleane.*'—

the reference being to Macleane's only observation, instead

Chapter V                    143

Miss Elizabeth Ashe, of whom we are told ¹
that she was said ' to have been of very high
parentage ', and Lady Caroline Petersham, a
daughter of the Duke of Grafton, figure more
pleasantly in another letter of Walpole, which
gives a glimpse of some of those diversions with
which he was wont to relieve the gothicising of
his villa by the Thames.   In a sentence that
proves how well he understood his own qualities,
he says he tells the story—' to show the manners
of the age, which are always as entertaining to a
person fifty miles off as to one born an hundred
and fifty years after the time '.   We have long
passed the latter limit ; but there is little doubt
as to the interest of Walpole's account of his visit
in the month of June 1750, to the famous gardens
of Mr. Jonathan Tyers.   He got a card, he says,
from Lady Caroline to go with her to Vauxhall.
He repairs accordingly to her house, and finds her
' and the little Ashe, or the Pollard Ashe,² as they
call her ', having ' just finished their last layer of
red, and looking as handsome as crimson could

of the expected speech, after sentence was pronounced :
' My Lord, I *cannot speak.*'
    ¹ [Indirectly by Wraxall, and directly by Mrs. Piozzi.]
    ² [According to Mrs. Piozzi, she was ' particularly small
in her person '.]

make them '.   Others of the party are the Duke
of Kingston ;   Lord March of Thackeray's *Vir-
ginians ;*  Harry Vane, soon to be Earl of Darling-
ton ;  Mr. Whithed ;  a 'pretty Miss Beauclerc ',
and a 'very foolish Miss Sparre'.   As they sail
up the Mall, they encounter cross-grained Lord
Petersham (my lady's husband) shambling along
after his wont,[1] and 'as sulky as a ghost that
nobody will speak to first'.   He declines to
accompany his wife and her friends, who, getting
into the best order they can, march to their barge,
which has a boat of French horns attending, and
'little Ashe' sings.   After parading up the river,
they 'debark' at Vauxhall, where at the outset
they narrowly escape the excitement of a quarrel.
For a certain Mrs. Lloyd of Spring Gardens,
afterwards married to Lord Haddington, observ-
ing Miss Beauclerc and her companion following
Lady Caroline, says audibly, 'Poor girls, I am
sorry to see them in such bad company', a remark
which the 'foolish Miss Sparre' (she is but fifteen),
for the fun of witnessing a duel, endeavours to
make Lord March resent.   But my Lord, who
is not only 'very lively and agreeable', but also
of a nice discretion, laughs her out of 'this charm-

---

[1] He was popularly known as 'Peter Shamble'.   He
afterwards became Earl of Harrington.

ing frolic with a great deal of humour'. Next they pick up Lord Granby, arriving very drunk from 'Jenny's Whim' at Chelsea, where he has left a mixed gathering of thirteen persons of quality playing at Brag. He is in the sentimental stage of his malady, and makes love to Miss Beauclerc and Miss Sparre alternately until the tide of champagne turns, and he remembers that he is married. 'At last', says Walpole, and at this point the story may be surrendered to him entirely—'we assembled in our booth, Lady Caroline in the front, with the visor of her hat erect, and looking gloriously jolly and handsome. She had fetched my brother Orford from the next box, where he was enjoying himself with his *petite partie*, to help us to mince chickens. We minced seven chickens into a china dish, which Lady Caroline stewed over a lamp with three pats of butter and a flagon of water, stirring, and rattling, and laughing, and we every minute expecting to have the dish fly about our ears. She had brought Betty, the fruit girl,[1] with hampers of strawberries

[1] Elizabeth Neale, here referred to, was a well-known personage in St. James's Street, where, for many years, she kept a fruit shop. From Lady Mary Coke's *Letters and Journals*, 1889, vol. ii, p. 427, Betty appears to have assiduously attended the Debates in the House of Commons, being characterized (15 Dec. 1763) as a 'violent Politician,

L

and cherries from Rogers's, and made her wait upon us, and then made her sup by us at a little table.    The conversation was no less lively than the whole transaction.    There was a Mr. O'Brien arrived from Ireland, who would get the Duchess of Manchester from Mr. Hussey, if she were still at liberty.    I took up the biggest hautboy in the dish, and said to Lady Caroline, " Madam, Miss Ashe desires you will eat this O'Brien strawberry " ;  she replied immediately, " I won't, you hussey."    You may imagine the laugh this reply occasioned.    After the tempest was a little calmed, the Pollard said, " Now, how anybody would spoil this story that was to repeat it, and say, I won't, you jade."    In short, the whole air of our party was sufficient, as you will easily imagine, to take up the whole attention of the garden ;  so much so, that from eleven o'clock till half an hour after one we had the whole concourse round our booth : at last, they came into the little gardens of each booth on the sides of our's, till Harry Vane took up a bumper, and drank their healths and was proceeding to treat them with still greater freedom.    It

& always in the opposition '.   In Mason's *Heroic Epistle to Sir William Chambers, Knight,* she is spoken of as ' Patriot Betty '.   She survived until 1797, when her death, at the age of 67, is recorded in the *Gentleman's Magazine.*

was three o'clock before we got home.' He adds
a characteristic touch to explain Lord Granby's
eccentricities.  He had lost eight hundred pounds
to the Prince of Wales at Kew the night before, and
this had ' a little ruffled ' his lordship's temper.[1]

Early in 1753, Edward Moore, the author of
some *Fables for the Female Sex*, once popular
enough to figure, between Thomson and Prior,
in Goldsmith's *Beauties of English Poesy*, established the periodical paper called *The World*,
which, to quote a latter-day definition, might
fairly claim to be ' written by gentlemen for
gentlemen '.  Soame Jenyns, Cambridge of the
*Scribleriad* (Walpole's Twickenham neighbour),
Hamilton Boyle, Sir Charles Hanbury Williams,
and Lord Chesterfield were all contributors.  That
Walpole should also attempt this ' bow of Ulysses,
in which it was the fashion for men of rank and
genius to try their strength ', goes without saying.
His gifts were exactly suited to the work, and his
productions in the new journal [2] are by no means
its worst.  His first essay [3] was a bright little piece
of persiflage upon what he calls the return of
nature, and proceeds to illustrate by the introduc-

---

[1] *Walpole to Montagu*, 23 June 1750.
[2] [His contributions are reprinted in *Works of Lord Or-
ord*, i. 146–204.]         [3] [No. vi (8 Feb. 1753).]

tion of ' real water ' on the stage, by Kent's landscape gardening, and by the fauna and flora of the
dessert table.　A second [1] effort was devoted to
that extraordinary adventurer, Baron Neuhoff,
otherwise Theodore, King of Corsica, who, with
his realm for his only assets, was at this time a
tenant of the King's Bench prison.　Walpole,
with genuine kindness, proposed a subscription
for this bankrupt Belisarius, and a sum of fifty
pounds was collected.　This, however, proved so
much below the expectations of His Corsican
Majesty, that he actually had the effrontery to
threaten Dodsley, the printer of the paper, with
a prosecution for using his name unjustifiably.
' I have done with countenancing kings,' wrote
Walpole to Mann. [2]　Others of his *World* essays

[1] [No. viii (22 Feb. 1753).]

[2] [27 Apr. 1753.]—Nevertheless, when this ' *Roi en Exil* '
shortly afterwards died, Walpole erected a tablet in St.
Anne's Churchyard, Soho, to his memory, with the following inscription :

Near this Place is interred

Theodore, King of Corsica ;

Who died in this Parish, December 11, 1756,

Immediately after leaving the King's-Bench-Prison

By the Benefit of the Act of Insolvency ;

In Consequence of which He Registered

His Kingdom of Corsica

For the Use of his Creditors.

are on the Glastonbury Thorn;[1] on Letter-Writing,[2] a subject of which he might claim to speak with authority; on old women as objects of passion;[3] and on politeness,[4] wherein occurs the already quoted anecdote of Maclean the highwayman. His light hand and lighter humour made him an almost ideal contributor to Moore's pages, and it is not surprising to find that such judges as Lady Mary approved his performances, or that he himself regarded them with a complacency which peeps out now and again in his letters. ' I met Mrs. Clive two nights ago ', he says, ' and told her I had been in the meadows, but would walk no more there, for there was all the world. "Well," says she, "and don't you

> The Grave, great Teacher, to a Level brings,
> Heroes and Beggars, Galley-slaves and Kings.
> But Theodore this Moral learn'd, ere dead ;
> Fate pour'd its Lessons on his *living* Head,
> Bestow'd a Kingdom, and deny'd him Bread.

Theodore's Great Seal, and ' that very curious piece by which he took the benefit of the Act of Insolvency ', and in which he was only styled Theodore Stephen, Baron de Neuhoff, were among the treasures of the Tribune. (See Chapter VIII.)—[The epitaph on King Theodore was subsequently (Sept. 1757) printed at Strawberry Hill, in two dozen copies only.]        [1] [No. x (8 Mar. 1753).]
  [2] [No. xiv (5 Apr. 1753).]   [3] [No. xxviii (12 July 1753).]
  [4] [No. ciii (19 Dec. 1754).]

like *The World?*    I hear it was very clever last
Thursday." ' ¹   ' Last Thursday ' had appeared
Walpole's paper on elderly ' flames '.

During the period covered by this chapter the
*redintegratio amoris* with Gray, to which reference
has been made, became confirmed.   Whether the
attachment was ever quite on the old basis, may
be doubted.   Gray always poses a little as the
aggrieved person who could not speak first, and
to whom unmistakable overtures must be made
by the other side.   He as yet ' neither repents,
nor rejoices over much, but is pleased '—he tells
Chute.²   On the other hand, Walpole, though
he appears to have proffered his palm branch with
very genuine geniality and desire to let by-gones
be by-gones, was not above very candid criticism
of his recovered friend.   ' I agree with you most
absolutely in your opinion about Gray,' he writes
to Montagu, September 3rd, 1748 : ' he is the
worst company in the world.   From a melancholy
turn, from living reclusely, and from a little too
much dignity, he never converses easily—all his
words are measured and chosen, and formed into
sentences ;   his writings are admirable ;   he himself is not agreeable.'   Meantime, however, the

¹ [*Walpole to Montagu,* 17 July 1753.]
² [*Gray to Chute,* 23 Nov. 1746.]

THOMAS GRAY

revived connection went on pleasantly. Gray made
flying visits to Strawberry and Arlington Street,
and prattled to Walpole from Pembroke between
whiles. And certainly, in a measure, it is to Walpole
that we owe Gray. It was Walpole who induced
Gray to allow Dodsley to print in 1747, as an
attenuated *folio* pamphlet,[1] the *Ode on a Distant
Prospect of Eton College;* and it was the tragic end
of one of Walpole's favourite cats in a china tub of
gold-fish (of which, by the way, there was a large
pond called Poyang at Strawberry) which prompted
the delightful occasional verses by Gray beginning :—

> ' 'Twas on a lofty vase's side,
> Where China's gayest art had dy'd
>     The azure flow'rs, that blow ;
> Demurest of the tabby kind,
> The pensive Selima reclin'd,
>     Gaz'd on the lake below,'—

a stanza which, with trifling verbal alterations,
long served as a label for the ' lofty vase '[2] in the
Strawberry Hill collection. To Walpole's offi-
cious circulation in manuscript of the famous

[1] [Price sixpence.]

[2] [It was actually a ' large blue and white china tub ',
which stood in the Little Cloister at Strawberry Hill ; it
was bought at the sale in 1842 (lot 32 of nineteenth day)
by Lord Derby for £42, and is now at Knowsley.]

*Elegy written in a Country Church-Yard* must indirectly be attributed its publication by Dodsley [1] in February 1751 ; to Walpole also is due that typical piece of *vers de société*, the *Long Story*, which originated in the interest in the recluse poet of Stoke Poges with which Walpole's well-meaning (if unwelcome) advocacy had inspired Lady Cobham and some other lion-hunters of the neighbourhood.   But his chief enterprise in connection with his friend's productions was the edition of them put forth in March 1753, with illustrations by Richard Bentley, the youngest child of the famous Master of Trinity.   Bentley possessed considerable attainments as an amateur artist, and as a scholar and connoisseur had just that virtuoso *finesse* of manner which was most attractive to Walpole, whose guest and counsellor he frequently became during the progress of the Strawberry improvements.   Out of this connection, which, in its hot fits, was of the most confidential character, grew the suggestion that Bentley should make, at Walpole's expense, a series of designs for Gray's poems.   These, which are still in existence,[2] were engraved with great

[1] [Price sixpence.]

[2] A copy of the poems, ' illustrated with the original designs of Mr. Richard Bentley, elaborately executed by

delicacy by two of the best engravers of that time,
Müller and Charles Grignion; and the *Poëmata
Grayo-Bentleiana,* as Walpole christened them,
became and remains one of the most remarkable
of the illustrated books of the eighteenth century.
Gray, as may be imagined, could scarcely oppose
the compliment; and he seems to have grown
minutely interested in the enterprise, rewarding
the artist by some commendatory verses, in which
he certainly does not deny himself—to use a phrase
of Mr. Swinburne—' the noble pleasure of praising '.[1]   But even over this book the sensitive liga-
ment that linked him to Walpole was perilously
strained.   Without consulting him, Walpole had
his likeness engraved as a frontispiece, a step
which instantly drew from Gray a wail of nervous
expostulation so unmistakably heartfelt [2] that the

him with pen and ink, and also with Mr. Gray's original
sketch of Stoke House, from which Mr. Bentley made his
finished pen drawing ', was sold at the Strawberry Hill sale
(lot 1044 of eighth day of sale of prints, &c.) of 1842 to
H. G. Bohn for £8 8s.

[1] The verses include this magnificent stanza :—

'   But not to one in this benighted age
      Is that diviner inspiration giv'n,
   That burns in Shakespeare's or in Milton's page,
      The pomp and prodigality of heav'n.'

[2] [*Gray to Walpole,* 13 Feb. 1753.]

plate had to be withdrawn.[1]   Thus it came about that *Designs by Mr. R. Bentley for Six Poems by Mr. T. Gray* made its appearance without the portrait of the poet.

Bentley's ingenious son was not the only person whom the decoration of Strawberry pressed into the service of its owner.   Selwyn, the wit, George James (or 'Gilly') Williams, a connoisseur of considerable ability, and Richard, later second Lord Edgcumbe, occasionally sat as a committee of taste, a function commemorated by Reynolds in a conversation-piece which afterwards formed one of the chief ornaments of the Refectory;[2] and upon Bentley's recommendation Walpole invited from Jersey a humbler guest in the person of a Swiss artist named Müntz—' an inoffensive, good creature', who would ' rather ponder over a foreign gazette than a pallet ',[3] but whose services kept him domiciled for some time at the Gothic castle.

[1] [Mason speaks of the plate as being unfinished in consequence of Gray's protest, but the prints from it in the Storer Collection at Eton, in the Hope Collection at Oxford, and in the British Museum, show that he was mistaken.]

[2] [See *Walpole to Montagu*, 30 Dec. 1761.]—It is copied in Cunningham, vol. iii, p. 475.   It was sold for £157 10s. at the Strawberry Hill sale of 1842 (lot 43 of twenty-first day), and passed into the collection of the late Lord Taunton.

[3] [*Walpole to Bentley*, 6 Jan. 1756.]

Müntz executed many views of the neighbourhood, which are still, like that of Twickenham
already referred to,[1] preserved in contemporary
engravings.   And besides the persons whom Walpole drew into his immediate circle, the ' village ',
as he called it, was growing steadily in public
favour.   ' Mr. Muntz '—writes Walpole in July
1755—' says we have more coaches than there
are in half France.   Mrs. Pritchard has bought
Ragman's Castle, for which my Lord Litchfield
could not agree.   We shall be as celebrated as
Baiae or Tivoli; and if we have not such sonorous
names as they boast, we have very famous people :
Clive and Pritchard, actresses ;  Scott and Hudson,
painters ;  my Lady Suffolk, famous in her time ;
Mr. H[ickey], the impudent Lawyer, that Tom
Hervey wrote against ;  Whitehead, the poet—
and Cambridge, the everything.' [2]   Cambridge
has already been referred to as a contributor to
the *World*, and the Whitehead was the one mentioned in Churchill's stinging couplet :—

' May I (can worse disgrace on manhood fall ?)
Be born a Whitehead, and baptiz'd a Paul,'—

who then lived on Twickenham Common.
Hickey, a jovial Irish attorney, was the legal

[1] See p. 134 n.
[2] [*Walpole to Bentley*, 5 July 1755.]

adviser of Burke and Reynolds, and the ' blunt, pleasant creature ' of Goldsmith's ' Retaliation '. Scott was Samuel Scott, the ' English Canaletto '; Hudson, Sir Joshua's master, who had a house on the river near Lord Radnor's. But Walpole's best allies were two of the other sex. One was Lady Suffolk, the whilom friend (as Mrs. Howard) of Pope and Swift and Gay, whose home at Marble Hill is celebrated in the Walpole-cum-Pulteney poem ; the other was red-faced Mrs. Clive, who occupied a house known familiarly as ' Clive-den ' and officially as Little Strawberry. She had not yet retired from the stage. Lady Suffolk's stories of the Georgian Court and its scandals,[1] and Mrs. Clive's anecdotes of the greenroom, and of their common neighbour at Hampton, the great ' Roscius ' himself [2] (with whom she was always at war), must have furnished Walpole with an inexhaustible supply of just the particular description of gossip which he most appreciated.

[1] [See *Reminiscences of Horace Walpole,* together with his *Notes of Conversations with Lady Suffolk* (ed. Toynbee), 1924.]

[2] David Garrick.

# CHAPTER VI

*Gleanings from the ' Short Notes ' ; ' Letter from Xo Ho ' ;
the Strawberry Hill Press ; Robinson the Printer ; Gray's
' Odes ' ; other works ; ' Catalogue of Royal and Noble Authors ' ; 'Anecdotes of Painting ' ; humours of the Press ;
' The Parish Register of Twickenham ' ; Lady Fanny Shirley, Fielding ; ' The Castle of Otranto '.*

# VI

IN order to take up the little-variegated thread
of Walpole's life, we must again resort to the
*Short Notes,* in which, as already stated, he has
recorded what he considered to be its most important occurrences. In 1754, he had been chosen
member, in the new Parliament of that year, for
Castle Rising in Norfolk. In March 1755, he
says, he was very ill-used by his nephew Lord
Orford [1] upon a contested election in the House
of Commons, ' on which I wrote him a long
letter, with an account of my own conduct in
politics'. This letter does not seem to have been
preserved, and it is difficult to conceive that its
theme could have involved very lengthy explana-
tions. In February 1757, he vacated his Castle
Rising seat for that of Lynn, and about the same
time, he tells us, used his best endeavours, although
in vain, to save the unfortunate Admiral Byng,
who was executed *pour encourager les autres* in
the following March. But with the exception
of his erection of a tablet to Theodore of Corsica,

[1] [George, 3rd Earl of Orford, who had succeeded his
father (Walpole's elder brother) in 1751.]

and the dismissal in 1759 of Mr. Müntz, with whom his connection seems to have been exceptionally prolonged, his record for the next decade, or until the publication of the *Castle of Otranto*, is almost exclusively literary, and deals with the establishment of his private printing press at Strawberry Hill, his publication thereat of Gray's *Odes* and other works, his *Catalogue of Royal and Noble Authors*, his *Anecdotes of Painting*, and his above-mentioned romance.[1]   This accidental absorption of his chronicle by literary production will serve as a sufficient reason for devoting this chapter to those efforts of his pen which, from the outset, were destined to the permanence of type.

Already, as far back as March 1751, he had begun the work afterwards known as the *Memoires of the last Ten Years of the Reign of George II*, to the progress of which there are scattered references in the *Short Notes*.   He had intended at first to confine them to the history of one year, but they grew under his hand.   His first definite literary effort in 1757, however, was the clever little squib, after the model of Montesquieu's *Lettres Persanes*, entitled *A Letter from Xo Ho, a Chinese Philosopher at London, to his friend Lien Chi, at*

[1] [*The Castle of Otranto* was printed in London, not, as were the other works named, at Strawberry Hill.]

*Peking,* in which he ingeniously satirizes the ' late political revolutions' and the inconstant disposition of the English nation, not forgetting to fire off a few sarcasms *à-propos* of the Byng tragedy. The piece, he tells Mann,[1] was written ' in an hour and a half' (there is always a little of Oronte's *Je n'ai demeuré qu'un quart d'heure à le faire* about Walpole's literary efforts), was sent to press next day, and ran through five editions in a fortnight.[2] Mrs. Clive was of opinion that the rash satirist would be sent to the Tower,[3] but he himself regarded it as ' perhaps the only political paper ever written, in which no man of any party can dislike or deny a single fact ' ; [4] and Henry Fox, to whom he sent a copy, may be held to confirm this view, since his only objection seems to have been that it did not hit some of the *other* side a

[1] [19 May 1757.]

[2] [See Walpole's note to the reprint in *Works of Lord Orford,* i. 205.]—It may be observed that when Walpole's letter was published, it was briefly noticed in the *Monthly Review,* where at this very date Oliver Goldsmith was working as the hind of Griffiths and his wife. It is also notable that the name of Xo Ho's correspondent, Lien Chi, seems almost a foreshadowing of Goldsmith's Lien Chi Altangi. Can it be possible that Walpole supplied Goldsmith with his first idea of the *Citizen of the World?*

[3] [*Walpole to Montagu,* 27 May 1757.]

[4] [*Walpole to Mann,* 19 May 1757.]

M

little harder.   It would be difficult now without long notes to make it intelligible to modern readers, but the following outburst of the Chinese philosopher respecting the variations of the English climate has the merit of enduring applicability. ' The English have no sun, no summer as we have, at least their sun does not scorch like ours. They content themselves with names : at a certain time of the year they leave their capital, and that makes summer ;  they go out of the city, and that makes the country.   Their monarch, when he goes into the country, passes in his calash [1] by a row of high trees, goes along a gravel walk, crosses one of the chief streets, is driven by the side of a canal between two rows of lamps, at the end of which he has a small house,[2] and then he is supposed to be in the country.   I saw this ceremony yesterday :  as soon as he was gone, the men put on under vestments of white linen, and the women left off those vast draperies, which they call *hoops*, and which I have described to thee; and then all the men and all the women said *it was hot*.   If thou wilt believe me I am now [3] writing to thee before a fire.' [4]

[1] A  four-wheeled  carriage  with  a  movable  hood.   Cf. Prior's *Down Hall :*—' Then answer'd Squire Morley : Pray get a *calash*, That in summer may burn, and in winter may splash,' etc.                              [2] Kensington Palace.

[3] 12 May 1757.          [4] [*Works of Lord Orford*, i. 208.]

In the following June Walpole had betaken himself to the place he ' loved best of all ', and was amusing himself at Strawberry with his pen. The next work which he records is the publication of a Catalogue and Description of King Charles the First's Capital Collection of Pictures, Statues, etc., for which he prepared 'a little introduction '. To this he added subsequently ' prefaces or advertisements ' to the Catalogues of the Collections of James the Second, and the Duke of Buckingham.[1] But the great event of 1757 is the establishment of the *Officina Arbuteana*, or private printing press of Strawberry Hill.[2] ' Elzevir, Aldus, and Stephens ', he tells Chute in July, ' are the freshest personages in his memory,' [3] and he jestingly threatens [4] to assume as his motto (with a slight variation) Pope's couplet :

' Some have at first for wits, then poets pass'd ;
Turn'd *printers* next, and proved plain fools at last.' [5]

' I am turned printer,' he writes somewhat later,[6] ' and have converted a little cottage here

[1] [All these are printed in *Works of Lord Orford*, i. 234–41.]

[2] [Since this *Memoir* was written, Horace Walpole's own journal of his private press has come to light, and has been published : *Journal of the Printing-Office at Strawberry Hill* (ed. Paget Toynbee), Lond., and Boston, Mass., 1923.]

[3] [*To Chute*, 12 July 1757.]    [4] [*To Chute*, 26 July 1757.]

[5] [*Essay on Criticism*, 36–7.]    [6] [*To Mann*, 4 Aug. 1757]

into a printing-office. My abbey is a perfect college or academy.   I keep a painter [1] in the house,
and a printer—not to mention Mr. Bentley, who
is an academy himself.' William Robinson, the
printer, an Irishman with noticeable eyes which
Garrick envied ('they are more Richard the
Third's than Garrick's own', says Walpole), must
have been a rather original personage, to judge by
a copy of one of his letters which his patron encloses to Mann.   He says he found it in a drawer
where it had evidently been placed to attract his
attention.   After telling his correspondent that he
dates from the ' shady bowers, nodding groves, and
amaranthine shades' of Twickenham—' Richmond's near neighbour, where great George the
King resides '—Robinson goes on to speak of his
employer as ' the Hon. Horatio Walpole, son to
the late great Sir Robert Walpole, who is very
studious, and an admirer of all the liberal arts and
sciences ;   amongst the rest he admires printing.
He has fitted out a complete printing-house at this
his country seat, and has done me the favour to
make me sole manager and operator (there being
no one but myself).   All men of genius resorts his
house, courts his company, and admires his understanding—what with his own and their writings,

[1] [Müntz (see above, p. 154).]

I believe I shall be pretty well employed. I have pleased him, and I hope to continue so to do.' Then after reference to the extreme heat—a heat by which fowls and quarters of lamb have been roasted in the London Artillery grounds ' by the help of glasses '—so capricious was the climate over which Walpole had made merry in May,— he proceeds to describe Strawberry. ' The place I am in now is all my comfort from the heat— the situation of it is close to the Thames, and is Richmond Gardens (if you were ever in them) in miniature, surrounded by bowers, groves, cascades, and ponds, and on a rising ground, not very common in this part of the country—the building elegant, and the furniture of a peculiar taste, magnificent and superb.' At this date poor Robinson seems to have been delighted with the place, and the fastidious master whom he hoped ' to continue to please '. But Walpole was nothing if not mutable, and two years later he had found out that Robinson of the remarkable eyes was ' a foolish Irishman, who took himself for a genius ', and they parted, with the result that the *Officina Arbuteana* was temporarily at a standstill.[1]

For the moment, however, things went smoothly enough. It had been intended that the maiden

[1] [*Walpole to Zouch,* 15 Mar. 1759.]

effort of the Strawberry types should have been a translation by Bentley of Paul Hentzner's curious account of England in 1598.   But Walpole suddenly became aware that Gray had put the penultimate, if not the final, touches to his painfully-elaborated Pindaric Odes, the *Bard* and the *Progress of Poesy*, and he pounced upon them forthwith—Gray as usual half expostulating, half overborne.   ' You will dislike this as much as I do '—he writes to Mason—' but there is no help.' ' You understand ', he adds, with the air of one resigning himself to the inevitable, ' it is he that prints them, not for me, but for Dodsley.' [1]   However, he persisted in refusing Walpole's not entirely unreasonable request for notes.   ' If a thing cannot be understood without them ', he said characteristically, ' it had better be not understood at all.' [2]   Consequently, while describing them as ' Greek, Pindaric, sublime ', Walpole confesses under his breath that he fears they are a little obscure.[3]   Dodsley paid Gray forty guineas for the book, which was a large, thin quarto, entitled *Odes by Mr. Gray . . . Printed at Strawberry-Hill, For R. and J. Dodsley in Pall-Mall.*   It

[1]  [*Gray to Mason*, 1 Aug. 1757.]
[2]  [*Gray to Walpole*, 11 July 1757.]
[3]  [*Walpole to Mann*, 4 Aug. 1757.]

was published on August 8th, and the price was
a shilling.   On the title-page was a vignette of
the Gothic castle at Twickenham.[1]   From a
letter [2] of Walpole to Lord Lyttelton it would
seem that his apprehensions as to the poems being
' understanded of the people' proved well-founded.
'The age . . . have cast their eyes over them, found
them obscure, and looked no farther, yet perhaps
no compositions ever had more sublime beauties
than are in each,'—and he goes on to criticise
them minutely in a fashion which shows that his
own appreciation of them was by no means un-
qualified.   But Warburton, and Garrick, and the
' word-picker' Hurd were enthusiastic.   Lyttelton [3] and Shenstone followed more moderately.
Upon the whole, the success of the first venture
was encouraging, and the share in it of ' Elzevir
Horace', as Conway called his friend, was not
forgotten.

Gray's *Odes* were succeeded by Hentzner's
*Travels*, or, to speak more accurately, by that
portion of Hentzner's *Travels* which refers to

[1] [Designed by Bentley, and engraved by Charles Grignion.]                    [2] [25 Aug. 1757.]
[3] [See *Lyttelton to Walpole*, 31 Aug. 1757, in *Supplement*
(vol. ii, pp. 100–2) to *Letters of Horace Walpole* (ed.
Toynbee).]

England. In England Hentzner was little known, and the 220 copies which Walpole printed in October 1757, were prefaced by an Advertisement from his pen and a dedication to the Society of Antiquaries, of which he was a member. After this came, in 1758, his *Catalogue of Royal and Noble Authors* ; a collection of *Fugitive Pieces* (which included his essays in the *World*) dedicated to Conway ; [1] and seven hundred copies of Lord Whitworth's *Account of Russia*. Then followed, in 1759, a book by Joseph Spence, the *Parallel of Magliabechi and Mr. Hill*,[2] the object of which was to benefit Hill, an end which must have been attained, as six out of seven hundred copies were sold in a fortnight, and the book was reprinted in London. In 1761 Bentley's *Lucan*, a quarto of 500 copies, succeeded Spence ; and then, in 1762 and 1764, came three other quartos of *Anecdotes of Painting* by Walpole himself. The only other notable products of the press during this period are the Autobiography of Lord Herbert of Cherbury, 4to, 1764, and 100 copies of the *Poems* of Lady

[1] These, though printed in 1758, were not circulated until 1759. See at end,—' Appendix of Books printed at the Strawberry Hill Press,' which contains ample details of all these publications.

[2] One Robert Hill, a self-educated tailor of Buckingham.

Temple. This, however, is a very fair record for seven years' work, when it is remembered that the Strawberry Hill staff never exceeded a man and a boy.[1] As already stated, the first printer, Robinson, was dismissed in 1759. His place, after a short interval of ' occasional hands ',[2] was taken by Thomas Kirgate,[3] whose name thenceforth appears on all the Twickenham issues, with which it is indissolubly connected. Kirgate continued, with greater good fortune than his predecessors, to perform his duties until Walpole's death.

In the above list there are two volumes which, in these pages, deserve a more extended notice than the rest. *The Catalogue of Royal and Noble*

[1] [This was an apprentice, Joseph Forrester, who was engaged in July 1759.]

[2] [Walpole had no less than three printers between Mar. 29 and July 16, 1759, the first of whom stayed a couple of months ; the second a week only ; while the third, Thomas Farmer, stayed till Dec. 1761, when he ran away and was never heard of again. He was succeeded by William Pratt, who stayed (save for a brief interval in 1762) till the end of 1764.]

[3] [Kirgate, the sixth printer, was first engaged in Mar. 1765, and stayed till the following August, when he was discharged on Walpole's going abroad ; he was re-engaged in Apr. 1768 and remained, first, as printer (till July 1789), and afterwards, as amanuensis and secretary, till Walpole's death in 1797.]

*Authors* had at least the merit of novelty, and certainly a better reason for existing than some of the works to which its author refers in his preface. Even the performances of Pulteney, Earl of Bath, and the English rondeaus of Charles of Orleans are more worthy of a chronicler than the lives of physicians who had been poets, of men who had died laughing, or of Frenchmen who had studied Hebrew.  Walpole took considerable pains in obtaining information, and his book was exceedingly well received [1]—indeed, far more favourably than he had any reason to expect.  A second edition, which was not printed at Strawberry Hill, speedily followed the first, with no diminution of its prosperity.  For an effort which made no pretensions to symmetry, which is often meagre where it might have been expected to be full, and is everywhere prejudiced by a sort of fine-gentleman disdain of exactitude—this was certainly as much as he could anticipate.  But he seems to have been more than usually sensitive to criticism, and some of the amplest of his *Short Notes* are devoted to the discussion of the adverse opinions which were expressed.  From these we learn that he was

[1] [He records in his *Journal* that he sold the copyright for *two years* to Graham and Dodsley for £200, for the benefit of Bentley.]

abused by the *Critical Review* for disliking the
Stuarts, and by the *Monthly* for liking his father.
Further, that he found an apologist in Dr. Hill
(of the *Inspector*), whose gross adulation was worse
than abuse; and lastly, that he was seriously
attacked in a Pamphlet of *Remarks on Mr. Walpole's ' Catalogue of Royal and Noble Authors '* by
a certain Carter, concerning whose antecedents
his irritation goes on to bring together all the
scandals he can collect. As the *Short Notes* were
written long after the events, it shows how his
soreness against his critics continued. What it
was when still fresh may be gathered from the
following quotation from a letter to the Rev.
Henry Zouch, to whom he was indebted for many
new facts and corrections, especially in the second
edition, and who afterwards helped him in the
*Anecdotes of Painting :*—' I am sick of the character of author; I am sick of the consequences of
it; I am weary of seeing my name in the newspapers; I am tired with reading foolish criticisms
on me, and as foolish defences of me; and I trust
my friends will be so good as to let the last abuse
of me pass unanswered. It is called " Remarks "
on my Catalogue, asperses the Revolution more
than it does my book, and, in one word, is written
by a nonjuring preacher, who was a dog-doctor.

Of me he knows so little, that he thinks to punish me by abusing King William ! ' [1]

In a letter of a few months earlier to the same correspondent, he refers to another task [2] upon which, in despite of the sentence just quoted, he continued to employ himself. ' Last summer ', —he says,—' I bought of Vertue's widow forty volumes of his MS. collections relating to English painters, sculptors, gravers, and architects. He had actually begun their lives : unluckily he had not gone far, and could not write grammar. I propose to digest and complete this work.' [3] The purchases referred to had been made subsequent to 1756, when Mrs. Vertue applied to Walpole, as a connoisseur, to buy from her the voluminous notes and memoranda which her husband had accumulated with respect to art and artists in England. Walpole also acquired at Vertue's sale in May 1757, a number of copies from Holbein and two or three other pictures. He seems to have almost immediately set about arranging and digesting this unwieldy and chaotic heap of material,[4]

[1] *Walpole to Zouch*, 14 May 1759.

[2] [His *Anecdotes of Painting in England*.]

[3] *Walpole to Zouch*, 12 Jan. 1759.

[4] ' Mr. Vertue's Manuscripts, in 28 vols.'—were sold at the Sale of Rare Prints and Illustrated Works from the Strawberry Hill Collection on Tuesday, 21 June 1842 (lot

much of which, besides being illiterate, was also illegible. More than once his patience gave way under the drudgery; but he nevertheless persevered in a way that shows a tenacity of purpose foreign, in this case at all events, to his assumption of dilettante indifference. His progress is thus chronicled. He began in January 1760, and finished the first volume on August 14. The second volume was begun on September 5 and completed on October 23. On January 4 in the following year he set about the third volume, but laid it aside after the first day, not resuming it until the end of June. On August 22, however, he finished it. Two volumes were published in 1762, and a third, which is dated 1763, in 1764. As usual, he affected more or less to undervalue his own share in the work; but he very justly laid stress in his 'Preface' upon the fact that he was little more than the arranger of data not collected by his own exertions. 'I would not', he said to Zouch,[1] 'have the materials of forty years, which was Vertue's case, depreciated in compliment to the work of four months, which is almost

1,110), for £26 10s. [to Dawson Turner, from whose collection they were acquired by the British Museum]. Walpole says in the *Short Notes* that he paid £100.

[1] [20 Mar. 1762.]

my whole merit.'   Here, again, the tone is a little
in the Oronte manner ;  but, upon the main point,
the interest of the work, his friends did not share
his apprehensions, and Gray especially was ' violent about it '.[1]   Nor did the public show themselves less appreciative, for there was so much that
was new in the dead engraver's memoranda, and
so much which was derived from private galleries
or drawn from obscure sources, that the work
could scarcely have failed of readers even if the
style had been hopelessly corrupt, which, under
Walpole's revision, it certainly was not.   In 1762,
he began a *Catalogue of Engravers*, which he
finished in about nine weeks as a supplementary
volume ; [2] and in 1763–5, still at the Strawberry
Press, he printed a second edition [3] of the first
three volumes, and the *Catalogue.*   [In 1771 a
fourth volume of the *Anecdotes of Painting* [4] was

[1] [*Walpole to Montagu*, 24 Nov. 1760.  For the notes
Walpole was very largely indebted to Gray—see *Gray to
Walpole*, 2 Sept., and Nov. 1760, in *Correspondence of Gray,
Walpole, West, and Ashton*, ii. 186–207.]

[2] [This was published in Feb. 1764, together with the
third volume of the *Anecdotes of Painting*, both being dated
1763.  The price of the four volumes was £3.]

[3] [This was dated 1765, but was not published till June
1767.]

[4] *The Anecdotes of Painting* was enlarged by the Rev.
James Dallaway in 1826–8, and again revised, with ad-

printed at Strawberry Hill, but was not published till October 1780 ; of this no second edition was printed by Walpole.]

After the printing of the second edition of the *Anecdotes of Painting,* a silence fell upon the *Officina Arbuteana* for three years, during ten months of which Walpole was at Paris, as will be narrated in the next chapter. His press, as may be guessed, was one of the sights of his Gothic castle, and there are several anecdotes showing how his ingenious fancy made it the vehicle of adroit compliment. Once,[1] not long after it had been established, my Lady Rochford, Lady Townshend (the witty Ethelreda or Audrey Harrison),[2] Sir John Bland's sister, and Earl Waldegrave, 'the new Knight of the Garter', were carried after dinner into the printing room to see Mr. Robinson at work. He immediately struck off some verse which was already in type, and presented it to Lady Townshend :—

THE PRESS SPEAKS :

From Me Wits and Poets their glory obtain ;
Without Me their Wit & their Verses were vain :
Stop, Townshend ! and let me but Print what You say ;
You, the fame I on others bestow, will repay.

ditional notes, by Ralph N. Wornum in 1849. The revised edition (1888) of this last in three volumes, 8vo, is the accepted edition.          [1] [On 19 Aug. 1757.]

    [2] She was married to Charles, 3rd Viscount Townshend,

The visitors then asked, as had been anticipated, to see the actual process of setting up, and Walpole ostensibly gave the printer four lines out of Rowe's *Fair Penitent*. But, by what would now be styled a clever feat of prestidigitation, the forewarned Robinson struck off the following, this time to Lady Rochford :—

### THE PRESS SPEAKS :

In vain from your properest name you have flown,
And exchang'd lovely Cupid's for Hymen's dull throne ;
By my art shall your beauties be constantly sung,
And in spite of yourself, you shall ever be YOUNG.

Lady Rochford's maiden name, it should be explained, was ' Young '. Such were what their inventor calls *les amusements des eaux de Straberri* in the month of August and the year of grace 1757.[1]

Beyond the major efforts already mentioned, the *Short Notes* contain references to various fugitive pieces which Walpole composed, some of which he printed, and some others of which have been published since his death. One of these,

in 1723, and was the mother of Charles Townshend, the statesman. She died in 1788, aged 85. There was an enamel of her by Zincke after Vanloo in the Tribune at Strawberry Hill, which is engraved at p. 150 of Cunningham's second volume.

    [1] [*Walpole to Montagu*, 25 Aug. 1757.]

*The Magpie and her Brood,*[1] was a pleasant little fable from the French of Bonaventure Despériers, rhymed for Miss Hotham, the youthful great-niece of his neighbour Lady Suffolk ; another a *Dialogue between two Great Ladies.*[2] In 1761 he wrote a poem on the King entitled *The Garland,* which first saw the light in the *Quarterly* for 1852 (No. CLXXX.). Besides these were several epigrams, mock sermons, and occasional verses. But perhaps the most interesting of his productions in this kind are the octosyllabics which he wrote in August 1759, and called *The Parish Register of Twickenham.* This is a metrical list of all the remarkable persons who ever lived there, for which reason it may find a place in these pages :—

> ' Where silver Thames round Twit'nam meads
> His winding current sweetly leads ;
> Twit'nam, the Muses' fav'rite seat,
> Twit'nam, the Graces' lov'd retreat ;
> There polish'd Essex wont to sport,
> The pride and victim of a court !
> There Bacon tun'd the grateful lyre
> To soothe Eliza's haughty ire ;
> —Ah ! happy had no meaner strain
> Than friendship's dash'd his mighty vein !
> Twit'nam, where Hyde, majestic sage,
> Retir'd from folly's frantic stage,
> While his vast soul was hung on tenters

[1] [Oct. 1764.]        [2] [Mar. 1760.]

To mend the world, and vex dissenters :
Twit'nam, where frolic Wharton revel'd,
Where Montague with locks dishevel'd
(Conflict of dirt and warmth divine),
Invok'd—and scandaliz'd the Nine ;
Where Pope in moral music spoke
To th' anguish'd soul of Bolingbroke,
And whisper'd, how true genius errs,
Preferring joys that pow'r confers ;
Bliss, never to great minds arising
From ruling worlds, but from despising :
Where Fielding met his bunter muse,
And, as they quaff'd the fiery juice,
Droll Nature stamp'd each lucky hit
With inimaginable wit ·
Where Suffolk sought the peaceful scene,
Resigning Richmond to the queen,
And all the glory, all the teasing,
Of pleasing one not worth the pleasing :
Where Fanny, ever-blooming fair,
Ejaculates the graceful pray'r,
And, 'scap'd from sense, with nonsense smit,
For Whitfield's cant leaves Stanhope's wit :
Amid this choir of sounding names
Of statesmen, bards, and beauteous dames,
Shall the last trifler of the throng
Enroll his own such names among ?
—Oh ! no—Enough if I consign
To lasting types their notes divine :
Enough, if Strawberry's humble hill
The title-page of fame shall fill.' [1]

[1] *Works of Lord Orford,* iv. 382–3.

In 1784, Walpole added a few lines to cele-
brate a new resident and a new favourite, Lady
Di Beauclerk, the widow of Johnson's famous
friend.[1]  Most of the other names which occur
in the *Twickenham Register* are easily identified.
' Fanny, " ever-blooming fair," ' was the beautiful Lady Fanny Shirley of Philips' ballad and
Pope's epistle, aunt of that fourth Earl Ferrers,
who in 1760 was hanged at Tyburn for murder-
ing his steward.  Miss Hawkins remembered her
as residing at a house now called Heath Lane
Lodge with her mother, ' a very ancient Countess
Ferrers ', widow of the first Earl.  Henry Fielding, to whom Walpole gives a quatrain, the second
couplet of which must excuse the insolence of the
first, had for some time lodgings in Back Lane,
whence was baptised in February 1748, the elder
of his sons by his second wife, the William Fielding, who, like his father, became a Westminster
magistrate.  It is more likely that *Tom Jones* was
written at Twickenham than at any of the dozen
other places for which that honour is claimed,
since the author quitted Twickenham late in
1748, and his great novel was published early in
the following year.  Walpole had only been resident for a short time when Fielding left, but even

[1] See Chapter IX.

had this been otherwise, it is not likely that, between the master of the Comic Epos (who was also Lady Mary's cousin !) and the dilettante proprietor of Strawberry, there could ever have been much cordiality.   Indeed, for some of the robuster spirits of his age Walpole shows an extraordinary distaste, which with him generally implies unsympathetic, if not absolutely illiberal, comment. Almost the only important anecdote of Fielding in his correspondence [1] is one of which the distorting bias is demonstrable ; [2]  and to Fielding's contemporary Hogarth, although as a connoisseur he was shrewd enough to collect his works, he scarcely ever refers but to place him in a ridiculous aspect, a course which contrasts curiously with the extravagant praise he gives to Bentley, Bunbury, Lady Di Beauclerk, and some other of the very minor artistic lights in his own circle.

It is, however, possible to write too long an excursus upon the *Twickenham Parish Register,* and the last paragraphs of this chapter belong of right to another and more important work, *The Castle of Otranto.*   According to the *Short Notes,* this ' Gothic story ' was begun in June 1764, and

[1] [See *Walpole to Montagu,* 18 May 1749.]
[2] Cf. chapter vi of *Fielding,* by the present writer, in the *Men of Letters* series, 2nd edition, 1889, pp. 145–7.

finished on the 6th August following. From another account we learn that it occupied eight nights of this period from ten o'clock at night until two in the morning, to the accompaniment of coffee. In a letter to Cole, the Cambridge antiquary, with whom Walpole commenced to correspond in 1762, he gives some further particulars, which, because they have been so often quoted, can scarcely be omitted here :—' Shall I even confess to you, what was the origin of this romance ? I waked one morning in the beginning of last June, from a dream, of which, all I could recover was, that I had thought myself in an ancient castle (a very natural dream for a head filled like mine with Gothic story), and that on the uppermost banister of a great staircase I saw a gigantic hand in armour. In the evening I sat down, and began to write, without knowing in the least what I intended to say or relate. The work grew on my hands, and I grew fond of it— add, that I was very glad to think of anything, rather than politics—in short, I was so engrossed with my tale, which I completed in less than two months, that one evening, I wrote from the time I had drunk my tea, about six o'clock, till half an hour after one in the morning, when my hand and fingers were so weary, that I could not hold the pen to finish the sentence, but left Matilda and Isabella talking, in the middle of a paragraph.' [1]

The work of which the origin is thus described was published in a limited edition [2] on the 24th December 1764, with the title of *The Castle of Otranto, a Story, translated by William Marshal, Gent. from the original Italian of Onuphrio Muralto, Canon of the Church of St. Nicholas at Otranto.* The name of the alleged Italian author is sometimes described as an anagram for Horace Walpole —a misconception which is easily demonstrated by counting the letters. The book was printed, not for Walpole, but for Lownds of Fleet Street, and it was prefaced by an introduction in which the author described and criticised the supposed original, which he declared to be a black-letter printed at Naples in 1529. Its success was considerable. It seems at first to have excited no suspicion as to its authenticity, but it is clear that Gray, to whom a copy was sent immediately after publication, was in the secret from the first.[3]  ' I

[1] *Letter to Cole,* 9 March 1765.

[2] [500 copies.]

[3] [Walpole writes to Mason on 17 Apr. 1765 : ' The *Castle of Otranto* . . . was begun and finished in less than two months, and then I showed it to Mr. Gray, who encouraged me to print it.']

have received the *Castle of Otranto* ',—he says,—
' and return you my thanks for it. It engages our
attention here,[1] makes some of us cry a little, and
all in general afraid to go to bed o' nights.' In the
second edition,[2] which followed in April 1765,
Walpole dropped the mask, disclosing his author-
ship in a second preface of great ability, which,
among other things, contains a vindication of
Shakespeare's mingling of comedy and tragedy
against the strictures of Voltaire—a piece of
temerity which some of his French friends feared
might prejudice him with that formidable critic.
But what is even more interesting is his own
account of what he had attempted. He had en-
deavoured to blend ancient and modern romance—
to employ the old supernatural agencies of Scudéry
and La Calprenède as the background to the adven-
tures of personages modelled as closely upon ordinary life as the personages of *Tom Jones*. These
are not his actual illustrations, but they express his
meaning. ' The actions, sentiments, conversations, of the heroes and heroines of ancient days
were as unnatural as the machines employed to
put them in motion.' He would make his heroes
and heroines natural in all these things, only

[1] At Cambridge.
[2] [Also of 500 copies.]

borrowing from the older school some of that imagination, invention, and fancy which, in the literal reproduction of life, he thought too much neglected.

His idea was novel, and the moment a favourable one for its development. Fluently and lucidly written, the *Castle of Otranto* set a fashion in literature. But, like many other works produced under similar conditions, it had its day. To the pioneer of a movement which has exhausted itself, there comes often what is almost worse than oblivion—discredit and neglect. A generation like the present, for whom fiction has unravelled so many intricate combinations, and whose Gothicism and Mediævalism are better instructed than Walpole's, no longer feels its soul harrowed up in the same way as did his hushed and awe-struck readers of the days of the third George. To the critic the book is interesting as the first of a school of romances which had the honour of influencing even the mighty ' Wizard of the North ', who, no doubt in gratitude, wrote for *Ballantyne's Novelist's Library* a most appreciative study of the story. But we doubt if that many-plumed and monstrous helmet, which crashes through stone walls and cellars, could now give a single shiver to the most timorous Cambridge don, while we suspect that the majority of modern students would, like the author, leave Matilda and Isabella talking, in the middle of a paragraph, but from a different kind of weariness. *Autres temps, autres mœurs,*—especially in the matter of Gothic romance.

# CHAPTER VII

HORACE WALPOLE

# VII

WHEN, towards the close of 1765, Walpole made the first of several visits to Paris,[1] the society of the French capital, and indeed French society as a whole, was showing signs of that coming *culbute générale* which was not to be long deferred. The upper classes were shamelessly immoral, and, from the King downwards, *liaisons* of the most open character excited neither censure nor comment. It was the era of Voltaire and the Encyclopædists; it was the era of Rousseau and the Sentimentalists; it was also the era of confirmed Anglomania. While we, on our side, were beginning to copy the *comédies larmoyantes* of La Chaussée and Diderot, the French in their turn were acting *Romeo and Juliet* and raving over Richardson. Richardson's chief rival in their eyes was Hume, then a *chargé d'affaires*, and in spite of his plain face and bad French, the idol of the freethinkers. He 'is treated here', writes Walpole,[2] 'with perfect veneration,' and we learn from other sources that no lady's toilette was complete without his attendance. 'At the Opera',—

[1] [The first since he was there with Gray in 1739.]
[2] [*To Montagu*, 22 Sept. 1765.]

says Lord Charlemont,—'his broad, unmeaning face was usually seen *entre deux jolis minois* ; the ladies in France gave the *ton,* and the *ton* was Deism.'    Apart from literature, irreligion, and philosophy, the chief occupation was cards.  'Whisk and Richardson' is Walpole's later definition of French society;  'Whisk and disputes,' that of Hume.    According to Walpole, a kind of pedantry and solemnity was the characteristic of conversation, and ' laughing was as much out of fashion as pantins or bilboquets.    Good folks, they have no time to laugh.    There is God and the King to be pulled down first ;  and men and women, one and all, are devoutly employed in the demolition.' [1]  How that enterprise eventuated history has recorded.

It is needless, however, to rehearse the origins of the French Revolution, in order to make a background for the visit of an English gentleman to Paris in 1765.    Walpole had been meditating this journey for two or three years, but the state of his health among other things (he suffered much from gout) had from time to time postponed it.  In 1763, he had been going next spring ; [2]  but

[1] [*To Brand,* 19 Oct. 1765.]

[2] It is curious to note in one of his letters at this date a *mot* which may be compared with the famous ' Good Ameri-

when next spring came he talked of the beginning
of 1765. Nevertheless, in March of that year,
Gilly Williams writes to Selwyn : ' Horry Walpole has now postponed his journey till May,' and
then he goes on to speak of the *Castle of Otranto*
in a way which shows that all the author's friends
were not equally enthusiastic respecting that ingenious romance. ' How do you think he has
employed that leisure which his political frenzy
has allowed of ? In writing a novel, . . . and such
a novel, that no boarding-school Miss of thirteen
could get through without yawning. It consists
of ghosts and enchantments ; pictures walk out
of their frames, and are good company for half an
hour together ; helmets drop from the moon, and
cover half a family. He says it was a dream, and
I fancy one when he had some feverish disposition
in him.' [1] May, however, had arrived and passed,
and the *Castle of Otranto* was in its second edition,
before Walpole at last set out, on Monday, the
9th September 1765.[2] After a seven hours' pas-

cans, when they die, go to Paris '. Walpole is more sar-
donic. ' Paris ', he says, . . . ' like the description of the
grave, is the way of all flesh ' (*Walpole to Mann*, 30 June
1763).

[1] *Gilly Williams to Selwyn*, 19 Mar. 1765.

[2] [Horace Walpole's (as yet unpublished) *Journals* of this
and his subsequent visits to Paris, formerly in the Waller

sage, he reached Calais from Dover. Near Amiens he was refreshed by a sight of one of his favourites, Lady Mary Coke,[1] ' in pea-green and silver ' ;[2] at Chantilly he was robbed of his portmanteau. By the time he reached Paris on the 13th, he had already ' fallen in love with twenty things, and in hate with forty '.[2] The dirt of Paris, the narrowness of the streets, the ' trees clipped to resemble

Collection, are now in the possession of Mr. Percival Merritt, of Boston, Mass. An article on them by the present writer was published in *The Times* of 16 Aug. 1924.]

[1] Lady Mary Coke, to whom the second edition of the Gothic romance was dedicated, was the youngest daughter of John, Duke of Argyll and Greenwich. At this date, she was a widow,—Lord Coke having died in 1753. Two volumes of her *Letters and Journals*, with a reprint of Lady Louisa Stuart's entertaining memoir of Lady Mary, and introductions by the editor, Hon. James A. Home, were printed privately at Edinburgh in 1889 from MSS. in the possession of the Earl of Home. A third volume, which includes a number of epistles addressed to her by Walpole, found among the papers of the late Mr. Drummond Moray of Abercairny, was issued in 1892 ; and a fourth in 1896. Walpole's tone in these documents is one of fantastic adoration ; but the pair ultimately (and inevitably) quarrelled. There is a well-known mezzotint of Lady Mary by McArdell after Allan Ramsay, in which she appears in white satin, holding a tall theorbo. The original painting is at Mount Stuart, and belongs to Lord Bute.

[2] [*Walpole to Conway*, 11–13 Sept. 1765.]

brooms, and planted on pedestals of chalk ', disgust him.   But he is enraptured with the *treillage* and fountains, ' and will prove it at Strawberry'.   He detests the French opera, though he loves the French *opéra comique* with its Italian comedy and his passion—'his dear favourite harlequin'.   Upon the whole, in these first impressions he is disappointed.   Society is duller than he expected, and with the staple topics of its conversation, philosophy, literature, and freethinking, he is (or says he is) out of sympathy.   ' Freethinking is for one's self, surely not for society. . . . I dined to-day with a dozen *savans,* and though all the servants were waiting, the conversation was much more unrestrained, even on the Old Testament, than I would suffer at my own table in England, if a single footman was present.   For literature, it is very amusing when one has nothing else to do. I think it rather pedantic in society ;   tiresome when displayed professedly—and, besides, in this country one is sure it is only the fashion of the day.'   And then he goes on to say that the reigning fashion is Richardson and Hume.[1]

One of his earliest experiences was his presentation at Versailles to the royal family, a ceremony which luckily involved but one operation instead of

[1] *Walpole to Montagu,* 22 Sept. 1765.

O

several as in England, where the Princess Dowager of Wales, the Duke of Cumberland, and the Princess Amelia had all their different levees.   He gives an account of this to Lady Hervey ; [1] but repeats it on the same day with much greater detail in a letter to Chute.   ' You perceive [he says] that I have been presented.   The Queen took great notice of me ; [2] none of the rest said a syllable. You are let into the King's bed-chamber just as he has put on his shirt ; he dresses and talks good-humouredly to a few, glares at strangers, goes to mass, to dinner, and a-hunting.   The good old Queen, who is like Lady Primrose in the face, and Queen Caroline in the immensity of her cap, is at her dressing-table, attended by two or three old ladies. . . . Thence you go to the Dauphin, for all is done in an hour.   He scarce stays a minute ; indeed, poor creature, he is a ghost, and cannot possibly last three months.[3]   The Dauphiness is in her bedchamber, but dressed and standing ; looks cross, is not civil, and has the true West-phalian grace and accents.   The four Mes-

---

[1] [3 Oct. 1765.]

[2] For which reason, in imitation of Madame de Sévigné, he tells Lady Hervey that she is *le plus grand roi du monde*.

[3] He died, in fact, within this time, on the 20th December.

dames [1] who are clumsy plump old wenches, with
a bad likeness to their father, stand in a bedchamber
in a row, with black cloaks and knotting-bags, looking good-humoured, [and] not knowing what to
say. . . . This ceremony is very short; then you
are carried to the Dauphin's three boys, who you
may be sure only bow and stare. The Duke of
Berry [2] looks weak and weak-eyed: the Count
de Provence [3] is a fine boy; the Count d'Artois [4]
well enough. The whole concludes with seeing
the Dauphin's little girl dine, who is as round and
as fat as a pudding.' [5] Such is Walpole's account
of the royal family of France on exhibition. In
the Queen's ante-chamber he was treated to a
sight of the famous *bête du Gévaudan*, a hugeous
wolf of which a highly sensational representation
had been given in the *St. James's Chronicle* for
June 6–8. It had just been shot, after a pros-
perous but nefarious career, and was exhibited by
two chasseurs ' with as much parade as if it was
Mr. Pitt '.[6]

[1] These were the *Graille, Chiffe, Coche,* and *Loque* of
history.

[2] Afterwards Louis XVI.           [3] Louis XVIII.

[4] Charles X.           [5] *Walpole to Chute,* 3 Oct. 1765.

[6] [*Walpole to Conway,* 6 Oct. 1765.] Madame de Genlis
mentions this fearsome monster in her *Mémoires* :—' Tout
le monde a entendu parler de la hyène de Gévaudan, qui a

When he had been at Paris little less than a month, he was laid up with the gout in both feet. He was visited during his illness by Wilkes, for whom he expresses no admiration.[1] From another letter [2] it appears that Sterne and Foote were also staying in the French capital at this time. In November he is still limping about, and it is evident that confinement in ' a bedchamber in a *hôtel garni* . . . when the court is at Fontainebleau ',[3] has not been without its effect upon his views of things in general. In writing to Gray (who replies [4] with all sorts of kindly remedies), he says, ' the charms of Paris have not the least attraction for me, nor would keep me an hour on their own account. For the city itself, I cannot conceive where my eyes were : it is the ugliest beastliest fait tant de ravages.' The point of Walpole's allusion to Pitt is explained in one of his letters to Lady Mary Coke at this date (15 Oct.) :—' I had the fortune to be treated with the sight of what, next to Mr. Pitt, has occasioned most alarm in France, the Beast of the Gevaudan.' In another letter to Pitt's sister Ann, maid of honour to Queen Caroline, he says (8 Oct.) :—' It is a very large wolf to be sure, and they say has twelve teeth more than any of the species, and six less than the Czarina.'

[1] [*Walpole to Montagu*, 16 Oct. 1765.]
[2] [*Walpole to Brand*, 19 Oct. 1765.]
[3] [*Walpole to Mann*, 16 Oct. 1765.]
[4] [13 Dec. 1765.]

town in the universe. I have not seen a mouth-
ful of verdure out of it, nor have they anything
green but their *treillage* and window shutters . . .
Their boasted knowledge of society is reduced to
talking of their suppers, and every malady they
have about them, or know of.' [1]   A day or two
later his gout and his stick have left him, and his
good humour is coming back. Before the month
ends, he is growing reconciled to his environment ;
and by January ' France is so agreeable, and England so much the reverse '—he tells Lady Hervey [2]
—' that he does not know when he shall return '. The great ladies, too, Madame de Brionne,
Madame d'Aiguillon, Marshal Richelieu's daughter, Madame d'Egmont (with whom he could fall
in love if it would break anybody's heart in England), begin to flatter and caress him. His ' last
new passion ' is the Duchess de Choiseul, who is
so charming that ' you would take her for the
queen of an allegory '. ' One dreads its finishing,
as much as a lover, if she would admit one, would
wish it should finish.' There is also a beautiful
Countess de Forcalquier, the ' broken music ' of
whose imperfect English stirs him into heroics
too Arcadian for the matter-of-fact meridian of

[1] [*Walpole to Gray,* 19 Nov. 1765.]
[2] [11 Jan. 1766.]

London, where Lady Hervey is cautioned not to exhibit them to the profane.[1]

In a letter of later date [2] to Gray, he describes some more of these graceful and witty leaders of fashion, whose ' *douceur* ' he seems to have greatly preferred to the pompous and arrogant fatuity of the men. ' They have taken up gravity '—he says of these latter—' thinking it was philosophy and English, and so have acquired nothing in the room of their natural levity and cheerfulness '. But with the women the case is different. He knows six or seven ' with very superior understandings ; some of them with wit, or with softness, or very good sense '. His first portrait is of the famous Madame Geoffrin, to whom he had been recommended by Lady Hervey, and who had visited him when imprisoned in his *chambre garnie*.[3] He lays stress upon her knowledge of character, her tact and good sense, and the happy

---

[1] Of Mad. de Forcalquier it is related that, entering a theatre during the performance of Gresset's *Le Méchant*, just as the line was uttered—' *La faute en est aux dieux, qui la firent si bête*,' some of the pit rapturously applauded her beauty, and, called to order by the rest of the audience, excused themselves by laying the blame on the powers ' *qui la firent si belle* ' (Hawkins' *French Stage*, 1888, i. 398).

[2] [25 Jan. 1766.]

[3] [*Walpole to Lady Hervey*, 13 Oct. 1765.]

mingling of freedom and severity by which she preserved her position as ' an epitome of empire, subsisting by rewards and punishments '.   Then there is the Maréchale de Mirepoix, a courtier and an *intrigante* of the first order.   ' She is false, artful, and insinuating beyond measure when it is her interest, but indolent and a coward '—says Walpole, who does not measure his words even when speaking of a beauty and a Princess of Lorraine.   Others are the *savante*, Madame de Boufflers, who visited England and Johnson, and whom the writer hits off neatly by saying that you would think she was always sitting for her picture to her biographer; a second *savante*, Madame de Rochefort, ' the *decent* friend ' of Walpole's former guest at Strawberry, the Duc de Nivernois; 1 the already

¹ Louis-Jules-Barbon-Mancini-Mazarini, Duc de Nivernois (1716–98), who had visited Twickenham three years earlier, when he was Ambassador to England.   He was a man of fine manners ; and tastes so literary that his works fill eight volumes.   They include a translation of Walpole's *Essay on Modern Gardening* (see Appendix at end).   In his letters to Miss Ann Pitt at this date (8 Oct., 25 Dec. 1765), Walpole speaks of the Duke's clever fables, by which he is now best remembered.   Lord Chesterfield told his son in 1749 that Nivernois was ' one of the prettiest men he had ever known ', and in 1762 his opinion was unaltered.   ' *M. de Nivernois est aimé, respecté, et admiré par tout ce qu'il y a d'honnêtes gens à la cour et à la ville,*' he writes to Madame

mentioned Duchess de Choiseul, and Madame la Maréchale de Luxembourg, whose youth had been stormy, but who was now softening down into a kind of twilight melancholy which made her rather attractive. This last, with one exception, completes his list.

The one exception is a figure which henceforth played no inconsiderable part in Walpole's correspondence—that of the brilliant and witty Madame du Deffand. As Marie de Vichy-Chamrond, she had been married at one-and-twenty to the nobleman whose name she bore, and had followed the custom of her day by speedily choosing a lover, who had many successors. For a brief space she had captivated the Regent himself, and at this date, being nearly seventy and hopelessly blind, was continuing, from mere force of habit, a 'decent friendship' with the deaf President Hénault. At first Walpole was not impressed with her, and speaks of her, disrespectfully, as 'an old blind *débauchée* of wit '.[1] A little later, although he still refers to her as the ' old lady of the house ',

de Monconseil. The Duke's end was worthy of Chesterfield himself, for he spent some of his last hours in composing valedictory verses to his doctor, which are said to have been '*pleins de sentiments affectueux*'.

    1  [*To Conway*, 6 Oct. 1765.]

he says she is very agreeable.[1]  Later still,[2] she
has completed her conquest by telling him he has
*le feu mocqueur ;* and in the letter to Gray above
quoted,[3] it is plain that she has become an object
of absorbing interest to him, not unmingled with
a nervous apprehension of her undisguised partial-
ity for his society.  In spite of her affliction (he
says) she ' retains all her vivacity, wit, memory,
judgment, passions, and agreeableness.  She goes
to Operas, Plays, suppers, and Versailles ;  gives
suppers twice a week ;  has every thing new read
to her ;  makes new songs and epigrams, ay, admirably,[4] and remembers every one that has been
made these fourscore years.  She corresponds with
Voltaire, dictates charming letters to him, contradicts him, is no bigot to him or anybody, and
laughs both at the clergy and the philosophers.
In a dispute, into which she easily falls, she is very

[1] [*To Gray*, 19 Nov. 1765.]
[2] [*To Selwyn*, 2 Dec. 1765.]    [3] [25 Jan. 1766.]
[4] One of her *logogriphes* or enigmas, which Walpole sent
to Lady Hervey (21 Nov. 1765), is as follows :—

> ' *Quoique je forme un corps, je ne suis qu'une idée ;*
> *Plus ma beauté vieillit, plus elle est décidée :*
> *Il faut, pour me trouver, ignorer d'où je viens :*
> *Je tiens tout de lui, qui réduit tout à rien.*'

The answer is *noblesse*.  Lord Chesterfield thought it so
good that he sent it to his godson (Letter 166).

warm, and yet scarce ever in the wrong: her
judgment on every subject is as just as possible:
on every point of conduct as wrong as possible:
for she is all love and hatred, passionate for her
friends to enthusiasm, still anxious to be loved, I
don't mean by lovers, and a vehement enemy, but
openly.   As she can have no amusement but conversation, the least solitude and ennui are insup-
portable to her, and put her into the power of
several worthless people, who eat her suppers
when they can eat nobody's of higher rank;
wink to one another and laugh at her; hate
her because she has forty times more parts—and
venture to hate her because she is not rich.'   In
another letter to Mr. James Crawford,[1] of Auchi-
names (Hume's *Fish* Crawford), who was also
one of Madame du Deffand's admirers, he says,
in repeating some of the above details, that he is
not 'ashamed of interesting himself exceedingly
about her.   To say nothing of her extraordinary
parts, she is certainly the most generous friendly
being upon earth.'   Upon her side Madame du
Deffand seems to have been equally attracted by
the strange mixture of independence and effeminacy which went to make up Walpole's character.
Her attachment to him rapidly grew into a kind

[1] [6 March 1766.]

of infatuation. He had no sooner quitted Paris, which he did on the 17th April, than she began to correspond with him, and thenceforward, until her death in 1780, her letters, dictated to her faithful secretary Wiart, continued, except when Walpole was actually visiting her (and she sometimes wrote to him even then), to reach him regularly.[1] Not long after his return to England, she

[1] [The originals of these letters, to the number of 838, many of them annotated by Horace Walpole, together with ten written to him by Wiart, now form part of the Toynbee Collection in the Bodleian. A selection from them, consisting of 52 complete letters, and extracts from about 300 more, was published by Miss Berry in 1810 (Lond., 4 vols., 12mo). The whole collection, which had been lost sight of, was discovered some 25 years ago by the late Mrs. Paget Toynbee in the possession of Mr. W. R. Parker-Jervis, of Meaford, Stone, Staffs., and was transcribed and edited by her, and published in 1912 (*Lettres de la Marquise du Deffand à Horace Walpole*, Lond., 3 vols., demy 8vo). The originals of Walpole's letters to Madame du Deffand, with the exception of seven, which by some accident were preserved with those written by her to him, are no longer in existence. All that were written subsequently to Jan. 1775 were burned by Madame du Deffand by his express desire. The rest, save for the seven above mentioned, were returned to Walpole periodically, as occasion offered, at his request (see *Lettres*, ed. cit., vol. i, pp. xxv–viii). These were in existence in 1810, when Miss Berry published her edition, in which extracts from about 80 of them were printed as

made him the victim of a charming hoax. He
had, when in Paris, admired a snuff-box, which
bore a portrait of Madame de Sévigné, for whom
he professed an extravagant admiration. Madame
du Deffand procured a similar box, had the portrait copied, and sent it to him with a letter, purporting to come from the dateless Elysian Fields
and 'Notre Dame de Livry' herself, in which
he was enjoined to use his present always, and
to bring it often to France and the Faubourg St.
Germain. Walpole was completely taken in, and
imagined that the box had come from Madame de
Choiseul ; but he should have known at first that
no one living but his blind friend could have
written 'that most charming of all letters'.[1]
The box itself, the memento of so much old-

notes, but were destroyed by her shortly after, as there is
every reason to believe, in obedience to Walpole's own
directions. The seven letters already mentioned were printed
by Mrs. Toynbee in her edition of Walpole's *Letters* ; the
extracts printed by Miss Berry were reprinted in the *Supplement* (vol. i) to Mrs. Toynbee's edition, with eleven other
letters, which were first printed (from copies discovered in
the 'Cabinet Noir' of the Post Office in Paris) in Mrs.
Toynbee's edition of Madame du Deffand's letters to Walpole.]

[1] [The letter is printed in a note to Walpole's letter to
Lady Hervey of 28 June 1766 in Mrs. Toynbee's edition
(see also *Supplement*, vol. ii, p. 136).]

world ingenuity, was sold (with the pseudo-Sévigné epistle) at the Strawberry Hill sale for £28 7s. (lot 25 of fifteenth day). When witty Mrs. Clive heard of the last addition to Walpole's list of favourites, she delivered herself of a good-humoured *bon mot*. There was a new resident at Twickenham—the first Earl of Shelburne's widow. 'If the new Countess is but lame', quoth Clive (referring to the fact that Lady Suffolk was deaf and Madame du Deffand blind), 'I shall have no chance of ever seeing you.' [1] But there is nothing to show that he ever relaxed in his attentions to the delightful actress whom he somewhere styles *dimidium animæ meæ*.[2]

One of the other illustrious visitors to Paris during Walpole's stay there was Rousseau. Being no longer safe in his Swiss asylum, where the curate of Motiers had excited the mob against him, that

---

[1] [*Walpole to Montagu,* 25 May 1766.]

[2] He was malicious enough to add, 'a pretty round half' [*to Montagu,* 16 Dec. 1766]. In middle life Mrs. Clive, like her Twickenham neighbour, Mrs. Pritchard, grew excessively stout ; and there is a pleasant anecdote that, on one occasion, when the pair were acting together in Cibber's *Careless Husband,* the audience were regaled by the spectacle of two leading actresses, neither of whom could manage to pick up a letter which, by ill-luck, had been dropped upon the ground.

extraordinary self-tormentor, clad in his Armenian costume, had arrived in December at the French capital, and shortly afterwards left for England under the safe conduct of Hume, who had undertaken to procure him a fresh resting-place. He reached London on the 14th January 1766. Walpole had, to use his own phrase, ' a hearty contempt' for the fugitive sentimentalist and his grievances, and not long before Rousseau's advent in Paris, taking for his pretext an offer made by the King of Prussia, he had woven some of the light mockery at Madame Geoffrin's into a sham letter from Frederick to Jean-Jacques, couched in the true Walpolean spirit of persiflage. It is difficult to summarize, and may be reproduced here as its author transcribed it on the 12th January, for the benefit of Conway :—

LE ROI DE PRUSSE A MONS. ROUSSEAU

MON CHER JEAN JACQUES,

Vous avez renoncé à Geneve votre patrie ; vous vous êtes fait chasser de la Suisse, pays tant vanté dans vos écrits ; la France vous a decreté. Venez donc chez moi ; j'admire vos talens ; je m'amuse de vos reveries, qui (soit dit en passant) vous occupent trop, et trop long tems. Il faut à la fin être sage et heureux. Vous avez fait assez parler de vous par des singularités peu convenables à un veritable grand homme. Demontrez à vos ennemis que vous pouvez avoir quelquefois le sens commun : cela les fachera, sans vous faire tort. Mes états vous offrent une retraite paisible ; je vous veux du bien, et je vous en ferai, si vous le trouvez bon. Mais si vous vous obstiniez à rejetter mon secours, attendez vous que je ne le dirai à personne. Si vous persistez à vous creuser l'esprit pour trouver de nouveaux malheurs, choisissez les tels que vous voudrez. Je suis roi, je puis vous en procurer au grè de vos souhaits : et ce qui surement ne vous arrivera pas vis à vis de vos ennemis, je cesserai de vous persecuter quand vous cesserez de mettre votre gloire à l'être.

Votre bon ami,     FREDERIC.

This composition, the French of which was touched up by Helvétius, Hénault, and the Duc de Nivernois,[1] gave extreme satisfaction to all the anti-Rousseau party.[2] While Hume and his *protégé* were still in Paris, Walpole, out of delicacy to Hume, managed to keep the matter a secret, and he also abstained from making any overtures to Rousseau, whom, as he truly said, he could scarcely have visited cordially with a letter in his

[1] [*Walpole to Conway*, 12 Jan. 1766.]

[2] In a letter to Miss Ann Pitt, 19 Jan. 1766, Walpole makes reference to the popularity which this *jeu d'esprit* procured for him. 'Everybody would have a copy [of course he encloses one to his correspondent] ; the next thing was, everybody would see the author. . . . I thought at last I should have a box quilted for me like Gulliver, be set upon the dressing-table of a Maid of Honour and fed with bonbons. . . . If, contrary to all precedent, I should exist in vogue a week longer, I will send you the first statue that is cast of me in *bergamotte* or *biscuite porcelaine*.'

pocket written to ridicule him.   But Hume had
no sooner departed, than Frederick's sham invitation went the round, ultimately finding its way
across the Channel, where it was printed in the
*St. James's Chronicle.*   Rousseau, always on the
alert to pose as the victim of plots and conspiracies,
was naturally furious, and wrote angrily from his
retreat at Mr. Davenport's in Derbyshire to de-
nounce the fabrication.   The worst of it was,
that his morbid nature immediately suspected the
innocent Hume of participating in the trick.
'What rends and afflicts my heart [is] ',—he
told the *Chronicle,*[1]—' that the impostor hath his
accomplices in England,' and this delusion became
one of the main elements in that ' twice-told tale ',
—the quarrel of Hume and Rousseau.   Walpole
was called upon to clear Hume from having any
hand in the letter, and several communications,
all of which are printed at length in the fourth
volume of his works,[2] followed upon the same
subject.   Their discussion would occupy too large
a space in this limited memoir.[3]   It is however

[1] [The letter is printed in *Lettres de Mme du Deffand à
Horace Walpole* (ed. Toynbee), vol. i, p. 10 n.]

[2] *Works of Lord Orford,* iv. 247–69.

[3] Hume's narrative of the affair may be read in *A Concise
and Genuine Account of the Dispute between Mr. Hume and*

worth noticing that Walpole's instinct appears to have foreseen the trouble that fell upon Hume. ' I wish ', he wrote to Lady Hervey, in a letter which Hume carried to England when he accompanied his untunable *protégé* thither, ' I wish he may not repent having engaged with Rousseau, who contradicts and quarrels with all mankind, in order to obtain their admiration.' [1]   He certainly, upon the present occasion, did not belie this uncomplimentary character.

Before the last stages of the Hume-Rousseau controversy had been reached, Hume was back again in Paris, and Walpole had returned to London.  Upon the whole, he told Mann,[2] he liked France so well that he should certainly go there

*Mr. Rousseau : with the Letters that passed between them during their Controversy.  As also, the Letters of the Hon. Mr. Walpole, and Mr. D'Alembert, relative to this extraordinary Affair.  Translated from the French.  London. Printed for T. Becket and P. A. De Hondt, near Surry-street, in the Strand, MDCCLXVI.*

[1] *Walpole to Lady Hervey*, 2 Jan. 1766.  In a letter to Lady Mary Coke, dated two days later, he says :—' Rousseau set out this morning for England.  As he loves to contradict a whole nation, I suppose he will write for the present opposition. . . . As he is to live at Fulham, I hope his first quarrel will be with his neighbour the Bishop of London, who is an excellent subject for his ridicule.'

[2] [20 Apr. 1766.]

P

210 Horace Walpole: A Memoir

again. In September 1766, he was once more
attacked with gout,[1] and at the beginning of
October went to Bath, whose Avon (as compared
with his favourite Thames) he considers 'paltry
enough to be the Seine or Tyber'. Nothing
pleases him much at Bath, although it contained
such notabilities as Lord Chatham, Lord North-
ington, and Lord Camden ; [2] but he goes to hear
Wesley, of whom he writes rather flippantly to
Chute.[3] He describes him as 'a lean elderly man,
fresh-coloured, his hair smoothly combed, but
with a *soupçon* of curl at the ends'. 'Wondrous
clean (he adds), but as evidently an actor as Garrick. He spoke his sermon, but so fast, and with
so little accent, that I am sure he has often uttered
it, for it was like a lesson. There were parts and
eloquence in it ; but towards the end he exalted
his voice, and acted very ugly enthusiasm ; decried
learning, and told stories, like Latimer, of the fool
of his college, who said, 'I *thanks* God for everything'. He returned to Strawberry Hill in October. In August of the next year he again went
to Paris,[4] going almost straight to Madame du
Deffand's, where he finds Mademoiselle Clairon

---

[1] [*To Mann*, 9, 25 Sept. 1766.]
[2] [*To Conway*, 2 Oct. 1766.]      [3] [10 Oct. 1766.]
[4] [His first visit lasted from 14 Sept. 1765 till 17 Apr. 1766.]

(who had quitted the stage) invited to declaim
Corneille in his honour, and he sups in a distinguished company. His visit lasted nearly two
months,[1] but his letters for this period contain few
interesting particulars, while those of the lady
cease altogether, to be resumed again on the 9th
October, a few hours after his departure. Two
years later he travels once more to Paris [2] and his
blind friend, whom he finds in better health than
ever, and with spirits so increased that he tells her
she will go mad with age. 'When they ask her
how old she is, she answers, *J'ai soixante et mille
ans.*' [3] Her septuagenarian activity might well
have wearied a younger man. 'She and I, he
writes to Chute, went to the Boulevard last night
after supper, and drove about there till two in the
morning. We are going to sup in the country this
evening, and are to go to-morrow night at eleven
to the puppet-show.' [3] In a letter to George
Montagu, which adds some details to her portrait,
he writes :—'I have heard her dispute with all
sorts of people, on all sorts of subjects, and never
knew her in the wrong.[4] She humbles the learned,

[1] [23 Aug. to 9 Oct. 1767.]
[2] [This visit lasted from Aug. 18 till 5 Oct. 1769.]
[3] [*To Chute*, 30 Aug. 1769.]
[4] Lady Mary Coke (in her *Journal* for 6 Apr. 1770)

sets right their disciples, and finds conversation for everybody.   Affectionate as Madame de Sévigné, she has none of her prejudices, but a more universal taste ; and, with the most delicate frame, her spirits hurry her through a life of fatigue that would kill me, if I was to continue here. . . . I had great difficulty last night to persuade her, though she was not well, not to sit up till between two and three for the comet ;  for which purpose she had appointed an astronomer to bring his telescopes to the President Hénault's, as she thought it would amuse me.   In short, her goodness to me is so excessive, that I feel unashamed at producing my withered person in a round of diversions, which I have quitted at home.' [1]   One of the other amusements which she procured for him was the *entrée* of the famous convent of St. Cyr, of which he gives an interesting account.[2]   He inspects the pensioners, and the numerous portraits of the foundress, Madame de Maintenon. In one class-room he hears the young ladies sing

testifies to the charm of her conversation :—' In the evening I made a visit to Madame du Deffan.  She talks so well that I wish'd to write down every thing She said, as I thought I should have liked to have read it afterwards.'  (*Letters and Journals,* iii. 233.)          [1] *To Montagu,* 7 Sept. 1769.
   [2] [*To Montagu,* 17 Sept. 1769.]

the choruses in *Athalie ;* in another sees them
dance minuets to the violin of a nun who is not
precisely St. Cecilia.   In the others they act *pro-
verbes* or conversations.   Finally, he is enabled to
enrich the archives of Strawberry with a piece of
paper containing a few sentences of Madame de
Maintenon's handwriting.

Walpole's literary productions for this date (in
addition to the letter from the King of Prussia to
Rousseau) are scheduled in the *Short Notes* with
his usual minuteness.   In June 1766, shortly after
his return from Paris, he wrote a squib upon Captain Byron's description of the Patagonians, entitled *An Account of the Giants lately discovered,*
which was published on the 25th August.[1]   On
18 August, he began his *Memoirs of the Reign of
King George the Third ;* and, in 1767, the detec-
tion of a work published at Paris in two volumes
under the title of the *Testament Politique du
Chevalier Robert Walpoole,* and ' stamped in that
mint of forgeries, Holland '.   This, which is
printed in the second volume of his works,[2] re-

[1] [It is printed in *Works of Lord Orford,* ii. 91–102.   It
was translated into French by the Chevalier de Redmond
(see *Lettres de Mme du Deffand à Horace Walpole,* i. 174),
whose MS., which has never been published, is in the
Toynbee Collection in the Bodleian.]

[2] *Works of Lord Orford,* ii. 323–38.

mained unpublished during his lifetime, as no English translation of the *Testament* was ever made.    His next deliverance was a letter, written on 13 March 1767, and subsequently printed in the *St. James's Chronicle* for 28 May, in which he announced to the Corporation of Lynn, in the person of their Mayor, Mr. Langley, that he did not intend to offer himself again as the representative in Parliament of that town.    A wish to retire from all public business and the declining state of his health are assigned as the reasons for his thus breaking his Parliamentary connection, which had now lasted for five-and-twenty years. Following upon this comes the already mentioned account of his action in the Hume and Rousseau quarrel, and a couple of letters on *Political Abuse in Newspapers*.    These appeared in the *Public Advertiser*.    But the chief results of his leisure in 1766–8 are to be found in two efforts more ambitious than any of those above indicated, the *Historic Doubts on Richard the Third*, and the tragedy of *The Mysterious Mother*.    The *Historic Doubts* was begun in the winter of 1767 and published in February 1768;[1] the tragedy in December 1766, and published in March 1768.

The *Historic Doubts* was an attempt to vindi-

---

[1] [It was reprinted in *Works of Lord Orford*, ii. 103–84.]

cate Richard III from his traditional character, which Walpole considered had been intentionally blackened in order to whiten that of Henry VII. ' *Vous seriez un excellent attornei général,*'—wrote Voltaire [1] to him,—' *vous pesez toutes les probabilités.*' He might have added that they were all weighed on one side. Gray admits the clearness with which the principal part of the arguments was made out; but he remained unconvinced, especially as regards the murder of Henry VI.[2] Other objectors speedily appeared, who were neither so friendly nor so gentle. *The Critical Review* attacked him for not having referred to Guthrie's *History of England,* which had in some respects anticipated him; and he was also criticised adversely by the *London Chronicle.* Of these attacks Walpole spoke and wrote very contemptuously; but he seems to have been considerably nettled by the conduct of a Swiss named Deyverdun, who, giving an account of the book in a work called *Mémoires Littéraires de la Grande Bretagne* for 1768, declared his preference for the views which Hume had expressed in certain notes to

[1] [At Voltaire's request, Walpole had sent him a copy of the work. See *Walpole to Voltaire,* 21 June 1768.]

[2] [*Gray to Walpole,* 14 Feb. 1768. Gray had given Walpole some assistance.]

the said account.   Deyverdun's action appears to
have stung Walpole into a supplementary defence
of his theories, in which he dealt with his critics
generally.   This he did not print, but set aside to
appear as a postscript in his works.[1]   In 1770,
however, his arguments were contested by Dr.
Milles, Dean of Exeter, to whom he replied ; [2]
and later still, another antiquary, the Rev. Mr.
Masters,[3] came forward.   The last two assailants
were members of the Society of Antiquaries, from
which body Walpole, in consequence, withdrew.
But he practically abandoned his theories in a final
postscript written in February 1793, which is to
be found in the second volume of his works.[4]

Concerning the second performance above referred to, *The Mysterious Mother*, most of Walpole's
biographers are content to abide in generalities.
That the proprietor of Gothic Strawberry should
have produced *The Castle of Otranto* has a certain
congruity, but one scarcely expects to find the
same person indulging in a blank-verse tragedy
sombre enough to have taxed the powers of Ford

[1] [*Works of Lord Orford*, ii. 185–220.]
[2] [*Works of Lord Orford*, ii. 221–44.]
[3] [His reply to Masters is printed in *Works of Lord
Orford*, ii. *245–*251.]
[4] [*Works of Lord Orford*, ii. *251–*252.]

or Webster. It is a curious example of literary reaction, and his own words respecting it are doubtful-voiced. To Montagu and to Madame du Deffand he writes apologetically. ' *Il ne vous plairoit pas assurément ;* '—he informs the lady —' *il n'y a pas de beaux sentiments ; il n'y a que des passions sans enveloppe ; des crimes, des repentirs, et des horreurs ;* ' [1] and he lays his finger on one of its gravest defects when he goes on to say that its interest languishes from the first act to the last. Yet he seems, too, to have thought of its being played, for he tells Montagu a month later [2] that though he is not yet intoxicated enough with it to think it would do for the stage, yet he wishes to see it acted,—a wish which must have been a real one,—since he says further that he has written an epilogue for Mrs. Clive to speak in character. The postscript which is affixed to the printed piece contradicts the above utterances considerably, or, at all events, shows that fuller consideration has materially revised them. He admits that *The Mysterious Mother* would not be proper to appear upon the boards. ' The subject is so horrid, that I thought it would shock rather than give satisfaction to an audience. Still I found it so truly tragic

[1] [*Lettres de Mme du Deffand à Horace Walpole* (ed. Toynbee), i. 407, n. 3.]      [2] [15 Apr. 1768.]

in the two essential springs of terror and pity, that I could not resist the impulse of adapting it to the scene, though it should never be practicable to produce it there.' [1] After his criticism to Madame du Deffand upon the plot, it is curious tŏ find him later claiming that ' every scene tends to bring on the catastrophe, and [that] the story is never interrupted or diverted from its course '. Notwithstanding its imaginative power, it is impossible to deny that the author's words as to the repulsiveness of the subject are just. But it is needless to linger longer upon a dramatic work which had such grave defects as to render its being acted impossible, and concerning the literary merit of which there will always be different opinions. Byron spoke of it as ' a tragedy of the highest order ', a judgment which has been traversed by Macaulay and Scott ; Miss Burney shuddered at its very name ; while Lady Di Beauclerk illustrated it enthusiastically with a series of seven

[1] [Mason made alterations in it, in order to adapt it for the stage, which Walpole inserted in his own copy of the play (see *Walpole to Mason*, 11 May 1769). This copy was sold at Hodgson's at the Milnes-Gaskell sale (lot 97) on Feb. 28, 1924, for £29 10*s*. None of Mason's alterations were adopted by Walpole when the play was reprinted ; but they have been printed recently in an edition by Montague Summers.]

designs in ' sut-water ' [1] for which the enraptured author erected a special gallery.[2]   Meanwhile, we may quote, from the close of the above postscript, a passage where Walpole is at his best.   It is a rapid and characteristic *aperçu* of tragedy in England :—

' The excellence of our dramatic writers is by no means equal in number to the great men we have produced in other walks.   Theatric genius lay dormant after Shakespeare ;  waked with some bold and glorious, but irregular and often ridiculous flights in Dryden ;  revived in Otway ;  maintained a placid pleasing kind of dignity in Rowe, and even shone in his *Jane Shore*.   It trod in sublime and classic fetters in *Cato*, but void of nature, or the power of affecting the passions.   In Southern it seemed a genuine ray of nature and Shakespeare ;  but falling on an age still more Hottentot, was stifled in those gross and barbarous productions, tragicomedies.   It turned to tuneful nonsense in the *Mourning Bride ;* grew stark mad in Lee ;  whose cloak, a little the worse for wear, fell on Young ;  yet in both was still a poet's cloak.

[1] i.e. Soot-water [*Walpole to Mason*, 18 Feb. 1776]. There were two landscapes in soot-water by Mr. Bentley in the Green Closet at Strawberry.
[2] See Chapter IX.

It recovered its senses in Hughes and Fenton, who
were afraid it should relapse, and accordingly kept
it down with a timid, but amiable hand—and then
it languished.  We have not mounted again above
the two last.' [1]

The original editions of the *Castle of Otranto*
and the *Historic Doubts* were not printed by Mr.
Robinson's latest successor, Mr. Kirgate.[2]  But
the Strawberry Press had by this time resumed its
functions, for *The Mysterious Mother*, of which
50 copies were struck off in 1768, was issued from
it.[3]  Another book which it produced in the same
year was *Cornélie*, a youthful tragedy by Madame
du Deffand's friend, President Hénault.  Walpole's
sole reason for giving it the permanence of his type

[1] *Works of Lord Orford*, i. 129.

[2] [They were both reprinted by Kirgate in the (unfinished) edition of Walpole's *Works*, which he began to
print in 1768, and finally abandoned in 1787—see Walpole's *Journal of the Printing-Office at Strawberry Hill* (ed.
Toynbee), p. 89.]

[3] [A second edition was published in London by Dodsley
in 1781, in order to stop the issue of an unauthorised edition ; a pirated edition was issued in Dublin in 1791.
A third edition was actually begun by Woodfall, the
famous printer of the letters of Junius, in 1783, but Walpole managed ' to buy himself out of his claws '.—See
*Supplement* (vol. iii, pp. 447–8) *to Letters of Horace Walpole*
(ed. Toynbee).]

appears to have been gratitude to the venerable
author, then fast hastening to the grave, for his
kindness to himself in Paris. To Paris three-
fourths of the impression [1] went. More important reprints were Grammont's *Memoirs*,[2] a small
quarto, and a series of *Letters of Edward VI*,[3]
both printed in 1772. The list for this period
is completed by *Hoyland's Poems*,[4] 1769, and the
well-known, but now rare *Description of the Villa
of Horace Walpole at Strawberry Hill*, 1774, 100
copies of which were printed, six being on large
paper.[5] To an account of this patchwork edifice,
the ensuing chapter will be chiefly devoted. The
present may fitly be concluded with a brief statement of that always-debated passage in Walpole's
life, his relations with the ill-starred Chatterton.

Towards the close of 1768, and early in 1769,
Chatterton, fretting in Mr. Lambert's office at
Bristol, and casting about eagerly for possible clues
to a literary life, had offered some specimens of the
pseudo-Rowley to James Dodsley of Pall-Mall,
but apparently without success. His next appeal

[1] [200 copies.]
[2] [100 copies, of which 25 went to France.]
[3] [200 copies.]                    [4] [300 copies.]
[5] [Two of the large-paper copies (Walpole's own copy
with his MS. notes, and that given by him to Cole) are in
Earl Waldegrave's collection at Chewton Priory.]

was made to Walpole, and mainly as the author of the *Anecdotes of Painting in England*. The documents he submitted to him are supposed to have contained an account of a sequence of native artists in oil (hitherto wholly undreamed of by the distinguished virtuoso he addressed), included in the notes to which were some examples of monkish verse. The packet was handed to Walpole at Arlington Street by Mr. Bathoe, his bookseller (also notable as the keeper of the first circulating library in London); and, incredible to say, Walpole was instantly ' drawn '. He despatched without delay to his unknown Bristol correspondent such a courteous note [1] as he might have addressed to Zouch or Ducarel, expressing interest, curiosity, and a desire for further particulars. Chatterton as promptly rejoined, forwarding more extracts from the Rowley MSS. But he also, from Walpole's recollection of his letter, in part unbosomed himself, making revelation of his position as a widow's son and lawyer's apprentice, who had ' a taste and turn for more elegant studies ', which inclinations, he suggested, his illustrious correspondent might enable him to gratify. Upon this, perhaps not unnaturally, Walpole's suspicions were aroused, the more so that Mason and Gray, to whom he

[1] [28 Mar. 1769.]

showed the papers, declared them to be forgeries. He made, nevertheless, some private enquiry from an aristocratic relative at Bath as to Chatterton's antecedents, and found that, although his description of himself was accurate, no account of his character was forthcoming. He accordingly—he tells us—wrote him a letter ' with as much kindness and tenderness as if he had been his guardian ', recommending him to stick to his profession, and adding, by way of postscript, that judges, to whom the manuscripts had been submitted, were by no means thoroughly convinced of their authenticity. Two letters from Chatterton followed,—one (the first) dejected and seemingly acquiescent; the other, a week later, curtly demanding the restoration of his papers, the genuineness of which he re-affirmed. These communications Walpole, by his own account, either neglected to notice, or over-looked. After an interval of some weeks arrived a final missive, the tone of which he regarded as 'singularly impertinent'.[1] Snapping up both poems

[1] [Walpole says he received this letter, which is dated July 24, soon after his return from France in 1769 ; but his memory played him false, for he did not leave England for Paris till Aug. 18, and did not return till Oct. 5 ; moreover he himself states that Chatterton's MSS. were returned to him on Aug. 4. (See *Works of Lord Orford*, iv. 223–4, 237.)]

and letters in a pet, he scribbled a hasty reply, but, upon reconsideration, enclosed them to their writer without comment, and thought no more of him or them.    It was not until about a year and a half afterwards that Goldsmith told him, at the first Royal Academy dinner, that Chatterton had come to London and destroyed himself [1]—an announcement which seems to have filled him with unaffected pity.    ' Several persons of honour and veracity ', he says, 'were present when I first heard of his death, and will attest my surprise and concern.' [2]

The apologists of the gifted and precocious Bristol boy, reading the above occurrences by the light of his deplorable end, have attributed to Walpole a more material part in his misfortunes than can justly be ascribed to him ; and the first editor of Chatterton's *Miscellanies* did not scruple to emphasize the current gossip which represented Walpole as ' the primary cause of his [Chatterton's] dismal catastrophe ',[3]—an aspersion which

[1] [*Works of Lord Orford*, iv. 224.]

[2] *Works*, iv. 219.   In the above summary of the story we have relied by preference on the fairly established facts of the case, which is full of difficulties—difficulties which naturally present themselves in widely differing aspects to the ardent and not always impartial advocates of Walpole and Chatterton.

[3] An example of this is furnished by Miss Seward's

drew from the Abbot of Strawberry the lengthy letter on the subject which was afterwards reprinted in his *Works*.[1] So long a vindication, if needed then, is scarcely needed now. Walpole, it is obvious, acted very much as he might have been expected to act. He had been imposed upon, and he was as much annoyed with himself as with the impostor. But he was not harsh enough to speak his mind frankly, nor benevolent enough to act the part of that rather rare personage, the ideal philanthropist. If he had behaved less like an ordinary man of the world,—if he had obtained Chatterton's confidence instead of lecturing him, —if he had aided and counselled and protected him,—Walpole would have been different, and things might have been otherwise. As they were,

*Correspondence.* 'Do not expect (she writes) that I can learn to esteem that fastidious and unfeeling being, to whose insensibility we owe the extinction of the greatest poetic luminary [Chatterton], if we may judge from the brightness of its dawn, that ever rose in our, or perhaps in any other hemisphere' (*Seward to Hardinge,* 21 Nov. 1787).

[1] [*A Letter to the Editor of the Miscellanies of Thomas Chatterton* was printed at Strawberry Hill (200 copies) in Jan. 1779, and was reprinted in *Works of Lord Orford,* iv. 205–33, where it is followed (pp. 234–45) by *Papers relative to Chatterton,* in which is included part of the correspondence between Chatterton and Walpole.]

upon the principle that ' two of a trade can ne'er agree ', it is difficult to conceive of any abiding alliance between the author of the fabricated *Tragedy of Ælla* and the author of the fabricated *Castle of Otranto*.

# CHAPTER VIII

# VIII

IN 1774, when, according to its title-page, the *Description of Strawberry Hill* was printed, Walpole was a man of fifty-seven. During the period covered by the last chapter, many changes had taken place in his circle of friends. Mann and George Montagu (until, in October 1770, his correspondence with the latter suddenly ceased) [1] were still the most frequent recipients of his letters, and next to these, Conway and Cole the antiquary. But three of his former correspondents, his deaf neighbour at Marble Hill, Lady Suffolk,[2] Lady Hervey (Pope's and Chesterfield's Molly Lepel,

[1] [In a letter announcing Montagu's death to Cole, Walpole writes (11 May 1780) : 'He had dropped me, partly from politics and partly from caprice, for we never had any quarrel.']

[2] Henrietta Hobart, Countess Dowager of Suffolk, died in July 1767, aged 86. Her portrait by Charles Jervas, with Marble Hill in the background, hung in the Round Bedchamber at Strawberry Hill. [This painting, now in the possession of the Earl of Buckinghamshire, once belonged to Pope, who left it to Martha Blount ; at her sale it was bought by Lady Suffolk by whom it was given to Walpole. A reproduction of it forms the frontispiece to *Horace Walpole's Notes of his Conversations with Lady Suffolk*, in Walpole's *Reminiscences* (ed. Toynbee), Oxford, 1924.]

to whom he had written much from Paris), and Gray, were dead. On the other hand, he had opened what promised to be a lengthy series of letters with Gray's friend and biographer, the Rev. William Mason, Rector of Aston in York-shire; with Madame du Deffand; and with the divorced Duchess of Grafton, who, in 1769, had married his Paris friend, John Fitzpatrick, second Earl of Upper Ossory. There were changes, too, among his own relatives. By this time his eldest brother's widow, Lady Orford, had lost her second husband, Sewallis Shirley, and was again living, not very reputably, on the continent. Her son George, who since 1751 had been third Earl of Orford, and was still unmarried, was eminently unsatisfactory. He was shamelessly selfish, and by way of complicating the family embarrass-ments, had taken to the turf. Ultimately he had periodical attacks of insanity, during which time it fell to Walpole's fate to look after his affairs. With Sir Edward Walpole, his second brother, he seems never to have been on terms of real cordiality; but he made no secret of his pride in his beautiful nieces, Edward Walpole's natural daughters, whose charms and amiability had vic-toriously triumphed over every prejudice which could have been entertained against their birth.

Laura, the eldest, had married a brother of Lord Albemarle, Frederick Keppel, Canon of Windsor, subsequently Bishop of Exeter, and Dean of Windsor; Charlotte, the third, became Lady Huntingtower, and afterwards Countess of Dysart; while Maria, the *belle* of the trio, was more fortunate still. After burying her first husband, Lord Waldegrave,[1] she had succeeded in fascinating H.R.H. William Henry, Duke of Gloucester, the King's own brother, and so contributing to bring about the Royal Marriage Act of 1772. They were married in 1766; but the fact was not formally announced to His Majesty until September 1772.[2] Another marriage which must have given Walpole almost as much pleasure was that of General Conway's daughter to Mr. Damer, Lord Milton's eldest son, which took place in 1767.[3] After the unhappy death of her husband, who shot himself in a tavern ten years later,[4]

[1] [2nd Earl Waldegrave, d. April 1763.]

[2] 'The Duke of Gloucester',—wrote Gilly Williams to Selwyn, as far back as December 1764,—'has professed a passion for the Dowager Waldegrave. He is never from her elbow. This flatters Horry Walpole not a little, though he pretends to dislike it.'

[3] [*Walpole to Mann*, 19 Mar. 1767.]

[4] [*Walpole to Lady Ossory*, 16 Aug. 1776; *to Mann*, 20 Aug.]

Mrs. Damer developed considerable talents as a sculptor, and during the last years of Walpole's life was a frequent exhibitor at the Royal Academy. *Non me Praxiteles finxit, at Anna Damer*—wrote her admiring relative under one of her works, a wounded eagle in terra cotta,[1] and in the fourth volume of the *Anecdotes of Painting*, he likens ' her shock dog, large as life ', to such masterpieces of antique art as the Tuscan boar and the Barberini goat.

It is time, however, to return to the story of Strawberry itself, as interrupted in Chapter V. In the introduction to Walpole's *Description* of 1774 a considerable interval occurs between the building of the Refectory and Library in 1753–4, and the subsequent erection of the Gallery, Round Tower, Great Cloister, and Cabinet or Tribune, which, already in contemplation in 1759, were, according to the same authority, erected in 1760 and 1761.   But here, as before, the date must rather be that of the commencement than the completion of these additions.   In May 1763, he tells Cole that the Gallery is fast advancing, and in July, it is ' almost in the critical minute of con-

---

[1] The idea was borrowed from an inscription upon a statue at Milan :—' Non me Praxiteles, sed Marcus finxit Agrati ! '   [(*Walpole to Lady Ossory*, 14 June 1787.)]

summation '.¹  In August, 'all the earth is beg-
ging to come to see it '.²  A month afterwards,
he is 'keeping an inn; the sign, "The Gothic
Castle "'.  His whole time is passed in giving
tickets of admission to the Gallery, and hiding
himself when it is on view.  'Take my advice,'
he tells Montagu,³ 'never build a charming house
for yourself between London and Hampton-court:
everybody will live in it but you.'  Next summer
he is giving a great fête to the French and Spanish
Ambassadors, March, Selwyn, Lady Waldegrave,
and other distinguished guests, which finishes
in the new room.  'During dinner there were
French horns and clarionets in the cloister,' and
after coffee, the guests were treated with 'a sylla-
bub milked under the cows that were brought to
the brow of the terrace.  Thence they went to the
Printing-house, and saw a new fashionable French
song printed.  They drank tea in the Gallery, and
at eight went away to Vauxhall.' ⁴

This last entertainment, the munificence of
which, he says,⁴ the treasury of the Abbey will
feel, took place in June 1764; and it is not until
four years later that we get tidings of any fresh

¹ [*To Montagu*, 1 July 1763.]
² [*To Conway*, 9 Aug. 1763.]     ³ [3 Sept. 1763.]
⁴ [*To Montagu*, 18 June 1764.]

improvements.   In August 1768 he tells Cole that he is going on with the Round Tower, or Chamber, at the end of the Gallery, which, in another letter, he says ' has stood still these five years ', and he is besides ' *playing* with the little garden on the other side of the road ' which had come into his hands by Francklin's death.[1]   In May of the following year he gives another magnificent *festino* at Strawberry which will almost mortgage it,[2] but the Round Tower still progresses.[3]   In October 1770, he is building again, in the intervals of gout ;  this time it is the Great Bedchamber—a ' sort of room which he seems likely to inhabit much time together '.[4]   Next year the whole piecemeal structure is rapidly verging to completion.   ' The Round Tower is finished, and magnificent ;  and the State Bedchamber proceeds fast.' [5]   In June, he is writing to Mann from the delicious bow window of the former, with Vasari's Bianca Capello (Mann's present) over against him, and the setting sun behind, ' throwing its golden rays all around.' [6]

[1] [*To Cole*, 20 Aug. 1768.]
[2] [*To Montagu*, 11 May 1769.]
[3] [*To Mann*, 14 June 1769.]
[4] [*To Mann*, 4 Oct. 1770.]  [5] [*To Mann*, 8 June 1771.]
[6] [*To Mann*, 19 June 1771.]

Further on, he is building a tiny brick chapel in the garden, mainly for the purpose of receiving ' two valuable pieces of antiquity ',—one being a painted window from Bexhill of Henry III and his Queen, given him by Lord Ashburnham ; the other Cavallini's Tomb of Capoccio from the Church of Santa Maria Maggiore at Rome, which had been sent to him by Sir William (then Mr.) Hamilton, the English Minister at Naples.[1]   In August 1772, the Great Bedchamber is finished, the house is complete, and he has ' at last exhausted all his hoards and collections '.[2]   Nothing remains but to compile the *Description and Catalogue,* concerning which he had written to Cole as far back as 1768,[3] and which, as already stated, he ultimately printed in 1774.[4]

[1] [*To Cole,* 23 Oct. 1771 ; *to Mason,* 9 May 1772 ; for the materials of the tomb (a shrine), see *to Hamilton,* 22 Sept. 1768 (in *Supplement* (vol. iii, pp. 13–14) to *Letters of Horace Walpole* (ed. Toynbee).]

[2] [*To Mann,* 29 Aug. 1772.  For details of the progress and cost of the various additions to Strawberry Hill, see *Strawberry Hill Accounts* (ed. Toynbee).]

[3] Aug. 20.

[4] [In the same year (apparently) he also printed a few copies of a shortened *Description,* ' for the use of the Servants in showing the house ' ; of this issue, which is excessively rare, there are copies in the Storer collection at Eton, and in Earl Waldegrave's collection at Chewton

As time went on, his fresh acquisitions obliged him to add several *Appendices* to this issue, and the copy before us, although dated 1774, has supplements which bring the record down to 1786. A fresh edition, in royal quarto, with twenty-seven plates, was printed in 1784,[1] and this, or an expansion of it, reappears in Vol. ii of his *Works*.[2] With these later issues we have little to do ; but with the aid of that of 1774, may essay to give some brief account of the long, straggling, many-pinnacled building, with its round tower at the end, the east and south fronts of which are figured in the black-looking vignette upon the title-page. The entrance was on the north side, from the Teddington and Twickenham road, here shaded by lofty trees ; and once within the embattled boundary wall, covered by this time

Priory (see *Journal of the Printing-Office at Strawberry Hill* (ed. Toynbee), p. 61.]

[1] [200 copies.] From a passage in a letter of 15 Sept. 1787, to Lady Ossory, it appears that this, though printed, was withheld, on account of certain difficulties caused by the overweening curiosity of Walpole's ' customers ' (as he called them), the visitors to Strawberry. According to the sheet of regulations for visiting the house, it was to be seen between the 1st of May and the 1st of October. Children were not admitted ; and only one company of four on one day.

[2] *Works of Lord Orford*, ii. 393–516.

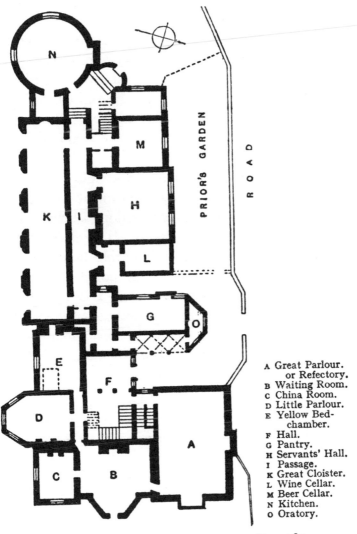

PRIOR'S GARDEN

ROAD

A Great Parlour.
 or Refectory.
B Waiting Room.
C China Room.
D Little Parlour.
E Yellow Bed-
 chamber.
F Hall.
G Pantry.
H Servants' Hall.
I Passage.
K Great Cloister.
L Wine Cellar.
M Beer Cellar.
N Kitchen.
O Oratory.

STRAWBERRY HILL : GROUND PLAN—1781

with ivy, the first thing that struck the spectator
was a small oratory inclosed by iron rails, with
saint, altar, niches, and holy-water basins designed
*en suite* by Mr. Chute.   On the right hand,—its
gaily-coloured patches of flower-bed glimmering
through a screen copied from the tomb of Roger
Niger, Bishop of London, in old St. Paul's,—was
the diminutive Abbot's, or Prior's Garden, which
extended in front of the offices to the right of the
principal entrance.[1]  This was along a little cloister
to the left, beyond the oratory.  The chief decoration of this cloister was a marble bas-relief, inscribed ' Dia Helionora ', the portrait of a lady
identified by Walpole with that Eleanora d'Este
who turned the head of Tasso.[2]   At the end was
the door, which opened into ' a small gloomy hall '
united with the staircase, the balustrades of which,
designed by Bentley, were decorated with ante-

[1] ' It is not much larger than an old lady's flower-knot
in Bloomsbury '—said Lady Morgan in 1826.

[2] [Hamilton, who sent Walpole the bas-relief from Italy,
calls the lady ' Diana d'Este '.   The portrait is now held
to be that of Eleanora of Aragon, Duchess of Ferrara,
whom Castiglione eulogises in his *Cortegiano*.  (See *Supplement* (vol. iii, p. 24) to *Letters of Horace Walpole* (ed.
Toynbee).   In the same cloister as the bas-relief was the
' vase ' in which Walpole's cat was drowned (see above,
p. 151, n. 2).]

lopes, the Walpole supporters. In the well of the staircase was a Gothic lantern of japanned tin, also due to Bentley's fertile invention. If, instead of climbing the stairs, you turned out of the hall into a little passage on your left, you found yourself in the Refectory or Great Parlour, where were accumulated the family portraits. Here, over the chimney-piece, was the 'conversation' by Sir Joshua Reynolds representing the triumvirate of Selwyn, Williams, and Richard Edgcumbe, already referred to ; [1] here also were Sir Robert Walpole and his two wives, Catherine Shorter and Maria Skerret ; Robert Walpole the second, and his wife in a white riding-habit ; Horace himself by Richardson ; Dorothy Walpole, his aunt, who became Lady Townshend ; [2] his sister, Lady Maria Churchill,[3] and a number of others.[4] In the Waiting Room,[5] into which the Refectory

[1] See p. 154.  [2] See p. 7.

[3] [This portrait (by Eckardt), in which Lady Mary is depicted wearing the 'very large diamond, but with a great flaw in it ' (*Walpole to Mann*, 8 Jan. 1784), bequeathed to her by her father, to whom it had been given by George II, is now (1926) in the possession of Mr. W. S. Lewis, of Farmington, Connecticut.]

[4] [Among them one of Sir Horace Mann.]

[5] [Formerly the kitchen, built by Walpole in 1748 (see above, p. 127, n. 4).]

opened, was a stone head of John Dryden, whom Catherine Shorter claimed as great uncle; next to this again was the China Closet, neatly lined with blue and white Dutch tiles, and having its ceiling painted by Müntz, after the ceiling of a villa at Frascati, with convolvuluses on poles. In this China Room, among great stores of Sèvres and Chelsea, and oriental china, perhaps the greatest curiosity was a couple of Saxon tankards, exactly alike in form and size, which had been presented to Sir Robert Walpole at different times by the mistresses of the first two Georges, the Duchess of Kendal and the Countess of Yarmouth. To the left of the China Closet, with a bow window looking to the south, was the Little Parlour, which was hung with stone-coloured 'gothic paper' in imitation of mosaic, and decorated with the 'wooden prints' already referred to, the chiaroscuros of Jackson;[1] and at the side of this came the Yellow Bedchamber, known later, from its numerous feminine portraits, as the Beauty Room. The other spaces on the ground floor were occupied towards the Prior's Garden, by the kitchen cellars, and servants' hall, and, at the back, by the Great Cloister which went under the Gallery.

Returning to the staircase where, in later years,

[1] See p. 131 n.

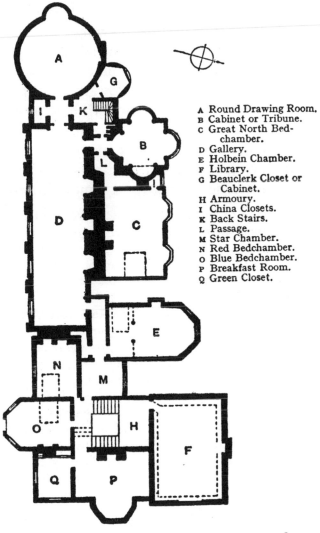

A Round Drawing Room.
B Cabinet or Tribune.
C Great North Bed-
   chamber.
D Gallery.
E Holbein Chamber.
F Library.
G Beauclerk Closet or
   Cabinet.
H Armoury.
I China Closets.
K Back Stairs.
L Passage.
M Star Chamber.
N Red Bedchamber.
O Blue Bedchamber.
P Breakfast Room.
Q Green Closet.

STRAWBERRY HILL : PRINCIPAL FLOOR—1781

hung Bunbury's original drawing [1] for his well-
known caricature of ' Richmond Hill ', you entered the Breakfast Room [2] on the first floor, the
window of which looked towards the Thames.
It was pleasantly furnished with blue paper, and
blue and white linen, and contained many miniatures and portraits, notable among which were
Carmontelle's picture of Madame du Deffand and
the Duchess de Choiseul ; [3] a print of Madame du

[1] It was exhibited in the Royal Academy of 1781, and
was Bunbury's acknowledgment of the praise given him by
Walpole in the ' Advertisement ' to the fourth volume of
the *Anecdotes of Painting*, 1 Oct. 1780. A copy of it was
shown at the Exhibition of English Humourists in Art,
June 1889.

[2] [Otherwise known as the Blue Room, which must not
be confounded with the Blue Bedchamber (sometimes also
called the Blue Room by Walpole) on the same floor.]

[3] In a note to Madame du Deffand's *Letters*, 1810, i. 201,
the editor, Miss Berry, thus describes this picture :—It was
' a washed drawing of Mad. la Duchesse de Choiseul and
Mad. du Deffand, under their assumed characters of grandmother and grand-daughter ; Mad. de Choiseul giving
Mad. du Deffand a doll. The scene the interior of Mad.
du Deffand's sitting-room. It was done by M. de Car-
montel, an amateur in the art of painting. He was reader
to the Prince of Condé, and author of several little Theatrical
pieces.' It is engraved as the frontispiece of vol. vii of
Walpole's *Letters*, by Cunningham, 1857–9. Mad. du Deffand's portrait [which is reproduced as the frontispiece to

Deffand's room and cats, given by the President Hénault; and a view painted by Raguenet for Walpole in 1766 of the Hôtel de Carnavalet, the whilom residence of Madame de Sévigné.[1]

The Breakfast Room opened into the Green Closet, over the door of which was a picture by Samuel Scott of Pope's house at Twickenham, showing the wings added after the poet's death by Sir William Stanhope. On the same side of the room hung Hogarth's portrait of Sarah Malcolm the murderess, painted at Newgate on the day preceding her execution in Fleet Street.[2] Here also was ' Mr. Thomas Gray; etched from his shade [silhouette]; by Mr. W. Mason '. There were many other portraits in this room, besides

vol. i of Mrs. Toynbee's *Lettres de Mme du Deffand à Horace Walpole*] was said to be extremely like; that of the Duchess was not good.

[1] ' It is now the Musée Carnavalet, and contains numberless souvenirs of the Revolution, notably a collection of china plates, bearing various dates, designs, and inscriptions applicable to the Reign of Terror ' (*Century Magazine*, Feb. 1890, p. 600). A washed drawing of Mad. de Sévigné's country house at Les Rochers, ' done on the spot by Mr. Hinchcliffe, son of the Bishop of Peterborough, in 1786 ', was afterwards added to this room.

[2] Both these pictures are in existence. The Scott, which belongs (1910) to Lady Freake, was exhibited in the Pope Loan Museum of 1888.

some water colours (one on ivory) by Horace himself. In a line with the Green Closet, and looking east, was the Library; and at the back of it, the Blue Bedchamber, the toilette of which was worked by Mrs. Clive, who since her retirement from the stage in 1769, had lived wholly at Twickenham. The chief pictures in this room were Eckardt's portraits of Gray in a Van Dyck dress and of Walpole himself in similar attire.[1] There were also by the same artist pictures of Walpole's father and mother, and of General Conway and his wife, Lady Ailesbury.

Facing the Blue Bedchamber was the Armoury, a vestibule of three Gothic arches, in the left-hand corner of which was the door opening into the Library, a room twenty-eight feet by nineteen feet six, lighted by a large window looking to the east, flanked by a small rose-window on each side of it. The books, arranged in Gothic arches of pierced work, went all round it. The chimney-piece was imitated from the tomb of John of Eltham in Westminster Abbey, and the stone work from another tomb at Canterbury. Over

[1] [These are now in the National Portrait Gallery. That of Gray is reproduced here; and also, with that of Walpole, in vol. ii of the *Correspondence of Gray, Walpole, West, and Ashton.*]

the chimney-piece was a picture (which is engraved in the *Anecdotes of Painting*) representing
the marriage of Henry VI. Walpole and Bentley
had designed the ceiling, a gorgeous heraldic med-
ley surrounding a central Walpole shield.[1] Above
the bookcases were pictures. One of the greatest
treasures of the room was a clock given by
Henry VIII to Anne Boleyn.[2] Of the books
it is impossible to speak in detail. Noticeable
among them, however, was a Thuanus in fourteen volumes, a very extensive set of Hogarth's
prints, and all the original drawings for the *Aedes
Walpolianae*. Vertue, Hollar and Faithorne were
also largely represented. Among special copies,
were the identical *Iliad* and *Odyssey* from which
Pope made his translations of Homer,[3] a volume
containing Bentley's original designs for Gray's

[1] [The painting of the ceiling was executed by the
French decorative artist, Clermont, at the cost of £73 10s.
(see *Strawberry Hill Accounts*, p. 5).]

[2] [This clock, which formed lot 48 of the seventeenth
day of the Strawberry Hill sale in 1842, was bought by
Queen Victoria for £110 5s.]

[3] This was the Amsterdam edition of 1707, in 2 vols.
12mo, inscribed ' E libris, A. Pope, 1714 ' ; and lower
down, ' Finished ye translation in Feb. 1719–20, A. Pope '.
It also contained a pencil sketch by the poet of Twickenham Church. [It sold in 1842 (lot 74 of sixth day) for
£11 0s. 6d.]

*Poems*,[1] and a black morocco pocket-book of sketches by Jacques Callot.[2]   In a rosewood case in this room was also a fine collection of coins, which included the rare silver medal struck by Gregory XIII on the Massacre of St. Bartholomew.

Concerning the Red Bedchamber, the Star Chamber, and the Holbein Chamber, which intervened between the rest of the first floor and the latest additions—there is little to say.   In the Red Bedchamber were some sketches of Pope and his parents by Cooper and the elder Richardson,[3] [and a copy of Princess Amelia's portrait of Sophia Dorothea, wife of George I.[4]]   In the Holbein Chamber, so called from a number of copies on oil-paper by Vertue from the drawings of Holbein in Queen Caroline's Closet at Kensington, were two of those 'curiosities' which represent the Don Saltero, or Madame Tussaud side of Strawberry, viz., a tortoise-shell comb studded with silver hearts and roses which was said to have

[1] See above, p. 152, n. 2.

[2] [This was sold in 1842 (lot 46 of sixth day) to Thomas Grenville for £43 1s.]

[3] [Sold in 1842 (lot 72 of twenty-second day) for £4 10s. to 'Mr. Young of Pope's Villa'.]

[4] [See *Walpole to Lord Duncannon*, 29 Nov. 1786, and notes, in *Supplement* (vol. iii, pp. 46–7) *to Letters of Horace Walpole* (ed. Toynbee).]

belonged to Mary, Queen of Scots, and (later) the red hat of Cardinal Wolsey.[1] The pedigree of the hat, it must, however, be admitted, was unimpeachable. It had been found in the great wardrobe by Bishop Burnet when Clerk of the Closet. From him it passed to his son the Judge (author of that curious squib on Harley known as the *History of Robert Powel the Puppet-Show-Man*), and thence to the Countess Dowager of Albemarle, who gave it to Walpole. A carpet in this room was worked by Mrs. Clive, who seems to have been a most industrious decorator of her friend's mansion museum.[2] The Star Chamber was but an ante-room powdered with gold stars in mosaic, the chief glory of which was a stone bust of Henry VII by Torrigiano.

With these three rooms, the first floor of Strawberry, as it existed previous to the erection

---

[1] [Sold in 1842 (lot 73 of seventeenth day) for £21 to Charles Kean.]

[2] Walpole wrote an epilogue—not a very good one—for Mrs. Clive when she quitted the stage ; and in the same year, 1769, the *Town and Country Magazine* linked their names in its ' *Tête-à-Têtes* ' as ' Mrs. Heidelberg ' (Clive's part in the *Clandestine Marriage*) and ' Baron Otranto ', a name under which Chatterton subsequently satirized Walpole in this identical periodical. (See *Memoirs of a Sad Dog*, Pt. 2, July 1770.)

of the additions mentioned in the beginning of this chapter, namely, the Gallery, the Round Tower, the Tribune, and the Great North Bedchamber, came to an end. But it was in these newer parts of the house that some of its rarest objects of art were assembled. The Gallery, which was entered from a gloomy little passage in front of the Holbein Chamber, was a really spacious room, fifty-six feet by thirteen, seventeen feet high, and lighted from the south by five high windows. Between these were tables laden with busts, bronzes, and urns; on the opposite side, fronting the windows, were recesses, finished with gold network over looking-glass, between which stood couch-seats covered, like the rest of the room, with crimson Norwich damask.[1] The ceiling[2] was copied from one of the side aisles of Henry VII's Chapel; the great door at the western end, which led into the Round Tower, was taken from the north door of St. Albans. A long carpet, made at Moorfields,[3] traversed the room from end to end. In one of the recesses, that to the left of the chimney-piece,

[1] [This cost Walpole £102 16s. (see *Strawberry Hill Accounts*, p. 10).]

[2] [For the work on this, which was executed by Bromwich, the fashionable decorator, Walpole paid £115 (*op. cit.*, p. 9).]

[3] [This and the carpet for the Tribune cost £87 19s. (*op. cit.*, p. 11).]

which was designed by Mr. Chute and Mr. Thomas Pitt of Boconnoc, stood one of the finest surviving pieces of Greek sculpture, the Boccapadugli eagle,[1] found in the precinct of the Baths of Caracalla, a *chef-d'œuvre* from which Gray is said to have borrowed the 'ruffled plumes, and flagging wing' of the *Progress of Poesy* ; to the right was a noble bust in basalt of Vespasian,[2] which had been purchased from the Ottoboni collection. Of the pictures it is impossible to speak at large ; but two of the most notable were Sir George Villiers,[3] the father of the Duke of Buckingham, and Mabuse's *Marriage of Henry VII and Elizabeth of York*.[4] Of Walpole's own relatives, there were portraits by Ramsay of his nieces,[5] Mrs. Keppel (the Bishop's wife) and Lady Dysart, and of the Duchess of Gloucester (then Lady Waldegrave) by Reynolds.[6]

[1] [This was sold in 1842 (lot 86 of twenty-third day) for £210 to Lord Leicester, and is now at Holkham.]

[2] [This fetched £220 10*s*. in 1842 (lot 73 of twenty-third day).]

[3] [By Cornelis Janssens—sold in 1842 (lot 54 of twenty-first day) for £33 2*s*.]

[4] [Fetched £178 10*s*. in 1842 (lot 52 of twenty-first day).]

[5] [This, for which Walpole paid Ramsay £84 in 1765 (see *Strawberry Hill Accounts*, p. 10), was bought in by Lord Waldegrave in 1842 (lot 51 of twenty-first day) for £52 10*s*.]

[6] [Bought in by Lord Waldegrave in 1842 (lot 72 of twenty-first day) for £735 ; it is now at Chewton Priory.]

There were also portraits of Henry Fox, Lord Holland, of George Montagu, of Lord Walde-grave,[1] and of Horace's uncle, Lord Walpole of Wolterton.[2]

Issuing through the great door of the Gallery, and passing on the left a glazed closet containing a quantity of china which had once belonged to Walpole's mother, a couple of steps brought you into the pleasant Drawing Room in the Round Tower, the bow window of which looked to the south-west. Like the Gallery this room was hung with Norwich damask. Its chief glory was the picture of Bianca Capello,[3] by Vasari, which was given to Walpole by Mann. To the left of this room, at the back of the Gallery, and consequently in the front of the house, was the Cabinet, or Tribune, a curious square chamber with semicircular recesses, in two of which, to the north and west,

[1] [Walpole paid Reynolds £21 for this in 1765 (see *Strawberry Hill Accounts*, p. 11); it was bought in by Lord Waldegrave in 1842 (lot 71 of twenty-first day) for £73 10s., and is now at Chewton Priory.]

[2] Horatio, brother of Sir Robert Walpole, created Baron Walpole of Wolterton in 1756. He died in 1757. His *Memoirs* were published by Coxe in 1802.

[3] [See *Walpole to Mann*, 6 Dec. 1753, and note. It was afterwards in the Great North Bedchamber; it fetched £16 16s. in 1842 (lot 92 of twentieth day).]

were stained windows. In the roof, which was modelled on the chapter house at York, was a star of yellow glass throwing a soft golden glow over all the room. Here Walpole had amassed his choicest treasures, miniatures by Oliver and Cooper, enamels by Petitot and Zincke,[1] bronzes from Italy, ivory bas-reliefs, seal-rings and reliquaries, caskets and cameos and filigree-work. Here, with Madame du Deffand's letter inside it,[2] was the 'round white snuff box' with Madame de Sévigné's portrait; here, carven with masks and flies and grasshoppers, was Cellini's silver bell from the Leonati Collection, at Parma, a masterpiece[3] against which he had exchanged 'some very scarce Roman medals of great bronze' with the Marquis of Rockingham. A bronze bust of

[1] 'The chief boast of my collection', he told Pinkerton, 'is the portraits of eminent and remarkable persons, particularly the miniatures, and enamels; which, so far as I can discover, are superior to any other collection whatever. The works I possess of Isaac and Peter Oliver are the best extant; and those I bought in Wales for 300 guineas [i.e., the Digby Family in the Breakfast Room] are as well preserved as when they came from the pencil' (*Walpoliana*, ii, 2nd ed., 159).

[2] It is printed in both the Catalogues.

[3] [It was bought in by Lord Waldegrave in 1842 (lot 83 of fifteenth day) for £252; for a description of it see *Walpole to Mann*, 14 Feb. 1772.]

Caligula with silver eyes; [1] a missal with miniatures by Raphael; [2] a dagger of Henry VIII,[3]
and a mourning ring given at the burial of
Charles I, were among the other show objects
of the Tribune, the riches of which occupy more
space in their owner's catalogue than any other
part of his collections.

With the Great North Bedchamber, which
adjoined the Tribune, and filled the remaining
space at the back of the Gallery, the account of
Strawberry Hill, as it existed in 1774, comes to
an end, for the Round Bedchamber [4] over the
Round Drawing-Room in the Tower, and ' Mr.
Walpole's Bedchamber, two pair of stairs ' (which
contained the Warrant for beheading King
Charles I inscribed ' Major Charta ', so often
referred to by Walpole's biographers),[5] may be

[1] [Given by Mann ; in 1842 (lot 68 of fifteenth day) it
fetched £48 6s.]

[2] [Bought in by Lord Waldegrave in 1842 (lot 77 of
fifteenth day) for £115 10s.]

[3] [Bought by Charles Kean in 1842 (lot 79 of fifteenth
day) for £54 12s.

[4] [It was in this room that Jervas's portrait of Lady
Suffolk was hung (see above, p. 229, n. 2).]

[5] Here is his own reference to this, in a letter to Montagu
of 14 Oct. 1758 :—' The only thing I have done that can
compose a paragraph, and which I think you are Whig
enough to forgive me, is, that on each side of my bed I have

dismissed without further notice. The Beauclerk Closet, a later addition, will be described in its proper place. Over the chimney-piece in the Great North Bedchamber was a large picture of Henry VIII and his children, a recent purchase; [1] in the same room, 'over the glass', was afterwards hung the portrait of Catherine of Braganza, [2] sent from Portugal previous to her marriage with Charles II. Fronting the bed was a head of Niobe, by Guido, which in its turn subsequently made way for *la belle Jennings*. [3] Among the pictures on the north or window side of the room was the original sketch by Hogarth of the *Beggar's Opera*, [4] which Walpole had purchased at the sale of Rich, the fortunate manager who produced Gay's masterpiece at Lincoln's Inn Fields. It was exhibited at Manchester in 1857, being then

hung the *Magna Charta*, and the Warrant for King Charles's execution, on which I have written *Major Charta*; as I believe, without the latter, the former by this time would be of very little importance.'

[1] [It cost Walpole £84 (see his letter to Cole of 7 Apr. 1773). At the sale in 1842 (lot 86 of twentieth day) it fetched £220 10*s*.]

[2] [See *Walpole to Lady Ossory*, 30 June 1785; it sold for £33 12*s*. in 1842 (lot 94 of twentieth day).]

[3] See p. 8.

[4] [It fetched £4 4*s*. in 1842 (lot 113 of twentieth day).]

the property of Mr. Willett.    Another curious
oil painting in this room was the *Rehearsal of an
Opera* by Sebastian and Marco Ricci,[1] which
included caricature portraits of Nicolini (of *Spectator* celebrity), of the famous Mrs. Catherine
Tofts, and of Margherita de l'Épine.    In a nook
by the window there was a glazed china closet,
with a number of minor curiosities, among which
were conspicuous the speculum of cannel coal
with which Dr. Dee was in the habit of gulling
his votaries,[2] and an agate puncheon with Gray's
arms which his executors had presented to Walpole.

A few external objects claim a word.    In the
Great Cloister under the Gallery was originally
placed the blue and white china tub in which had
taken place that tragedy of the ' pensive Selima '
previously referred to as having prompted the
muse of Gray.[3]    The Chapel in the Garden

---

[1] [It was bought by Mr. Willett in 1842 (lot 114 of
twentieth day) for £57 15*s*.]

[2] ' Doctor Dee's black stone was named in the catalogue
of the collection of the Earls of Peterborough, whence it
went to Lady Betty Germaine.    She gave it to the last Duke
of Argyle, and his son, Lord Frederic, to me ' (*Walpole
to Lady Ossory*, 12 Jan. 1782).

[3] This was afterwards moved to the Little Cloister at the
entrance, where it appears in the later Catalogue (see above,
p. 151, n. 2).

has already been sufficiently described.[1] In the
Flower Garden across the road was a cottage
which Walpole had erected upon the site of the
building once occupied by Francklin the printer,
and which he used as a place of refuge when the
tide of sightseers became overpowering. It included a Tea-Room containing a fair collection
of china, and hung with green paper and engravings; and a little white and green Library of
which the principal ornament was a half-length
portrait of Milton.[2] A portrait of Lady Hervey
by Allan Ramsay was afterwards added to its
decorations.[3]

Many objects of interest, as must be obvious,

[1] (See above, p. 235.) Not far from the Chapel was 'a
large seat in the form of a shell, carved in oak, from a design
by Mr. Bentley'. It must have been roomy, for in 1759,
the Duchesses of Hamilton and Richmond, and Lady Ailesbury (the last two, daughter and mother), occupied it
together. 'There never was so pretty a sight as to see them
all three sitting in the shell'—says the delighted Abbot of
Strawberry (*Walpole to Montagu*, 2 June).

[2] In a note to the obituary notice of Walpole in the
*Gentleman's Magazine* for March 1797, p. 260, it is stated
that this library was 'formed of all the publications during
the reigns of the three Georges, or Mr. W's own time'.

[3] This was exhibited at South Kensington in 1867 by
Viscount Lifford, and is now (1892) at Austin House,
Broadway, Worcester.

have remained undescribed in the foregoing account, and those who seek for further information concerning what its owner called his ' paper fabric and assemblage of curious trifles ' must consult either the catalogue of 1774 itself, or that later and definitive version of it which is reprinted in the second volume of the *Works of Lord Orford* (1798).[1]   The intention in the main has here been to lay stress upon those articles which bear most directly upon Walpole's biography.   It will also be observed that, during the prolonged progress of the house towards completion, his experience and his views considerably enlarged, and the pettiness and artificiality of his first improvements disappeared.   The house never lost, and never could lose, its invertebrate character ;  but the Gallery, the Round Tower, and the North Bedchamber were certainly conceived in a more serious and even spacious spirit of Gothicism than any of the early additions.   That it must, still, have been confined and needlessly gloomy, may be allowed ;  but as a set-off to some of those accounts which insist so pertinaciously upon its ' paltriness ', its ' architectural solecisms ' and its lack of beauty and sublimity, it is only fair to recall a few sentences from the preface which its owner prefixed

[1] pp. 393–516.

to the *Description* of 1784. It was designed, he says of the catalogue, to exhibit 'specimens of Gothic architecture, as collected from standards in cathedrals and chapel-tombs', and to show 'how they may be applied to chimney-pieces, ceilings, windows, balustrades, loggias, etc.' Elsewhere he characterizes the building itself as candidly as any of its critics. He admits its diminutive scale and its unsubstantial character (he calls it himself, as we have seen, a 'paper fabric'); and he confesses to the incongruities arising from an antique design and modern decorations. 'In truth,' he concludes, 'I did not mean to make my house so Gothic as to exclude convenience, and modern refinements in luxury. . . . It was built to please my own taste, and in some degree to realise my own visions. I have specified what it contains : could I describe the gay but tranquil scene where it stands, and add the beauty of the landscape to the romantic cast of the mansion, it would raise more pleasing sensations than a dry list of curiosities can excite : at least the prospect would recall the good humour of those, who might be disposed to condemn the fantastic fabric, and to think it a very proper habitation of, as it was the scene that inspired, the author of the *Castle of Otranto*.'[1]

[1] *Works of Lord Orford*, ii. 395–8.

As one of his censors has remarked, this tone disarms criticism; and it is needless to accumulate proofs of peculiarities which are not denied by the person most concerned.

In spite of its charming situation, Strawberry Hill was emphatically a summer residence, and there is more than one account in Walpole's letters of the sudden floods which, when Thames flowed with a fuller tide than now, occasionally surprised the inhabitants of the pleasant-looking villas along its banks. It was decidedly damp, and its gouty owner had sometimes to quit it precipitately for Arlington Street, where, he says, 'after an hour', he revives ' like a member of parliament's wife '. One of his editors, Peter Cunningham, whose knowledge as an antiquary was exceptional,— for was he not the author of the *Handbook of London ?*—has amused himself, in an odd corner of one of his prefaces, by retracing the route taken in these townward flights. The extract is so packed with suggestive memories that no excuse is needed for reproducing it (with a few now-necessary notes) as the tail-piece of the present chapter.

' At twelve his [Walpole's] light bodied chariot was at the door with his English coachman and his Swiss valet [Philip Colomb] . . In a few minutes he left Lord Radnor's villa to the right, rolled over the grotto of Pope, saw on his left Whitton, rich with recollections of Kneller and Argyll, passed Gumley House, one of the country seats of his father's opponent and his own friend, Pulteney, Earl of Bath, and Kendal House,[1] the retreat of the mistress of George I, Ermengarde von der Schulenberg, Duchess of Kendal. At Sion, the princely seat of the Percys, the Seymours and the Smithsons, he turned into the Hounslow Road, left Sion on his right, and Osterley, not unlike Houghton, on his left, and rolled through Brentford—

"Brentford, the Bishopric of Parson Horne," [2]

then, as now, infamous for its dirty streets and famous for its white-legged chickens.[3] Quitting Brentford, he approached the woods that concealed the stately mansion of Gunnersbury, built by Inigo Jones and Webb, and then inhabited by the Princess Amelia, the last surviving child of King George II.[4] Here he was often a visitor,

[1] Kendal House now no longer exists.
[2] *An Heroic Epistle to Sir William Chambers, Knight*, 1773.
[3] ' —————— *Brandford's* tedious town,
For dirty streets, and white-leg'd chickens known.'
Gay's *Journey to Exeter.*
[4] Gunnersbury House (or Park), a new structure, now

and seldom returned without being a winner at silver loo.    At the Pack Horse [1] on Turnham Green he would, when the roads were heavy, draw up for a brief bait.    Starting anew, he would pass a few red brick houses on both sides, then the suburban villas of men well to do in the Strand and Charing Cross.    At Hammersmith, he would leave the church [2] on his right, call on Mr. Fox at Holland House, look at Campden House with recollections of Sir Baptist Hicks,[3] and not without an ill-suppressed wish to transfer some little part of it to his beloved Strawberry.    He was now at Kensington Church, then, as it still is, an ungraceful structure,[4] but rife with associations

(1910) belongs to Lord Rothschild.—[The Park has recently been acquired as a public recreation ground.]

[1] The Old Pack Horse, somewhat modernized by red-brick additions, still (1910) stands at the corner of Turnham Green.    It is mentioned in the *London Gazette* as far back as 1697.    The sign, a common one for posting inns in former days, is on the opposite side of the road.

[2] Hammersmith church was rebuilt in 1882–3.

[3] Sir Baptist Hicks, once a mercer in Cheapside, and afterwards Viscount Campden, erected it *circa* 1612.    At the time to which Cunningham is supposed to refer, it was a famous ladies' boarding-school kept by a Mrs. Terry and patronized by Selwyn and Lady Di Beauclerk.

[4] The (with all due deference to the writer) quaint and picturesque old Church of St. Mary the Virgin, in Ken-

which he would at times relate to the friend he
had with him. On his left he would leave the
gates of Kensington Palace, rich with reminiscences connected with his father and the first
Hanoverian kings of this country. On his right
he would quit the red brick house in which the
Duchess of Portsmouth lived,[1] and after a drive
of half a mile (skirting a heavy brick wall), reach
Kingston House,[2] replete with stories of Elizabeth
Chudleigh, the bigamist maid of honour, and
Duchess-Countess of Kingston and Bristol. At
Knightsbridge (even then the haunt of highway-
men less gallant than Maclean) he passed on his
left the little chapel [3] in which his father was
married. At Hyde Park Corner he saw the
Hercules Pillars ale-house of Fielding and Tom
Jones,[4] and at one door from Park Lane would

sington High Street, at which Macaulay, in his later days,
was a regular attendant, gave way in 1869 to a larger and
more modern edifice by Sir Gilbert Scott, R.A.

[1] Old Kensington House, as it was called, has also been
pulled down. One of its inmates, long after the days of
‘ Madam Carwell ’, was Elizabeth Inchbald, the author of
*A Simple Story*, who died there in 1821.

[2] Now (1910) Lord Listowel’s. It stands near the Prince’s
Gate into Hyde Park.

[3] Restored and remodelled in 1861, and now the Church
of the Holy Trinity.

[4] The Hercules Pillars, where Squire Western put up his

occasionally call on old " Q," for the sake of
Selwyn, who was often there.[1]   The trees which
now grace Piccadilly were in the Green Park in
Walpole's day; they can recollect Walpole, and
that is something.   On his left, the sight of
Coventry House [2] would remind him of the Gun-
nings, and he would tell his friend the story of
the " beauties ", with which (short story-teller
as he was) he had not completed when the chariot
turned into Arlington Street on the right, or
down Berkeley Street into Berkeley Square, on
the left.' [3]   In these last lines Cunningham anti-
cipates our story, for in 1774, Walpole had not yet
taken up his residence in Berkeley Square.

horses when he came to town, stood just east of Apsley
House, ' on the site of what is now the pavement opposite
Lord Willoughby's '.—[Walpole mentions it in his letter
to West of 2 Oct. 1740.]

[1] The Duke of Queensberry's house afterwards became
138 and 139 Piccadilly.

[2] This is No. 106,—the present St. James's Club.   It
was built in 1764 by George, sixth Earl of Coventry, some
years after the death of his first wife, the elder Miss Gunning.

[3] *Letters*, ed. Cunningham, 1857–9, vol. ix, pp. xx–xxi.

STRAWBERRY HILL

# CHAPTER IX

*Occupations and correspondence ; literary work ; Jephson and the stage ; ' Nature will Prevail' ; issues from the Strawberry Press ; fourth volume of the 'Anecdotes of Painting' ; the Beauclerk Tower and Lady Di ; George, third Earl of Orford ; sale of the Houghton pictures ; moves to Berkeley Square ; last visit to Madame du Deffand ; her death ; themes for letters ; death of Sir Horace Mann ; Pinkerton, Madame de Genlis, Miss Burney, Hannah More ; Mary and Agnes Berry ; their residence at Twickenham ; becomes fourth Earl of Orford ; 'Epitaphium vivi Auctoris' ; the Berrys again ; death of Marshal Conway ; last letter to Lady Ossory ; dies at Berkeley Square, 2 March 1797 ; his fortune and will ; the fate of Strawberry.*

AFTER the completion of Strawberry Hill and the printing of the *Catalogue*, Walpole's life grows comparatively barren of events. The volumes of his *Correspondence* from now take upon them imperceptibly the nature of *nouvelles à la main*, and are less fruitful in personal traits. Between his books and his prints, his time passes agreeably, ' but will not do to relate '. Indeed, from this period until his death in 1797, the most notable occurrences in his history are his friendship with the Miss Berrys in 1787–8, and his belated accession to the Earldom of Orford. Both at Strawberry and Arlington Street, his increasing years and his persistent malady condemn him more and more to seclusion and retirement. He is most at Strawberry, despite its dampness, for in the country he holds ' old useless people ought to live '. ' If you were not to be in London,' he tells Lady Ossory (6 April 1774), ' the spring advances so charmingly, I think I should scarce go thither. One is frightened with the inundation of breakfasts and balls that are coming on. Everybody is engaged to everybody for the next three weeks, and if one must hunt for a needle, I had rather look for it in a bottle of hay in the country than in a crowd.' ' By age and situation ', he writes from Strawberry in September, ' I live at this time of the year with nothing but old women. They do very well for me who have little choice left, and who rather prefer common nonsense to wise nonsense—the only difference I know between old women and old men. I am out of all politics, and never think of elections, which I think I should hate even if I loved politics ; just as if I loved tapestry I do not think I could talk over the manufacture of worsteds. Books I have almost done with too ; at least, read only such as nobody else would read. In short, my way of life is too insipid to entertain anybody but myself, and though I am always employed, I must say I think I have given up everything in the world only to be at liberty to be very busy about the most arrant trifles.' [1] His London life was not greatly different. ' How should I see or know anything ? ' he says a year later, apologizing for his dearth of news. ' I seldom stir out of my house [2] before seven in the evening, see very few persons, and go to fewer

---

[1] [*To Craufurd*, 26 Sept. 1774.]

[2] In Arlington Street.

places, make no new acquaintance, and have seen most of my old wear out.    Loo at Princess Amelie's, loo at Lady Hertford's, are the capital events of my history, and a Sunday alone, at Strawberry, my chief entertainment.    All this is far from gay; but as it neither gives me *ennui*, nor lowers my spirits, it is not uncomfortable, and I prefer it to being *déplacé* in younger company.' [1] Such is his account of his life in 1774–5, when he is nearing sixty, and it probably represents it with sufficient accuracy.    But a trifling incident easily stirs him into unwonted vivacity.    While he is protesting that he has nothing to say, his letters grow under his pen, and, almost as a neces- sary consequence of his leisure, they become more frequent and more copious.    In Mrs Toynbee's edition, including the three supplementary volumes, up to September 1774, they number seventeen hundred and sixty.    Speaking roughly, this repre- sents a period of nearly forty years.    During the two-and-twenty years that remained to him, he managed to swell them by what was, proportion- ately, a far greater number, the grand total in Mrs. Toynbee's edition (including the supplements as before) being 3420.[2]    Nevertheless, as stated

[1] [*To Lady Ossory*, 4 Dec. 1775.]
[2] [The nineteen volumes of the Toynbee edition contain

above, they more and more assume what he somewhere calls ' their proper character of newspapers '.

During the remainder of his life, they were his chief occupation, and his gout was seldom so severe but that he could make shift to scribble a line to his favourite correspondents, calling in his printer Kirgate as secretary in cases of extremity.[1] Of literature generally he professed to have taken

nearly eight hundred letters not included in Cunningham's last edition.]

[1] Kirgate, who will not be again mentioned, fared but ill at his master's decease, receiving no more than a legacy of £100, a circumstance which Pinkerton darkly attributes to ' his modest merit ' having been ' supplanted by intriguing impudence ' (*Walpoliana*, i. xxiv). [Pinkerton, however, makes no attempt to justify this statement. It is not improbable that an explanation is to be found in the fact, of which evidence exists, and of which Walpole may have been aware, that Kirgate, in his capacity of secretary, abused Walpole's confidence. This evidence will be found in a note to Mrs. Toynbee's preface to her edition of the *Letters* (vol. i, p. xiv, n. 1) ; see also *Journal of the Printing-Office at Strawberry Hill*, pp. 48–9.] There is a portrait of Kirgate engraved by William Collard, after Sylvester Harding, the Pall Mall miniature painter, who also wrote in 1797 for Kirgate some verses in which he is made to speak of himself as ' forlorn, neglected and forgot '. He had an unique collection of the Strawberry Press issues, which was dispersed at his death in 1810.

final leave. ' I no longer care about fame,' he tells Mason in 1774; ' I have done being an author.' Nevertheless, the *Short Notes* piously chronicle the production of more than one trifle, which are reprinted in his *Works*. When, in the above year, Lord Chesterfield's letters to his son were published, Walpole began a parody of that famous performance in a *Series of Letters from a Mother to a Daughter*, with the general title of the *New Whole Duty of Woman*.[1] He grew tired of the idea too soon to enable us to judge what his success might have been with a subject which, in his hands, should have been diverting as a satire, for, although he was a warm admirer of Chesterfield's parts, as he had shown in his character of him in the *Royal and Noble Authors*, he was thoroughly alive to the assailable side of what he styles his ' impertinent institutes of education '.[2]

[1] [See *Works of Lord Orford*, iv. 355–60.]

[2] This did not prevent his siding with Chesterfield in the difference of Johnson (one of his *bêtes noires*) with his patron. In his *Royal and Noble Authors* he says : ' The friendly patronage [i.e., of the Earl] was returned with ungrateful rudeness by the proud pedant ; and men smiled, without being surprised, at seeing a bear worry his dancing-master.'—[Walpole's antipathy to Johnson is further evidenced by his strictures on him in his recently published notes on Mason's later poems. See *Satirical Poems pub-*

Another work of this year was a reply to some remarks by Mr. Masters ¹ in the *Archæologia* upon the old subject of the *Historic Doubts*, which calls for no further notice. But early in 1775 he was persuaded into writing an epilogue ² for the *Braganza* of Captain Robert Jephson, a maiden tragedy of the *Venice Preserved* order which was produced at Drury Lane in February of that year with considerable success. In a correspondence which ensued with the author,³ Walpole delivered himself of his views on tragedy for the benefit of Mr. Jephson, who acted upon them, but not (as his Mentor thought) with conspicuous success, in his next attempt, the *Law of Lombardy*. Jephson's third play, however, the *Count of Narbonne*, which was well received in 1781, had a natural claim upon Walpole's good opinion, since it was based upon the *Castle of Otranto*.⁴ Besides the above

lished anonymously by William Mason with Notes by Horace Walpole, now first printed from his MS. (ed. Toynbee), pp. 32, 33, 54, 99, 114.]    ¹ See above, p. 216, n. 3.

² [Printed in *Works of Lord Orford*, iv. 400–1.]

³ [Reprinted in *Supplement* (vol. i, pp. 245–7) to *Letters of Horace Walpole* (ed. Toynbee).]

⁴ ' Jephson's " Count of Narbonne " has been more admired than any play I remember to have appeared these many years. It is still [Jan. 1782] acted with success to very full houses ' (*Malone to Charlemont, Hist. MSS. Com-*

letters on tragedy, Walpole wrote, 'in 1775 and
1776', a rather longer paper on comedy.¹ He
held, as he says, ' a good comedy, the *chef-d'œuvre*
of human genius', and it is manifest that his
keenest sympathies were on the side of comic
art. His remarks upon Congreve are full of
just appreciation. Yet, although he mentions
the *School for Scandal* ² (which by the way shows
that he must have written rather later than the
dates given above), he makes no reference to the
most recent development, in *She Stoops to Conquer*, of the school of humour and character, and
he seems rather to pose as the advocate of that
genteel or sentimental comedy which Foote and
Goldsmith and Sheridan had striven to drive from
the English stage. When his prejudices are
aroused he is seldom a safe guide, and in addition
to his personal contempt for Goldsmith,³ that

*mission*, 12*th Rept.*, *App.*, Pt. x, 1891, p. 395). Malone
wrote the epilogue.

¹ [*Works of Lord Orford*, ii. 315–22.]

² [First produced on 8 May 1777. Walpole's reference
to it occurs quite at the end of his paper, and was evidently
a later addition, Sheridan's play being coupled with Bur-
goyne's *Heiress*, which was written in 1786.]

³ ' Silly Dr. Goldsmith '—he calls him to Cole (27 April
1773). ' Goldsmith was an idiot, with once or twice a fit
of parts '—he says again to Mason (8 Oct. 1776).

writer had irritated him by his reference to the Albemarle Street Club, to which many of his friends belonged. It was an additional offence that the ' Miss Biddy [1] Buckskin ' of the comedy was said to stand for Miss Rachael Lloyd, long housekeeper at Kensington Palace, and one of the foundresses of the club, well known both to himself and to Madame du Deffand.[2]

In the second of the letters to Mr. Jephson, Walpole refers to his own efforts at comedy, and implies that he had made attempts in this direction even before the tragedy of *The Mysterious Mother*. He had certainly the wit, and much of the gift of direct expression, which comedy requires. But nothing of these earlier essays appears to have survived, and the only dramatic effort included among his *Works* (his tragedy excepted) is the little piece entitled *Nature will Prevail*, which, with its fairy machinery, has something of the character of such earlier productions of Mr.

---

[1] Originally ' Miss Rachael ' [see *Walpole to Lady Ossory*, 27 March 1773.]

[2] The rules of the so-called *Female Coterie* in Albemarle Street, together with the names of the members, are given in the *Gentleman's Magazine* for 1770, pp. 414–5. Besides Walpole and Miss Lloyd, Fox, Conway, Selwyn, the Waldegraves, the Damers, and many other ' persons of quality ' belonged to it [see *Walpole to Montagu*, 6 May 1770].

W. S. Gilbert as the *Palace of Truth.* This he wrote in 1773, and, according to the *Short Notes,* sent it anonymously to the elder Colman, then manager of Covent Garden. Colman (he says) was much pleased with it, but regarding it as too short for a farce, wished to have it enlarged.[1] This, however, its author thought too much trouble ' for so slight and extempore a performance '. Five years after (June 1778), it was produced at the little theatre in the Haymarket, and being admirably acted—says the *Biographia Dramatica*—met with considerable applause. But it is obviously one of those works to which the verdict of Goldsmith's critic, that it would have been better if the author had taken more pains, may judiciously be applied. It is more like a sketch for a farce than a farce itself; and it is not finished enough for a *proverbe.* Yet the dialogue is in parts so good that one almost regrets the inability of the author to nerve himself for an enterprise *de longue haleine.*

Between 1774 and 1780 the Strawberry Hill Press still now and then showed signs of vitality. In June 1775, it printed as a loose sheet some

[1] [See *Walpole to Colman,* 2 March 1778, in *Supplement* (vol. i, pp. 273-4) to *Letters of Horace Walpole* (ed. Toynbee).]

T

verses by Charles James Fox, celebrating, as Amoret, that lover of the Whigs, the beautiful Mrs. Crewe; and three hundred copies of an Eclogue by Mr. Fitzpatrick,[1] entitled *Dorinda*, which contains the couplet,—

'And oh! what Bliss, when each alike is pleas'd,
The Hand that squeezes, and the Hand that's squeez'd.'[2]

These were followed, in August 1778, by seventy-five copies of the *Sleep Walker*, a comedy from the French of Madame du Deffand's friend Pont-de-Veyle, translated by Lady Craven, afterwards Margravine of Anspach, and played for a charitable purpose at her house at Benham-Valence, near Newbury. A year later (Jan. 1779) came the vindication of his conduct to Chatterton, already mentioned;[3] and after this (Jan. 1780)

---

[1] The Hon. Richard Fitzpatrick, Lord Ossory's brother. He afterwards became a General and Secretary at War. At this time he was a captain in the Grenadier Guards. As a *littérateur* he had written *The Bath Picture; or, a Slight Sketch of its Beauties;* and he was later one of the chief contributors to the *Rolliad*. Besides being the life-long friend of Fox, he was a highly popular wit and man-of-fashion. Lord Ossory put him above Walpole and Selwyn; and Lady Holland is said to have thought him the most agreeable person she had ever known. He died in 1813.

[2] [See *Walpole to Mason*, 12 June 1775.]

[3] [See above, pp. 221-6.]

a sheet of verse by Mr. Charles Miller to Lady Horatia Waldegrave,[1] youngest daughter of the Duchess of Gloucester by her first husband. In October of this same year (1780) was issued the fourth volume of the *Anecdotes of Painting,* which had been printed as far back as 1771. This delay, the Advertisement informs us, arose ' from motives of tenderness '. The author was ' unwilling (he says) to utter even gentle censures, which might wound the affections, or offend the prejudices, of those related to the persons whom

---

[1] One of the three beautiful sisters painted by Reynolds, —Elizabeth Laura, afterwards Countess Waldegrave ; Charlotte Maria, afterwards Countess of Euston ; and Anna Horatia, who married Captain Hugh Conway. ' Sir Joshua Reynolds gets avaricious in his old age. My picture of the young ladies Waldegrave is doubtless very fine and graceful ; but it cost me 800 guineas ' (*Walpoliana*, 2nd ed., ii. 159).—[' 800 guineas ' was either a mistake of Pinkerton's, or a misprint ; the actual price was 300 guineas, as appears from Reynolds's receipt (formerly in the Waller collection), which is printed in *Supplement* (vol. ii, p. 165) to *Letters of Horace Walpole* (ed. Toynbee) (see also *Walpole to Harcourt,* 5 Aug. 1783). The picture was exhibited at the Royal Academy in 1781. Walpole's own copy (a proof) of Valentine Green's mezzotint engraving of it was sold at Christie's in June 1924 for 1,050 guineas ; at the Strawberry Hill sale in 1842 it fetched (with four other prints) no more than £4 10*s.*]

T 2

truth forbad him to commend beyond their merits'.[1]
But despite his unwillingness to ' dispense universal panegyric ', and the limitation of his theme to
living professors, he manages, in the same advertisement, to distribute a fair amount of praise to
some of his particular favourites.    Of H. W.
Bunbury, the husband of Goldsmith's ' Little
Comedy ', he says that he is the ' second Hogarth ',
and the ' first imitator who ever fully equalled
his original ', which is sheer extravagance.    He
lauds the miniature copying of Lady Lucan, as
almost depreciating the ' exquisite works ' of the
artists she follows—to wit, Cooper and the
Olivers ;  and he speaks of Lady Di Beauclerk's
drawings as ' not only inspired by Shakespeare's
insight into nature, but by the graces and taste
of Grecian artists '.    After this, the comparison
of Mrs. Damer with Bernini seems almost tame.
Yet her works ' from the life are not inferior to
the antique, and those . . . were not more like '.
One can scarcely blame Walpole severely for this
hearty backing of the friends who had added so
much to the attractions of his Gothic castle ;  but

---

[1] He was not successful as regards Hogarth, whose widow
was sorely and justly wounded by his coarse treatment of
*Sigismunda*, which is said to have been a portrait of herself.
The picture is now in the National Gallery.

the value of his criticisms, in many other instances sound enough, is certainly impaired by his loyalty to the old-new practice of ' log-rolling '.

[Several notable productions were yet to come from the Strawberry Hill Press, which continued its activities intermittently during the next nine years. In August 1781 were struck off 250 copies of William (afterwards Sir William) Jones's *Ode* on the marriage of Lord Althorp and the Hon. Lavinia Bingham. In 1784 the enlarged edition (200 copies) of the *Description of Straw-berry Hill* already mentioned [1] was printed. This was followed in the next year by Walpole's *Essay on Modern Gardening*, with the French translation by the Duc de Nivernois (400 copies, of which half were sent to the Duke in Paris); and by his *Hieroglyphic Tales*, ' some strange things, even wilder than the *Castle of Otranto* ',[2] of which ' only six copies, besides the revised copy ', were printed, and which is consequently one of the rarest of the productions of the *Officina Arbuteana*. In November 1786 a *Postscript to the Royal and Noble Authors* [3] (40 copies) was issued. A year later Walpole resumed, but finally abandoned, an undertaking which had been begun as far back as

---

[1] [See above, p. 236.]　　[2] [*To Cole*, 28 Jan. 1779.]
[3] [Otherwise known as *Christina*.]

1768, namely an edition in quarto of all his works. Of the portion actually completed, consisting of the first volume and part of the second, only one copy appears to be known.[1]    The list closes with Walpole's verses to Miss Mary and Miss Agnes Berry, printed in October 1788, and Hannah More's *Bishop Bonner's Ghost* (200 copies), printed in July 1789.[2]]

Lady Di Beauclerk, whose illustrations to Dryden's *Fables* are still a frequent item in second-hand catalogues, has a personal connection with Strawberry through the curious little closet bearing her name, which, with the assistance of Mr. Essex,[3] a Gothic architect from Cambridge, Walpole in 1776–8 managed to tuck in between the Cabinet and the Round Tower.    It was built on purpose to hold the 'seven incomparable drawings' executed in a fortnight, which her Ladyship prepared to illustrate *The Mysterious Mother*. These were the designs to which he refers in

[1] [This is in the collection of Mr. Percival Merritt, of Boston, Mass. ; for a collation of it, see *Journal of the Printing-Office at Strawberry Hill*, pp. 89–91.]

[2] [For further details of the books and pieces printed at Strawberry Hill, see *Appendix*.]

[3] [Essex was also architect of the new offices, which were built in 1790 at a cost of nearly £2,000 (see *Strawberry Hill Accounts*, p. 18).]

the *Anecdotes of Painting ;* and, in a letter to Lady Ossory,[1] says could not be surpassed by Guido and Salvator Rosa. They were hung on Indian blue damask, in frames of black and gold, and Clive's friend, Miss Pope, the actress, when she dined at Strawberry, was affected by them to such a degree that she shed tears, although she did not know the story,[2] an anecdote which may be regarded either as a genuine compliment to Lady Di, or a merely histrionic tribute to her entertainer. ' The drawings ', Walpole says, ' do not shock and disgust, like their original, the tragedy,' [3] but they were not to be shown to the profane. They were, nevertheless, probably exhibited pretty freely, as a copy of the play, carefully annotated in MS. by the author, and bound in blue leather to match the hangings, was always kept in a drawer of one of the tables for the purpose of explaining them.[4] Walpole afterwards

[1] [27 Dec. 1775.]    [2] [*To Mason*, 6 July 1777.]
[3] [*To Mann*, 31 Oct. 1779.]
[4] Miss Hawkins (*Anecdotes*, etc., 1822, p. 103) did not think highly of these performances :—' Unless the proportions of the human figure are of no importance in drawing it, these " Beauclerk drawings " can be looked on only with disgust and contempt.' But she praises the gipsies hereafter mentioned (p. 296) as having been copied by Agnes Berry.

added one or two curiosities to this closet.   It
contained, according to the last edition of the
*Catalogue*, a head in basalt of Jupiter Serapis, and
a book of Psalms illuminated by Giulio Clovio,
the latter purchased for £168 at the Duchess of
Portland's sale in May 1786.   There was also a
portrait by Powell, after Reynolds, of Lady Di
herself, who lived for some time at Twickenham
in a house now known as Little Marble Hill,
many of the rooms of which she decorated with
her own performances.   These were apparently
the efforts which prompted the already mentioned
postscript to the *Parish Register of Twickenham*:—

> ' Here Genius in a later hour
> Selected its sequester'd bow'r,
> And threw around the verdant room
> The blushing lilac's chill perfume.
> So loose is flung each bold festoon,
> Each bough so breathes the touch of noon ;
> The happy pencil so deceives,
> That Flora, doubly jealous, cries
> " The work 's not mine—yet trust these eyes,
> 'T is my own Zephyr waves the leaves." ' [1]

Mention has been made of the intermittent
attacks of insanity to which Walpole's nephew,
the third Earl of Orford, was subject.   At the
beginning of 1774, he had returned to his senses,

[1] See pp. 177-9.

and his uncle, on whom fell the chief care of his affairs during his illnesses, was, for a brief period, freed from the irksome strain of an uncongenial and a thankless duty. In April 1777, however, Lord Orford's malady broke out again with redoubled severity.[1] In August, he was still fluctuating ' between violence and stupidity ';[2] but in March 1778, a lucid interval had once more been reached, and Walpole was relieved of the care of his person. Of his affairs he had declined to take care, as his Lordship had employed a lawyer of whom Walpole had a bad opinion. 'He has resumed the entire dominion of himself,' says a letter to Mann in April, 'and is gone into the country, and intends to command the militia.'[3] One of the earliest results of this 'entire dominion' was a step which filled his relative with the keenest distress. He offered the famous Houghton collection of pictures to Catherine of Russia—'the most signal mortification to my idolatry for my father's memory, that it could receive', says Walpole to Lady Ossory.[4] By August 1779 the sale was completed. 'The sum stipulated', he tells Mann,

[1] [See Horace Walpole's letters to Sir Edward Walpole, in *Supplement* (vol. i, pp. 260–9) to *Letters* (ed. Toynbee).]
[2] [*To Mason*, 4 Aug. 1777.]
[3] [*To Mann*, 9 Apr. 1778.]    [4] [1 Feb. 1779.]

' is forty or forty-five thousand pounds,[1] I neither know nor care which ;  nor whether the picture-merchant ever receives the whole sum, which probably he will not do, as I hear it is to be discharged at three payments—a miserable bargain for a mighty empress ! . . . Well ! adieu to Houghton ! about its mad master I shall never trouble myself more. . . . Since he has stript Houghton of its glory, I do not care a straw what he does with the stone or the acres ! ' [2]

Not very long after the date of the above letter Walpole made what was, for him, an important change of residence.   The lease of his house in Arlington Street running out, he fixed upon a larger one in the then very fashionable district of Berkeley Square.[3]   But difficulties arose over the sale, and he found himself involved in a Chancery suit.   He was too adroit, however, to allow this to degenerate into an additional annoyance,

[1] The exact sum was £40,555.   Cipriani and West were the valuers.   Most of the family portraits were reserved ; but so many of the pictures were presents that it is not easy to estimate the actual profit over their first cost to the original owner.          [2] *To Mann*, 4 Aug. 1779.

[3] The house he selected was that now (1926) numbered 11 ; it was then 40, which, according to Harrison's *Memorable Houses*, 3rd ed., 1890, p. 62, is Lord Orford's number as given in *Boyle's Court Guide* for 1796.

and managed (by his own account) to turn what promised to be a tedious course of litigation into a combat of courtesy.[1]  Ultimately, in July 1779, he had won his cause, and was hurrying from Strawberry to pay his purchase money and close the bargain.[2]  Two months later, he is moving in, and is delighted with his acquisition.  He would not change his two pretty mansions for any in England, he says.[3]  On the 14th October, he took formal possession, upon which day— his ' inauguration day '—he dates his first letter ' Berkeley Square '.[4]  ' It is seeming to take a new lease of life,' he tells Mason.  ' I was born in Arlington Street, lived there about fourteen years, returned thither, and passed thirty-seven more ;  but I have sober monitors that warn me not to delude myself.' [5]  He had still a decade and a half before him.

Less than twelve months after he had settled down in his new abode, he lost the faithful friend [6] at Paris, to whom, for the space of fifteen years, he had written nearly once a week.  As early as

[1] [*To Lady Ossory*, 14 July 1779.]
[2] [*To Lady Ossory*, 24 July 1779.]
[3] [*To Mann*, 11 Oct. 1779.]
[4] [*To Lady Ossory*, 14 Oct. 1779.]
[5] [*To Mason*, 21 Oct. 1779.]
[6] [Mme du Deffand died 24 Sept. 1780.]

1769 he had become somewhat nervous about this accumulated correspondence in a language not his own.    For an Englishman, his French was good, and, as might be expected of anything he wrote, characteristic and vivacious.    But, almost of necessity, as he was well aware,[1] his letters contained many faults of phraseology, besides abounding in personal anecdote, mingled not infrequently with ' gronderies ' on account of what he termed his correspondent's ' indiscretions '; consequently he became apprehensive lest, after Madame du Deffand's death, his utterances should fall into alien hands.    He took measures, therefore, to secure that the letters should be returned to him.    Those down to 1759 he received back on the occasion of his third visit to Paris in the summer of that year. A second instalment, down to 1774, was brought back five years later by Conway.    The bulk of the remainder, save for a few which by some accident escaped, were burned by Madame du Deffand herself.    Such as were left at the time of her death were returned to Walpole by her secretary, Wiart.[2]    In August 1775 Walpole

---

[1] [See his letters to Conway of 28 Sept. 1774, and to Thomas Walpole of 6 Sept. 1780.]

[2] See above, p. 203 n.

made a fifth journey to visit his blind friend; and found her, as usual, impatiently expecting his arrival. She sat with him until half past two in the morning, and before his eyes were open again he had a letter from her. 'Her soul is immortal, and forces her body to keep it company.' [1] A little later he complains that he never gets to bed from her suppers before two or three o'clock. 'In short', he says, 'I need have the activity of a squirrel, and the strength of a Hercules, to go through my labours—not to count how many *démêlés* I have had to *raccommode*, and how many *mémoires* to present against Tonton,[2] who grows the greater favourite the more people

[1] [*To Lady Ailesbury*, 20 Aug. 1775.]

[2] Tonton was a snappish little dog belonging to Madame du Deffand which, when in its mistress's company, must have been extremely objectionable. In Jan. 1778, the Maréchale de Luxembourg presented her old friend with Tonton's portrait in wax on a gold snuff-box, together with the last six volumes of Madame du Deffand's favourite Voltaire, adding the following epigram by the Chevalier de Boufflers :—

> 'Vous les trouvez tous deux charmans,
> Nous les trouvons tous deux mordans ;
>     Voilà la ressemblance :
> L'un ne mord que ses ennemis,
> Et l'autre mord tous vos amis ;
>     Voilà la différence.'

he devours.' [1]    But Tonton's mistress is more
worth visiting than ever, he tells Selwyn,[2] and
she is apparently as tireless as of yore.   ' Madame
du Deffand and I (says another letter) set out last
Sunday at seven in the evening, to go fifteen miles
to a ball, and came back after supper ;  and another
night, because it was but one in the morning when
she brought me home, she ordered the coachman
to make the tour of the Quais, and drive gently
because it was so early.' [3]    At last, early in October, he tears himself away, to be followed almost
immediately by a letter of farewell.   Here it is :—

ADIEU, ce mot est bien triste ;  souvenez-vous que vous
laissez ici la personne dont vous êtes le plus aimé, et dont
le bonheur et le malheur consistent dans ce que vous pensez
pour elle.   Donnez-moi de vos nouvelles le plus tôt qu'il
sera possible.

Je me porte bien, j'ai un peu dormi, ma nuit n'est pas
finie ;  je serai très-exacte au régime, et j'aurai soin de moi,
puisque vous vous y intéressez.

Ce jeudi à 6 heures [12 Oct. 1775].

The correspondence thus resumed was continued for five years more, during which Walpole

At Madame du Deffand's death, both dog and box passed
to Walpole, the latter finding an honoured place among the
treasures of the Tribune.  (See *Description of Strawberry
Hill*, in *Works of Lord Orford*, ii. 485.)

[1] [*To Conway*, 8 Sept. 1775.]        [2] [16 Sept. 1775.]
[3] [*To Lady Ossory*, 9 Sept. 1775.]

did not visit Paris again. The references to Madame du Deffand in his general correspondence are not very frequent. Towards the middle of 1780, her life was plainly closing in. In July and August, she complained of being more than usually languid, and in a letter of the 22nd of the latter month intimates that it may be her last, as dictation grows painful to her. 'Ne vous devant revoir de ma vie '—she says pathetically—' je n'ai rien à regretter.' From this time she kept her bed, and on September 23rd Walpole tells Lady Ossory that he is trembling at every letter he gets from Paris. ' My dear old friend, I fear, is going ! . . . To have struggled twenty days at eighty-four shows such stamina that I have not totally lost hopes.' On the 24th, however, after a lethargy of several days, she died quietly ' without effort or struggle '. ' Elle a eu la mort la plus douce ' —says her faithful and attached secretary Wiart —' quoique la maladie ait été longue.' She was buried, at her own wish, in the parish church of St. Sulpice. By her will she made her nephew, the Marquis d'Aulan, her heir. Long since, she had wished Walpole to accept this character. Thereupon he had threatened that he would never set foot in Paris again if she carried out her intention ; and it was abandoned. But she left him the whole of her manuscripts,[1] as well as the gold box with Tonton's portrait on it mentioned above.[2]

As but few of his letters to her have been printed,[3] her death makes little difference in the amount of his correspondence. The war with the American Colonies, of which he foresaw the disastrous results, and the course of which he follows to Mann with the greatest keenness, fully absorbs as much of his time as he can spare from the vagaries of the Duchess of Kingston and the doings of the Duchess of Gloucester. Not many months before Madame du Deffand died had occurred the famous Gordon Riots, which, as he was in London most of the time, naturally occupy his pen.[4] It was General Conway who, as the author of *Barnaby Rudge* has not forgotten,

[1] The MSS., which included 838 of Madame du Deffand's letters, were sold in the Strawberry Hill sale of 1842 (lot 107 of sixth day) for £157 10*s*.—[The purchaser was D. O. Dyce-Sombre, at whose death in 1851 they passed to his widow, Hon. Mary Anne Jervis (afterwards Lady Forester) ; by her they were left to her nephew, the late W. R. Parker-Jervis, in whose possession they were discovered by Mrs. Paget Toynbee. Madame du Deffand's letters are now in the Bodleian (see above, p. 202 n.).]

[2] [See p. 285, n. 2.]        [3] [See above, p. 203 n.]

[4] [See letters to Lady Ossory, Mason, and Mann, of June 1780.]

so effectively remonstrated with Lord George
upon the occasion of the visit of the mob to the
House of Commons; and four days later Walpole chronicles from Berkeley Square the events
of the terrible ' Black Wednesday '. From the
roof of Gloucester House he sees the blazing
prisons—a sight he shall not soon forget. Other
subjects for which one dips in the lucky bag of
his records are the defence of Gibraltar,[1] the trial
of Warren Hastings,[2] the loss of the *Royal George*.[3]
But it is generally in the minor chronicle that he
is most diverting. The last *bon mot* of George
Selwyn or Lady Townshend, the newest ' royal
pregnancy ', the details of court ceremonial, the
most recent addition to Strawberry, the endless
stream of anecdote and tittle tattle which runs
dimpling all the way—these are the themes he
loves best—this is the element in which his easy
persiflage delights to disport itself. He is, above
all, a *rieur*. About his serious passages there is
sometimes a false ring, but never when he pours
out the gossip that he loves, and of which he has
so inexhaustible a supply. ' I can sit and amuse

[1] [See letters to Lady Ossory, and Mann of Oct. 1782.]
[2] [See letters to Mann of 3 Apr., 22 June, 1786 ; and
to Lady Ossory of 9 Feb. 1787.]
[3] [See to Lady Ossory, 31 Aug. 1782.]

U

myself with my own memory,' he says to Mann
(5 Feb. 1785), 'and yet find new stores at every audience that I give to it.    Then, for private episodes
[he has been speaking of his knowledge of public
events], varieties of characters, political intrigues,
literary anecdotes, &c., &c., the profusion that I remember is endless; in short, when I reflect on all I
have seen, heard, read, written, the many idle hours
I have passed, the nights I have wasted playing at
faro, the weeks, nay months, I have spent in pain,
you will not wonder that I almost think I have,
like Pythagoras, been Panthoides Euphorbus, and
have retained one memory in at least two bodies.'

He was sixty-eight when he wrote the above
letter.    Mann was eighty-four, and the long
correspondence—a correspondence 'not to be
paralleled in the annals of the Post Office' [1]—
was drawing to a close.    'What Orestes and
Pylades ever wrote to each other for four and
forty years without meeting'—Walpole asks.[2]    In
June 1786, however, the last letter of the eight
hundred and thirty-seven printed in the Oxford
edition of the *Letters of Horace Walpole* [3] was

[1] [*To Mann*, 25 Aug. 1784.]

[2] [*To Mann*, 30 Aug. 1782.]

[3] [Vols. i–xvi (1903–5), edited by Mrs. Paget Toynbee ;
vols. xvii–xix (*Supplement*, 1918, 1925), edited by Paget
Toynbee.]

despatched to Florence.[1]   In the following November, Mann died, after a prolonged illness.  He
had never visited England, nor had Walpole set
eyes upon him since he had left him at Florence in
May 1741.  His death followed hard upon that of
another faithful friend (whose gifts, perhaps, hardly
lay in the epistolary line [2]), bustling, kindly Kitty
Clive.  Her cheerful, ruddy face, ' all sun and ver-
milion,' [3] set peacefully in December 1785, leaving
Cliveden vacant, not, as we shall see, for long.[4]

[1] Walpole, as in the case of Madame du Deffand, had
taken the precaution of getting back his letters, and at his
friend's death, not more than a dozen of them were still in
Mann's possession.  The originals of Mann's letters to Walpole, which Cunningham pronounced to be ' absolutely
unreadable ', are in the possession of Mr. Richard Bentley.
An attempt to skim the cream of them (such as it is) was
made by Dr. Doran in two volumes entitled ' *Mann* ' *and
Manners at the Court of Florence*, 1740–1786, Bentley, 1876.

[2] [A letter from her to Walpole is printed in *Supplement*
(vol. iii, p. 139) to *Letters of Horace Walpole* (ed. Toynbee).]

[3] [*To Montagu*, 21 July 1766.]

[4] Mrs. Clive is buried at Twickenham, where a mural
slab was erected to her in the parish church by her *protégée*
and successor, Miss Jane Pope, the clever actress who shed
tears over the Beauclerk drawings (see p. 279).  Her portrait by Davison, which is engraved as the frontispiece to
Cunningham's fourth volume, hung in the Round Bedchamber at Strawberry.  It was given to Walpole by her
brother, James Raftor.

Earlier still had departed another old ally, Cole,[1] the antiquary, and the lapse of time had in other ways contracted Walpole's circle.  In 1781, Lady Orford had ended her erratic career at Pisa, leaving her son a fortune so considerable as to make his uncle regret vaguely that the sale of the Houghton pictures had not been delayed for a few months longer.[2]  Three years later,[3] she was followed by her brother-in-law, Sir Edward Walpole, an occurrence which had the effect of leaving between Horace Walpole and his father's title nothing but his lunatic and childless nephew.[4]

If his relatives and friends were falling away, however, their places—the places of the friends at least—were speedily filled again;  and, as a general rule, most of his male favourites were replaced by women.   Pinkerton, the antiquary, who afterwards published the *Walpoliana*, is one of the exceptions;  and several of Walpole's letters to him are contained in that book, and in the volumes of Pinkerton's own correspondence

[1] [He died 16 Dec. 1782.]

[2] [*Walpole to Mann*, 6 Feb. 1781.]

[3] [Jan. 1784. ]

[4] [His brother's death also had the effect of diminishing Walpole's income by £1,400 a year, derived from the sinecure place in the Customs which they held jointly (see *to Mason*, 2 Feb. 1784).]

published by Dawson Turner in 1830.[1] But Walpole's appetite for correspondence of the purely literary kind had somewhat slackened in his old age, and it was to the other sex that he turned for sympathy and solace.    He liked them best ; his style suited them ; and he wrote to them with most ease.    In July 1785, he was visited at Strawberry by Madame de Genlis, who arrived with her friend Miss Wilkes and the famous Pamela,[2] afterwards Lady Edward Fitzgerald.    Madame de Genlis at this date was nearing forty, and had lost much of her good looks.    But Walpole seems to have found her less *précieuse* and affected than he had anticipated,[3] and she was, on this occasion, unaccompanied by the inevitable harp.    A later visit was from Dr. Burney and his daughter Fanny —'Evelina-Cecilia' Walpole calls her,[4]—a young

[1] [These and others, some thirty in all, are printed in Mrs. Toynbee's edition of the *Letters*.]

[2] 'Whom she [Madame de Genlis] has educated to be very like herself in the face '—says Walpole, referring to a then current scandal.    At this date, however, it is but just to add that the investigations of Mr. J. G. Alger tend to show that it is by no means certain that Pamela was the daughter of the accomplished lady whom Philippe-Égalité entrusted with the education of his sons. (See *Dict. Nat. Biog.* xix. 142–3.)

[3] [*Walpole to Lady Ossory*, 23 July 1785.]

[4] [*To Lady Ossory*, 17 Sept. 1785.]

lady for whose good sense and modesty he expresses a genuine admiration.    Miss Burney had not as yet entered upon that court bondage which was to be so little to her advantage.    Another and more intimate acquaintanceship of this period was with Miss Burney's friend, Hannah More.    Hannah More became one of Walpole's correspondents, although scarcely 'so corresponding' as he wished; and they met frequently in society when she visited London as the guest of Mrs. Garrick.    On her side, she seems to have been wholly fascinated by his wit and conversational powers;  he, on his, was attracted by her mingled puritanism and vivacity.    He writes to her as 'St. Hannah';  [1] and she, in return, sighs plaintively over his lack of religion.    Yet (she adds) she ' must do him the justice to say, that except the delight he has in teasing me for what he calls over-strictness, I have never heard a sentence from him which savoured of infidelity '. [2]    He evidently took a

[1] [See Mrs. Toynbee's article *Horace Walpole and ' St. Hannah '*, in *Temple Bar* for Mar. 1897.]

[2] He is not explicit as to his creed.  'Atheism I dislike '— he said to Pinkerton.  ' It is gloomy, uncomfortable ; and, in my eye, unnatural and irrational.  It certainly requires more credulity to believe that there is no God, than to believe that there is ' (*Walpoliana*, 2nd ed., i. 78).  But Pinkerton must be taken with caution. (Cf. *Quarterly Review*, 1843, lxxii. 551.)

great interest in her works, and indeed in 1789 printed at his press (its last production under his auspices) one of her poems, ' Bonner's Ghost '.[1] His friendship for her endured for the remainder of his life, and not long before his death he presented her with a richly bound copy of Bishop Wilson's *Bible* with a complimentary inscription which may be read in the second volume of her *Life and Correspondence.*[2]

It was, however, neither the author of *Evelina* nor the author of *The Manners of the Great* who was destined to fill the void created by the death of Madame du Deffand. In the winter of 1787–8, he had first seen, and a year later he made the formal acquaintance of, ' two young ladies of the name of Berry '. They had a story. Their father, at this time a widower, had married for love, and had afterwards been supplanted in the good graces of a rich uncle by a younger brother who had the generosity to allow him an annuity of a thousand a year. In 1783, Mr. Berry had

[1] In 1786 she had dedicated to him her *Florio, A Tale,* etc., with a highly complimentary Preface, in which she says—' I should be unjust to your very engaging and well-bred turn of wit, if I did not declare that, among all the lively and brilliant things I have heard from you, I do not remember ever to have heard an unkind or an ungenerous one.'    [2] [Edited by W. Roberts, 4 vols., Lond., 1834.]

taken his daughters abroad to Holland, Switzerland, and Italy, whence, in June 1785, they had returned, being then highly cultivated and attractive young women of two-and-twenty and one-and-twenty respectively. Three years later, Walpole met them for the second time at the house of a Lady Herries, the wife of a banker in St. James's Street. The first time he saw them he ' would not be acquainted with them having heard so much in their praise that he concluded they would be all pretension '. But on the second occasion, ' in a very small company ', he sat next the elder, Mary, ' and found her an angel both inside and out '. ' Her face '—he tells Lady Ossory—' is formed for a sentimental novel, but it is ten times fitter for a fifty times better thing, genteel comedy '. The other sister was speedily discovered to be nearly as charming. ' They are exceedingly sensible, entirely natural and unaffected, frank, and, being qualified to talk on any subject, nothing is so easy and agreeable/as their conversation—not more apposite than their answers and observations. The eldest, I discovered by chance, understands Latin and is a perfect Frenchwoman in her language. The younger draws charmingly, and has copied admirably Lady Di's gipsies,[1] which I

[1] This (we are told) was Lady Di's *chef-d'œuvre*. It

lent, though for the first time of her attempting
colours. They are of pleasing figures; Mary,
the eldest, sweet, with fine dark eyes, that are
very lively when she speaks, with a symmetry of
face that is the more interesting from being pale ;
Agnes, the younger, has an agreeable sensible
countenance, hardly to be called handsome, but
almost. She is less animated than Mary, but
seems, out of deference to her sister, to speak
seldomer, for they dote on each other, and Mary
is always praising her sister's talents. I must even
tell you they dress within the bounds of fashion,
though fashionably ; but without the excrescences
and balconies with which modern hoydens over-
whelm and barricade their persons. In short, good
sense, information, simplicity, and ease character-
ize the Berrys ; and this is not particularly mine,
who am apt to be prejudiced, but the universal
voice of all who know them.' [1]

'This delightful family', he goes on to say,
'comes to me almost every Sunday evening'.
(They were at the time living on Twickenham
Common.) Of the father not much is recorded

was a water-colour drawing representing 'Gipsies telling
a country-maiden her fortune at the entrance of a beech-
wood ', and hung in the Red Bedchamber at Strawberry.

[1] *Walpole to Lady Ossory*, 11 Oct. 1788.

beyond the fact that he was 'a little merry man with a round face', and (as his eldest daughter reports) 'an odd inherent easiness in his disposition', who seems to have been perfectly contented in his modest and unobtrusive character of paternal appendage to the favourites.    Walpole's attachment to his new friends grew rapidly.    Only two days after the date of the foregoing letter, Mr. Kirgate's press was versifying in their honour,[1] and they themselves were already ' his two Straw Berries' whose praises he sang to all his friends. He delighted in devising new titles for them— they were his ' twin wives', his ' dear Both', his ' Amours'.    For them in this year he began writing the charming little volume of *Reminiscences*;[2] and in December 1789 [he presented them with a copy of his *Description of Strawberry Hill*, with a long inscription stating that it was offered to them ' from a heart overflowing with admiration, esteem, and friendship' ].[3]    It was not

[1] [*To Lady Ossory*, 19 Oct. 1788.]

[2] [*Reminiscences written in* 1788 *for the amusement of Miss Mary & Miss Agnes Berry*—first printed in *Works of Lord Orford*, iv. 273–318 ; first printed in full from the original MS. (now in possession of Mr. Pierpont Morgan) by Paget Toynbee, Oxford, 1924.]

[3] [See *Journals and Correspondence of Miss Berry*, i. 193. A misinterpretation of this inscription has given rise to the

long before he had secured them a home at Teddington, and finally, when, in December 1790, Cliveden became vacant,[1] he prevailed upon them to become his neighbours. He afterwards bequeathed the house to them, and for many years after his death, it was their summer residence. On either side the acquaintance was advantageous. His friendship at once introduced them to the best and most accomplished fashionable society of their day, while the charm of their ' company, conversation and talents ' must have inexpressibly sweetened and softened what, on his part, had begun to grow more and more a solitary, joyless, and painful old age.

His establishment of his ' wives ' in his immediate vicinity was not, however, accomplished without difficulty. For a moment some ill-natured newspaper gossip, which attributed the attachment of the Berry family to interested motives, so justly aroused the indignation of the elder sister that the whole arrangement threatened to collapse. But the slight estrangement thus caused

erroneous statement in *Dict. Nat. Biog.* (adopted by Austin Dobson and others) that Walpole *dedicated* the *Description* to the Miss Berrys.]

[1] [After the death of Mrs. Clive in Dec. 1785, it was occupied by Sir Robert Goodere till 25 Dec. 1790.]

soon passed away ; and at the close of 1791, they took up their abode in Mrs. Clive's old house, now doubly honoured.   On the 5th of the December in the same year, after a fresh fit of frenzy, Walpole's nephew died, and he became fourth Earl of Orford.   The new dignity was by no means a welcome one, and scarcely compensated for the cares which it entailed.   ' A small estate, loaded with debt, and of which I do not understand the management, and am too old to learn, a source of law suits amongst my near relations, though not affecting me ;   endless conversations with lawyers, and packets of letters every day to read and answer—all this weight of new business is too much for the rag of life that yet hangs about me, and was preceded by three weeks of anxiety about my unfortunate nephew, and a daily correspondence with physicians and mad-doctors, falling upon me when I had been out of order ever since July.' [1]   ' For the other empty metamorphosis ', he writes to Hannah More,[2] ' that has happened to the outward man, you do me justice in concluding that it can do nothing but tease me ;   it is being called names in one's old age.   I had rather be my Lord Mayor, for then I should

[1] *Walpole to Pinkerton,* 26 Dec. 1791.
[2] [1 Jan. 1792.]

keep the nickname but a year; and mine I may retain a little longer, not that at seventy-five I reckon on becoming my Lord Methusalem.' For a time he could scarcely bring himself to use his new signature; in two letters,[1] written before his nephew's funeral, he signed himself as 'The Uncle of the late Earl of Orford'. In 1792, he delivered himself, after the fashion of Cowley, of the following *Epitaphium vivi Auctoris* : [2]—

'An estate and an earldom at seventy-four !
Had I sought them or wish'd them, 'twould add one fear more,
That of making a countess when almost four-score.
But Fortune, who scatters her gifts out of season,
Though unkind to my limbs, has still left me my reason ;
And whether she lowers or lifts me, I'll try
In the plain simple style I have liv'd in, to die ;
For ambition too humble, for meanness [3] too high.'

The last line seems like another of the many echoes of Goldsmith's *Retaliation*. As for the fear indicated in the third, it is hinted that this at one time bade fair to be something more than a poetical apprehension. If we are to credit a

[1] [One dated Dec. 6 (to an unnamed correspondent), the other dated Dec. 8 (to the Duke of Bedford)—see *Supplement* (vol. ii, p. 54) to *Letters* (ed. Toynbee), and *Letters*, vol. xv, pp. 91–2.]

[2] [See *Works of Lord Orford*, iv. 407.]

[3] [Hitherto printed 'manners'.]

tradition handed down by Lord Lansdowne, he
had been willing to go through the form of marriage with either of the Berrys,[1] merely to secure
their society, and to enrich them, as he had the
power of charging the Orford estate with a join-
ture of £2000 per annum.   But this can only
have been a passing thought at some moment
when their absence, in Italy or elsewhere, left
him more sensitive to the loss of their gracious
and stimulating presence.   He himself was far
too keenly alive to ridicule, and too much in
bondage to *les bienséances*, to take a step which
could scarcely escape ill-natured comment, and
Mary Berry, who would certainly have been his
preference, was not only as fully alive as was he
to the shafts of the censorious, but, during the
greater part of her acquaintanceship with him,
was, apparently with his knowledge, warmly attached to a certain good-looking General O'Hara,
to whom she became engaged while on a visit to
Lady Ailesbury at Park Place in September 1795.[2]
He had been appointed Governor of Gibraltar in
this same year, and he wished Miss Berry to marry

[1] [On the authority of Miss Berry's maid, who survived
till 1896 or 1897, it is stated that Walpole, after he became
Earl of Orford, offered his ' hand and heart ' to Mary
Berry, and his ' hand and coronet ' to Agnes.]

[2] [See *Journals and Correspondence of Miss Berry*, ii. 2.]

him at once and go out with him. This, 'out of consideration for others', she declined to do, and consequently the engagement was broken off. O'Hara left England for Gibraltar in November 1796, and Miss Berry never again saw her soldier admirer. Whether Lord Orford's comfort went for anything in this renunciation of her happiness, does not clearly appear; but it is only reasonable to suppose that his tenacious desire for her companionship had its influence in a decision which, however much it may have been for the best (and there were those of her friends who regarded it as a providential escape), was nevertheless a lifelong source of regret to herself. When, in 1802, she heard suddenly at the Opera of O'Hara's death, she fell senseless to the floor.

The 'late Horace Walpole' never took his seat in the House of Lords. He continued, as before, to divide his time between Berkeley Square and Strawberry, to eulogize his 'wives' to Lady Ossory, and to watch life from his beloved Blue Room. Now and then he did the rare honours of his home to a distinguished guest—in 1793, it was the Duchess of York,[1] in 1795, Queen Charlotte[2] herself. In the latter year died his

---

[1] [See *to Miss Berry*, 8 Oct. 1793.]
[2] [See *to Conway*, 2, 7 July 1795.]

old friend Conway, by this time a Field-Marshal, and it was evident at the close of 1796 that his faithful correspondent would not long survive him. His ailments had increased, and in the following January, he wrote his last letter [1] to Lady Ossory :—

Jan. 9, 1797.

My Dear Madam :—

You distress me infinitely by showing my idle notes, which I cannot conceive can amuse anybody. My old-fashioned breeding impels me every now and then to reply to the letters you honour me with writing, but in truth very unwillingly, for I seldom can have anything particular to say ; I scarce go out of my own house, and then only to two or three very private places, where I see nobody that really knows anything, and what I learn comes from Newspapers, that collect intelligence from coffee-houses, consequently what I neither believe nor report. At home I see only a few charitable elders, except about fourscore nephews and nieces of various ages, who are each brought to me once a year, to stare at me as the Methusalem of the family, and they can only speak of their own cotemporaries, which interest me no more than if they talked of their dolls, or bats and balls. Must not the result of all this, Madam, make me a very entertaining correspondent ? And can such letters be worth showing ? or can I have any spirit when so old, and reduced to dictate ?

[1] [This letter, hitherto wrongly dated Jan. 15, is the last written to Lady Ossory ; a still later letter, addressed to Mark Noble, and dated Jan. 12, is printed in *Supplement* (vol. iii, pp. 339–40) to *Letters* (ed. Toynbee).]

Oh ! my good Madam, dispense with me from such a task, and think how it must add to it to apprehend such letters being shown. Pray send me no more such laurels, which I desire no more than their leaves when decked with a scrap of tinsel, and stuck on twelfth-cakes that lie on the shop-boards of pastry-cooks at Christmas. I shall be quite content with a sprig of rosemary thrown after me, when the parson of the parish commits my dust to dust. Till then, pray, Madam, accept the resignation of your

Ancient servant,

O.[1]

Within two months of the date of the above letter, he died at his house in Berkeley Square, to which he had been moved at the close of the previous year. During the latter days of his life, he suffered from a cruel lapse of memory, which led him to suppose himself neglected even by those who had but just quitted him. He sank gradually and expired without pain on the 2nd March 1797, being then in his eightieth year. He was buried at the family seat of Houghton.

His fortune, over and above his leases, amounted

[1] [The original of this letter, formerly in the Waller collection, is now (1926) in the possession of Mr. W. S. Lewis, of Farmington, Connecticut. Except for the date, one or two corrections, and the last line and signature (a very shaky ' O ', not ' Orford ' as hitherto printed), the letter is in the handwriting of Kirgate. See *Supplement* (vol. ii, pp. 194–5) to *Letters* (ed. Toynbee).]

to ninety-one thousand pounds. To each of the Miss Berrys he left the sum of £4000, and, for their lives jointly, the house and garden of ' Little Strawberry ' (Cliveden), the long meadow in front of it, and all the furniture. He also bequeathed to them and to their father his printed works and a certain number of his manuscripts, to be published at their discretion, and for their benefit. It was understood that the real editorship was to fall on the elder sister, who forthwith devoted herself to her task. The result was the edition, in five quarto volumes, of Lord Orford's *Works*, which has been so often referred to during the progress of these pages, and which appeared in 1798.[1] It was entirely due to Mary Berry's unremitting care, her father's share being confined to a final paragraph in the preface, in which she is eulogized.[2]

[1] [It is obvious that a large portion of the material had been prepared long before Lord Orford's death ; he himself had printed at Strawberry Hill one volume, and the greater part of a second, of his own works (see above, pp. 277–8).]

[2] Mary Berry died 20 Nov. 1852 ; Agnes Berry, Jan. 1852. They were buried in one grave in Petersham churchyard, ' amidst scenes '—says Lord Carlisle's inscription— ' which in life they had frequented & loved '. H. F. Chorley (*Autobiography*, etc., 1873, vol. i, p. 276) describes them as ' more like one's notion of ancient Frenchwomen than

Strawberry Hill passed to Mrs. Damer for life, together with £2000 to keep it in repair.  After living in it for some years, she resigned it, in 1811, to the Countess Dowager Waldegrave,[1] in whom the remainder in fee was vested.  It subsequently passed to George, seventh Earl Waldegrave, who sold its contents in 1842.  At his death, in 1846, he left it to his widow, Frances, Countess Waldegrave, who subsequently married (as her fourth husband) the Rt. Hon. Chichester S. Parkinson-Fortescue, afterwards Baron Carlingford.  Lady Waldegrave, who died in 1879, greatly added to and extended the original building, besides restoring many of the objects by which it had been decorated in Walpole's day.[2]

anything I have ever seen ; rouged, with the remains of some beauty, managing large fans like the Flirtillas, etc., etc., of Ranelagh '.  See also *Extracts from Miss Berry's Journals and Correspondence*, 1783–1852, edited by Lady Theresa Lewis, 1865 ; and Lady Ritchie, *Blackstick Papers*, 1908, No. VIII.

[1] [Widow of the fourth Earl.]

[2] [Strawberry Hill, which was sold after Lady Waldegrave's death, has now passed into the hands of the Roman Catholics, and has become a lay training college, under the title of St. Mary's College, Strawberry Hill ; extensive additions are projected, but it is understood that Horace Walpole's building will be preserved as far as possible intact.]

# CHAPTER X

## X

WHEN, in October 1833, Lord (then Mr.) Macaulay completed for the *Edinburgh* his review of Lord Dover's edition of Walpole's letters to Sir Horace Mann, he had apparently performed to his entire satisfaction the operation known, in the workmanlike vocabulary of the time, as 'dusting the jacket' of his unfortunate reviewee. 'I was up at four this morning to put the last touch to it,' he tells his sister Hannah. 'I often differ with the majority about other people's writings, and still oftener about my own; and therefore I may very likely be mistaken; but I think that this article will be a hit. . . . Nothing ever cost me more pains than the first half; I never wrote anything so flowingly as the latter half; and I like the latter half the best. [The latter half, it should be stated, was a rapid and very brilliant sketch of Sir Robert Walpole; the earlier, which involved so much labour, was the portrait of Sir Robert's youngest son.] I have laid it on Walpole [i.e., Horace Walpole] so unsparingly,' he goes on to say, 'that I shall not be surprised if Miss Berry should cut me. . .

Neither am I sure that Lord and Lady Holland will be well pleased.' [1]

His later letters show him to have been a true prophet. Macvey Napier, then the editor of the ' Buff and Blue ', was enthusiastic, praising the article ' in terms absolutely extravagant '. ' He says that it is the best that I ever wrote,' the critic tells his favourite correspondent, a statement which at this date must be qualified by the fact that he penned some of his most famous essays subsequent to its appearance. On the other hand, Miss Berry resented the review so much that Sir Stratford Canning advised its author not to go near her. But apparently her anger was soon dispelled, for the same letter which makes this announcement relates that she was already appeased. Lady Holland, too, was ' in a rage ', though with what part of the article does not transpire, while her good-natured husband told Macaulay privately that he quite agreed with him, but that they had better not discuss the subject. Lady Holland's irritation was probably prompted by her intimacy with the Waldegrave family, to whom the letters edited by Lord Dover belonged, and for whose benefit they were published. But, as Macaulay said justly, his article was surely not

[1] Trevelyan's *Life and Letters of Lord Macaulay*, ch. v.

calculated to injure the sale of the book. Her imperious ladyship's displeasure, however, like that of Miss Berry, was of brief duration. Macaulay was too necessary to her *réunions* to be long exiled from her little court.

Among those who occupy themselves in such enquiries, it has been matter for speculation what particular grudge Macaulay could have cherished against Horace Walpole when, to use his own expression, he laid it on him ' so unsparingly '. To this his correspondence affords no clue. Cunningham holds that he did it ' to revenge the dislike which Walpole bore to the Bedford faction, the followers of Fox and the Shelburne school '. It is possible, as another authority has suggested, that ' in the Whig circles of Macaulay's time, there existed a traditional grudge against Horace Walpole ', owing to obscure political causes connected with his influence over his friend Conway. But these reasons do not seem relevant enough to make Macaulay's famous onslaught a mere *vendetta*. It is more reasonable to suppose that between his avowed delight in Walpole as a letter-writer and his robust contempt for him as an individual, he found a subject to his hand, which admitted of all the brilliant antithesis and sparkle of epigram which he lavished upon it.

Walpole's trivialities and eccentricities, his whims
and affections, are seized with remorseless skill,
and presented with all the rhetorical advantages
with which the writer so well knew how to invest
them.  As regards his literary estimate, the truth
of the picture can scarcely be gainsaid; but the
personal character, as Walpole's surviving friends
felt, is certainly too much *en noir*.  Miss Berry, indeed, raised a gentle cry of expostulation [1] against
the entire representation.  She laid stress upon the
fact that Macaulay had not known Walpole in
the flesh (a disqualification to which too much
weight may easily be assigned); she dwelt upon
the warmth of Walpole's attachments; she contested the charge of affectation, and, in short,
made such a gallant attempt at a defence as her
loyalty to her old friend enabled her to offer.
Yet, if Macaulay had never known Walpole at
all, she herself, it might be urged, had only known
him in his old age.  Upon the whole, 'with due
allowance for a spice of critical pepper on one
hand, and a handful of friendly rosemary on the
other', as Croker says, both characters are 'sub-
stantially true'.  Under Macaulay's brush Walpole is depicted as he appeared to that critic's

---

[1] In her 'Advertisement' to vol. vi of Wright's edition
of the *Letters*.

masculine and (for the nonce) unsympathetic spirit; in Miss Berry's picture, the likeness is touched with a pencil at once grateful, affectionate, and indulgent. The biographer of to-day who is neither endeavouring to portray Walpole in his most favourable aspect, nor preoccupied (as Cunningham supposed the great Whig essayist to have been) with what would be thought of his work ' at Woburn, at Kensington, and in Berkeley Square ', may safely borrow details from the delineation of either artist.

Of portraits of Walpole (not in words) there is no lack. Besides that belonging to Mrs. Bedford, described elsewhere,[1] there is the enamel by Zincke painted in 1745.[2] There is another portrait of him by Nathaniel Hone, R.A., in the National Portrait Gallery.[3] A more characteristic presentment than any of these is the drawing by Müntz [4] which shows his patron sitting in the Library at Strawberry with the Thames and a passing barge seen through the open window. But his most

[1] See above, p. 12.

[2] [Reproduced as frontispiece to vol. iii of *Letters* (ed. Toynbee).]

[3] [Frontispiece to vol. vii of *Letters* (ed. Toynbee).]

[4] [The original is now (1926) in possession of Lt.-Col. Bruce Campbell Johnston ; it is reproduced as frontispiece to the present volume.]

interesting portraits are two which exhibit him in manhood and old age.   One is the half-length by J. G. Eckardt [1] which once hung in its black and gold frame in the Blue Bedchamber, near the companion pictures of Gray and Bentley.   Like these, it was ' from Vandyck ', that is to say it was in a costume copied from that painter, and depicts the sitter in a laced collar and ruffles, leaning upon a copy of the *Aedes Walpolianae*, with a view of part of the Gothic castle in the distance.   The canvas bears at the back the date of 1754, so that it represents him at the age of seven-and-thirty. [2] The shaven face is rather lean than thin, the forehead high, the brown hair brushed back and slightly curled.   The eyes are dark, bright, and intelligent, and the small mouth wears a slight smile.   The other, a drawing made for Samuel Lysons by Sir Thomas Lawrence, [3] is that of a much older man, having been executed in 1796. The eyelids droop wearily ;   the thin lips have a pinched, mechanical urbanity, and the features

[1] [Frontispiece to vol. v of *Letters* (ed. Toynbee).]

[2] [According to the *Catalogue* of the National Portrait Gallery, this and the companion portrait of Gray were painted in 1747.   The latter is reproduced in the present volume.]

[3] [Frontispiece to vol. i of *Works of Lord Orford* ; and to vol. xii of *Letters* (ed. Toynbee).]

July 1st 1793

HORACE WALPOLE, EARL OF ORFORD

are worn by years and ill-health. There are
other portraits by Bernard Lens,[1] Richardson,[1]
Rosalba,[1] Falconet,[1] Reynolds [2] (1757, which
McArdell and Reading engraved), Angelica
Kauffmann,[1] and Dance.[2]

Of the Walpole of later years there are more
descriptions than one, and among these, that given
by Miss Hawkins, the daughter of the pompous
author of the *History of Music*, is, if the most
familiar, also the most graphic. Sir John Hawkins was Walpole's neighbour at Twickenham
House, and the *History* is said to have been undertaken at Walpole's instance. Miss Hawkins's
description is of Walpole as she recalled him
before 1772. ' His figure ', she says, . . . ' was
not merely tall, but more properly *long* and slender
to excess; his complexion and particularly his
hands, of a most unhealthy paleness. . . . His eyes

---

[1] [Reproduced as frontispieces respectively to vols. i, ii,
iv, vi, x, of *Letters* (ed. Toynbee).]

[2] [Reproduced in the present volume.]—The writer of
the obituary notice in the *Gentleman's Magazine* for Mar.
1797, says that Dance's portrait of Walpole is ' the only
faithful representation of him [see also Joseph Farington's
*Diary* for 13 July 1793] '. Against this must be set the
fact that it was not selected by the editor of his works ;
and, besides being in profile, it is certainly far less pleasing
than the Lawrence.

were remarkably bright and penetrating, very dark and lively:—his voice was not strong, but his tones were extremely pleasant, and if I may so say, highly gentlemanly. I do not remember his common gait; [1] he always entered a room in that style of affected delicacy, which fashion had then made almost natural;—*chapeau bras* between his hands as if he wished to compress it, or under his arm—knees bent, and feet on tip-toe, as if afraid of a wet floor. His dress in visiting was most usually, in summer when I most saw him, a lavender suit, the waistcoat embroidered with a little silver or of white silk worked in the tambour, partridge silk stockings, and gold buckles, ruffles and frill generally lace. I remember when a child, thinking him very much under-dressed if at any time except in mourning, he wore hemmed cambric. In summer no powder, but his wig combed straight, and showing his very smooth pale forehead, and queued behind:—in winter powder.'[2]

Pinkerton, who knew Walpole from 1784

[1] It must, by his own account, have been peculiar. ' Walking is not one of my excellences,' he writes. ' In my best days Mr. Winnington said I tripped like a peewit ; and if I do not flatter myself, my march at present is more like a dabchick's ' (*Walpole to Lady Ossory*, 18 Aug. 1775).

[2] *Anecdotes, etc.*, by L. M. Hawkins, 1822, pp. 105–6.

until his death, and whose disappointment of a
legacy is supposed, in places, to have mingled a
more than justifiable amount of gall with his ink,
has nevertheless left a number of interesting particulars respecting his habits and personal characteristics. They are too long to quote entire ; but
are, at the same time, too picturesque to be greatly
compressed. He contradicts Miss Hawkins in
one respect, for he says Walpole was ' short and
slender ', but ' compact and neatly formed ', an
account which is confirmed by Müntz's full-
length. ' When viewed from behind, he had
somewhat of a boyish appearance, owing to the
form of his person, and the simplicity of his dress.'
None of his portraits, says Pinkerton, ' express
the placid goodness of his eyes,[1] which would
often sparkle with sudden rays of wit, or dart forth
flashes of the most keen and intuitive intelligence.
His laugh was forced and uncouth, and even his
smile not the most pleasing.'

' His walk was enfeebled by the gout ; which,

---

[1] ' I have lately become acquainted with your friend,
Mr. Walpole, and am quite charmed with him,'—writes
Malone to Lord Charlemont in 1782. ' There is an un-
affected benignity and good-nature in his manner that is,
I think, irresistibly engaging ' (*Hist. MSS. Commission*, 12th
*Rept., App.*, Pt. x, 1891, p. 395).

if the editor's memory do not deceive, he mentioned that he had been tormented with since the age of twenty-five; adding, at the same time, that it was no hereditary complaint, his father, Sir Robert Walpole, who always drank ale, never having known that disorder, and far less his other parent. This painful complaint not only affected his feet, but attacked his hands to such a degree that his fingers were always swelled and deformed, and discharged large chalk-stones once or twice a year: upon which occasions he would observe with a smile, that he must set up an inn, for he could chalk up a score with more ease and rapidity than any man in England.'

After referring to the strict temperance of his life, Pinkerton goes on :—

' Though he sat up very late, either writing or conversing, he generally rose about nine o'clock, and appeared in the breakfast-room, his constant and chosen apartment, with fine vistos towards the Thames. His approach was proclaimed, and attended, by a favourite little dog, the legacy of the Marquis [*sic*] du Deffand; [1] and which ease and attention had rendered so fat that it could hardly move. This was placed beside him on a small sofa; the tea-kettle, stand and heater, were

[1] Tonton.   See note to pp. 285–6.

brought in, and he drank two or three cups of that liquor out of most rare and precious ancient porcelain of Japan, of a fine white, embossed with large leaves. The account of his china-cabinet, in his description of his villa, will shew how rich he was in that elegant luxury. The loaf and butter were not spared . . . and the dog and the squirrel had a liberal share of his repast.[1]

' Dinner [his hour for which was four] was served up in the small parlour, or large dining-room, as it happened : in winter generally the former. His valet supported him down stairs ;[2] and he ate most moderately of chicken, pheasant, or any light food. Pastry he disliked, as difficult of digestion, though he would taste a morsel of venison pye. Never, but once that he drank two glasses of white-wine, did the editor see him taste any liquor, except ice-water. A pail of ice was placed under the table, in which stood a decanter

Another passage in the *Walpoliana* (2nd ed., i. 73–4) explains this :—' Regularly after breakfast, in the summer season, at least, Mr. Walpole used to mix bread and milk in a large bason, and throw it out at the window of the sitting-room, for the squirrels ; who, soon after, came down from the high trees, to enjoy their allowance.'

[2] ' I cannot go up or down stairs without being led by a servant. It is *tempus abire* for me : *lusi satis* ' (*Walpole to Pinkerton*, 15 May 1794).

of water, from which he supplied himself with his favourite beverage. . . .

' If his guest liked even a moderate quantity of wine, he must have called for it during dinner, for almost instantly after he rang the bell to order coffee upstairs.  Thither he would pass about five o'clock;  and generally resuming his place on the sofa, would sit till two o'clock in the morning, in miscellaneous chit-chat, full of singular anecdotes, strokes of wit, and acute observations, occasionally sending for books, or curiosities, or passing to the library, as any reference happened to arise in conversation.  After his coffee he tasted nothing; but the snuff box of *tabac d'étrennes*, from Fribourg's, was not forgotten, and was replenished from a canister lodged in an ancient marble urn of great thickness, which stood in the window seat, and served to secure its moisture and rich flavour.

' Such was a private rainy day of Horace Walpole.  The forenoon quickly passed in roaming through the numerous apartments of the house, in which, after twenty visits, still something new would occur;  and he was indeed constantly adding fresh acquisitions.  Sometimes a walk in the grounds would intervene, on which occasions he would go out in his slippers through a thick dew ; and he never wore a hat.  He said that, on his first visit to Paris, he was ashamed of his effeminacy, when he saw every little meagre Frenchman, whom even he could have thrown down with a breath, walking without a hat which he could not do, without a certainty of that disease, which the Germans say is endemial in England, and is termed by the natives *le-catch-cold*.[1] The first trial cost him a slight fever, but he got over it, and never caught cold afterwards : draughts of air, damp rooms, windows open at his back, all situations were alike to him in this respect. He would even show some little offence at any solicitude expressed by his guests on such an occasion, as an idea arising from a seeming tenderness of his frame ; and would say, with a half-smile of good-humoured crossness, ' My back is the same with my face, and my neck is like my nose '.[2] His

---

[1] ' I have persisted '—he tells Gray from Paris, 25 Jan. 1766—' through this Siberian winter in not adding a grain to my clothes, and in going open-breasted without an under waistcoat.'

[2] He was probably thinking of *Spectator*, No. 228,— ' The *Indian* answered very well to an *European*, who asked him how he could go naked ; I am all Face.' Lord Chesterfield wished his little godson to have the same advantage. ' I am very willing that he should be *all face*,'— he says in a letter to Arthur Stanhope of 19 Oct. 1762. Cf. also Montaigne's *Essays*, bk. i, ch. 35.

iced water he not only regarded as a preservative from such an accident, but he would sometimes observe that he thought his stomach and bowels would last longer than his bones; such conscious vigour and strength in those parts did he feel from the use of that beverage.' [1]

The only particular that Cunningham adds to this chronicle of his habits is one too characteristic of the man to be omitted. After dinner at Strawberry, he says, the smell was removed by ' a censer or pot of frankincense '. According to the *Description*, there was a small tripod of ormoulu kept in the Breakfast Room for this purpose. It is difficult to identify the ' ancient marble urn of great thickness' in which the snuff was stored; but it may have been that ' of granite, brought from one of the Greek Islands, and given to Sir Robert Walpole by Sir Charles Wager ' which was in the same room. [2]

Walpole's character may be considered in a fourfold aspect, as a man, a virtuoso, a politician, and an author. The first is the least easy to describe. What strikes one most forcibly is, that he was primarily and before all an aristocrat, or, as in his own day he would have been called,

[1]  *Walpoliana,* 2nd ed., i. xli–xlvi.
[2]  [*Works of Lord Orford,* ii. 427, 425.]

a ' person of quality ',[1] whose warmest sympathies
were reserved for those of his own rank.   Out of
the charmed circle of the peerage and baronetage,
he had few strong connections ;  and although in
middle life he corresponded voluminously with
antiquaries such as Cole and Zouch, and in the
languor of his old age turned eagerly to the reno-
vating society of young women such as Hannah
More and the Miss Berrys, however high his
heart may have placed them, it may be doubted
whether his head ever quite exalted them to the
level of Lady Caroline Petersham, or Lady Ossory,
or Her Grace of Gloucester.   In a measure, this
would also account for his unsympathetic attitude
to some of the great *literati* of his day.   With Gray
he had been at school and college, which made a
difference ;  but he no doubt regarded Fielding and
Hogarth and Goldsmith and Johnson,[2] apart from
their confessed hostility to ' high life ' and his beloved ' genteel comedy ', as gifted but undesirable
outsiders—' horn-handed breakers of the glebe '
in Art and Letters—with whom it would be
impossible to be as intimately familiar as one could
be with such glorified amateurs as Bunbury and

[1] [In his account of the funeral of George II (*to Montagu*, 13 Nov. 1760) he says he ' walked as a rag of quality '.]
[2] [For Walpole's opinion of Johnson, see above, p. 269 n.]

Lady Lucan and Lady Di Beauclerk, who were all more or less born in the purple. To the friends of his own class he was constant and considerate, and he seems to have cherished a genuine affection for Conway, George Montagu, and Sir Horace Mann. With regard to Gray, his relations, it would seem, were rather those of intellectual affinity and esteem than downright affection. But his closest friends were women. In them, that is in the women of his time, he found just that atmosphere of sunshine and *insouciance*,—those conversational ' lilacs and nightingales ',—in which his soul delighted, and which were most congenial to his restless intelligence and easily fatigued temperament. To have seen him at his best, one should have listened to him, not when he was playing the antiquary with Ducarel or Conyers Middleton, but gossipping of ancient greenroom scandals at Cliveden, or explaining the mysteries of the ' Officina Arbuteana ' to Madame de Boufflers or Lady Townshend, or delighting Mary and Agnes Berry, in the half-light of the Round Drawing Room at Strawberry, with his old stories of Lady Suffolk and Lady Hervey, and of the monstrous raven, under guise of which the disembodied spirit of His Majesty King George the First was supposed to have revisited the disconso-

late Duchess of Kendal.[1]   Comprehending thoroughly that cardinal precept of conversation—
' never to weary your hearer ', he was an admirable *raconteur* ;  and his excellent memory, shrewd
perceptions, and volatile wit—all the more piquant
for its never-failing mixture of well-bred malice—
must have made him a most captivating companion.   If—as Scott says—his temper was ' precarious ', it is more charitable to remember that
in middle and later life he was nearly always
tormented with a malady seldom favourable to
good humour, than to explain the less amiable
details of his conduct (as does Mr. Croker) by the
hereditary taint of insanity.   In a life of eighty
years many hot friendships cool, even with tem-
pers not ' precarious '.   As regards the charges
sometimes made against him of coldness and want
of generosity, very good evidence would be required before they could be held to be established ;
and a man is not necessarily niggardly because his
benefactions do not come up to the standard of
all the predatory members of the community.
It is besides clear, as Conway and Madame du
Deffand would have testified, that he could be
royally generous when necessity required.   That
he was careful rather than lavish in his expendi-

[1] [See his *Reminiscences* (ed. Toynbee), p. 27.]

ture must be admitted.    It may be added that he
was very much in bondage to public opinion, and
morbidly sensitive to ridicule.

As a virtuoso and amateur, his position is a
mixed one.    He was certainly widely different
from that typical art connoisseur of his day—
the butt of Goldsmith and of Reynolds—who
travelled the Grand Tour to litter a gallery at
home with broken-nosed busts and the rubbish
of the Roman picture-factories.    As the preface
to the *Aedes Walpolianae* showed, he really knew
something about painting, in fact was a capable
draughtsman himself, and besides, through Mann,
Sir William Hamilton, and others, had enjoyed
exceptional opportunities for procuring genuine
antiques.    But his collection was not so rich in
this way as might have been anticipated ;  and
his portraits, his china, and his miniatures were
probably his best possessions.    For the rest, he
was an indiscriminate rather than an eclectic
collector ;  and there was also considerable truth
in that strange ' attraction from the great to the
little, and from the useful to the odd ' which
Macaulay has noted.    Many of the marvels at
Strawberry would never have found a place in
the treasure-houses—say of Beckford or Samuel
Rogers.    It is difficult to fancy Bermingham's

fables in paper on looking-glass, or Hubert's card-cuttings, or the fragile mosaics of Mrs. Delany either at Fonthill or St. James's Place. At the same time, it should be remembered that several of the most trivial or least defensible objects were presents which possibly reflected rather the charity of the recipient than the good taste of the giver. All the articles over which Macaulay lingers, Wolsey's hat, Van Tromp's pipe case, and King William's spurs, were obtained in this way; and (with a laugher) Horace Walpole, who laughed a good deal himself, would probably have made as merry as the most mirth-loving spectator could have desired. But such items gave a heterogeneous character to the gathering, and turned what might have been a model museum into an old curiosity-shop. In any case, however, it was a memorable curiosity-shop, and in this modern era of *bric-à-brac* would probably attract far more serious attention than it did in those practical and pre-æsthetic days of 1842 when it fell under the hammer of George Robins.[1]

[1] See Mr. Robins's *Catalogue of the Classic Contents of Strawberry Hill*, etc. [1842], 4to. It is compiled in his well-known grandiloquent manner ; but includes an account of the Castle by Harrison Ainsworth, together with many interesting details. It gave rise to a humorous squib by Crofton Croker, entitled *Gooseberry Hall*, with ' Puffatory Remarks ', and cuts.

Walpole's record as a politician is a brief one, and if his influence upon the questions of his time was of any importance, it must have been exercised unobtrusively. During the period of the 'great Walpolean battle', as Junius styled the struggle that culminated in the downfall of Lord Orford, he was a fairly regular attendant in the House of Commons; and, as we have seen, spoke in his father's behalf when the motion was made for an enquiry into his conduct. Nine years later, he moved the address, and a few years later still, delivered a speech upon the employment of Swiss Regiments in the Colonies. Finally he resigned his 'senatorial dignity', quitting the scene with the valediction of those who depreciate what they no longer desire to retain. 'What could I see, but sons and grandsons playing over the same knaveries, that I have seen their fathers and grandfathers act? Could I hear oratory beyond my Lord Chatham's? Will there ever be parts equal to Charles Townshend's? Will George Grenville cease to be the most tiresome of beings?'[1] In his earlier days he was a violent Whig—'at times almost a Republican' (to which latter phase of his opinions must be attributed the transformation of King Charles's death-warrant into 'Major

[1] *To Montagu*, 12 Mar. 1768.

Charta '); [1] 'in his old and enfeebled age,' says Miss Berry, 'the horrors of the first French Revolution made him a Tory; while he always lamented, as one of the worst effects of its excesses, that they must necessarily retard to a distant period the progress and establishment of religious liberty.' He deplored the American War, and disapproved the Slave Trade; but, in sum, it is to be suspected that his main interest in politics, after his father's death, and apart from the preservation throughout an 'age of small factions' of his own uncertain sinecures, was the good and ill-fortune of the handsome and amiable, but moderately eminent statesman, General Conway. It was for Conway that he took his most active steps in the direction of political intrigue; and perhaps his most important political utterance is the *Counter Address to the Public on the late Dismission of a General Officer,*[2] which was prompted by Conway's deprivation of his command for voting in the opposition with himself in the debate upon the illegality of general warrants. Whether he would have taken office if it had been offered to him, may be a question; but his attitude, as disclosed by his letters, is a rather hesitating *nolo episcopari.* The most inter-

[1] [*To Montagu,* 14 Oct. 1756.]
[2] [Printed in *Works of Lord Orford,* ii. 547–76.]

esting result of his connection with public affairs
is the series of sketches of political men dispersed
through his correspondence, and through the post-
humous *Memoirs* published by Lord Holland, Sir
Denis Le Marchant, and Dr. Doran.    Making
every allowance for his prejudices and partisanship
(and of neither can Walpole be acquitted), it is
impossible not to regard these *Memoirs* as highly
important contributions to historical literature.
Even Mr. Croker admits that they contain ' a
considerable portion of voluntary or involuntary
truth ', and such an admission, when extorted
from Lord Beaconsfield's ' Rigby ', of whom no
one can justly say that he was ignorant of the
politics of Walpole's day, has all the weight which
attaches to a testimonial from the enemy.[1]

---

[1] The full titles of these memoirs are *Memoires of the last
Ten Years of the Reign of King George II*, edited by Lord
Holland.  2 vols. 4to, 1822 ;  *Memoires of the Reign of
King George III*, edited, with notes, by Sir Denis Le Marchant, Bart.  4 vols. 8vo, 1845 [(re-edited by G. F. Russell
Barker, 4 vols. 8vo, 1894) ;  and *Last Journals* (1771–
1783), edited by Dr. Doran.  2 vols. 8vo, 1859.  The
original MSS. of these *Memoirs* and *Journals* are in the
possession of Earl Waldegrave at Chewton Priory.]  The
first two series were reviewed, *more suo*, by Mr. Croker in
the *Quarterly*, with the main intention of proving that all
Walpole's pictures of his contemporaries were coloured and

This mention of the *Memoirs* naturally leads us to that final consideration, the position of Walpole as an author. Most of the productions which fill the five bulky volumes given to the world in 1798 by Miss Berry's pious care have been referred to in the course of the foregoing pages, and it is not necessary to recapitulate them here. The place which they occupy in English literature was never a large one, and it has grown smaller with lapse of time. Walpole, in truth, never took letters with sufficient seriousness. He was willing enough to

distorted by successive disappointments arising out of his solicitude concerning the patent places from which he derived his income,—in other words (Mr. Croker's words !), that ' the whole is " a copious polyglot of spleen " '. Such an investigation was in the favourite line of the critic, and might be expected to result in a formidable indictment. But the best judges hold it to have been exaggerated, and to-day the method of Mr. Croker is more or less discredited. Indeed, it is an instance of those quaint revenges of the whirligig of Time, that some of his utterances are really more applicable to himself than to Walpole. ' His [Walpole's] natural inclination (says Croker) was to grope an obscure way through mazes and *souterrains* rather than walk the high road by daylight. He is never satisfied with the plain and obvious cause of any effect, and is for ever striving after some tortuous solution.' This is precisely what unkind modern critics affirm of the Rt. Honourable John Wilson Croker.

obtain repute, but upon condition that he should be allowed to despise his calling and laugh at 'thoroughness'. If masterpieces could have been dashed off at a hand-gallop; if antiquarian studies could have been made of permanent value by the exercise of mere elegant facility; if a dramatic reputation could have been secured by the simple accumulation of horrors upon Horror's head, his might have been a great literary name. But it is not thus the severer Muses are cultivated; and Walpole's mood was too variable, his industry too intermittent, his fine-gentleman self-consciousness too inveterate to admit of his producing anything that (as one of his critics has said) deserves a higher title than '*opuscula*'. His essays in the *World* lead one to think that he might have made a more than respectable essayist, if he had not fallen upon days in which that form of writing was practically outworn; and it is manifest that he would have been an admirable writer of familiar poetry if he could have forgotten the fallacy (exposed by Johnson)[1] that easy verse is easy to write. Nevertheless, in the Gothic romance which was suggested by his Gothic castle—for, to speak paradoxically, Strawberry Hill is almost as much as Walpole the author of the *Castle of Otranto*—he managed to

[1] *Idler*, No. lxxvii (6 Oct. 1759).

initiate a new form of fiction ; and by decorating
' with gay strings the gatherings of Vertue ' he
preserved serviceably, in the *Anecdotes of Painting*,
a mass of curious, if sometimes uncritical information which, in other circumstances, must have
been hopelessly lost. If anything else of his professed literary work is worthy of recollection, it
must be a happy squib such as the *Letter of Xo
Ho*, a fable such as *The Entail*, or an essay such
as the pamphlet on Landscape Gardening, which
even Croker allows to be ' a very elegant history
and happy elucidation of that charming art '.[1]

But it is not by his professedly literary work
that he has acquired the reputation which he
retains and must continue to retain. It is as a

[1] See Appendix, p. 363. To the advocates of the rival
school Walpole's utterance, perhaps inevitably, appears in
a less favourable light. ' Horace Walpole published an
*Essay on Modern Gardening* in 1785, in which he repeated
what other writers had said on the subject. This was at
once translated and had a great circulation on the continent.
The *jardin à l'anglaise* became the rage ; many beautiful
old gardens were destroyed in France and elsewhere, and
Scotch and English gardeners were in demand all over
Europe to renovate gardens in the English manner. It is
not an exhilarating thought that in the one instance in
which English taste in a matter of design has taken hold on
the continent, it has done so with such disastrous results '
(*Formal Garden in England*, 2nd ed., 1892, p. 86).

letter-writer that he survives; and it is upon the vast correspondence, of which, even now, we seem scarcely to have reached the limits,[1] that is based his surest claim *volitare per ora virum.* The qualities which are his defects in more serious productions become merits in his correspondence; or, rather, they cease to be defects. No one looks for prolonged effort in a gossipping epistle; a weighty reasoning is less important than a light hand; and variety pleases more surely than symmetry of structure. Among the little band of those who have distinguished themselves in this way, Walpole is in the foremost rank; nay, if wit and brilliancy, without gravity or pathos, are to rank highest, he is first. It matters nothing whether he wrote easily or with difficulty; whether he did, or did not, make minutes of apt illustrations or descriptive incidents: the result is delightful. For diversity of interest and perpetual entertainment, for the constant surprises of an unique species of wit, for happy and unexpected turns of phrase, for graphic characterization and clever anecdote, for playfulness, pungency, irony, persiflage, there is nothing in English like his correspondence. And when one remembers that, in addition, this correspondence constitutes

[1] See above, p. 267.

a sixty-years' social chronicle of a specially picturesque epoch by one of the most picturesque of
picturesque chroniclers, there can be no need to
bespeak any further suffrage for Horace Walpole's
' incomparable letters '.

[As an epilogue may be printed the following
extracts from recollections of Horace Walpole,
written about the year 1820 by the third
Lord Holland, who was 24 when Lord Orford
died :—

' I was flattered by occasionally visiting Horace
Walpole in London and at Strawberry Hill, at
one or two letters I received from him, and at
the notice he took of me when I met him in
houses which he habitually frequented. His conversation, like his written compositions, displayed
a sprightly mind, and a memory stored with anecdotes, historical and literary, the result of much
antiquarian research, and the fruit of a long life
spent in the company of statesmen, authors, artists,
and wits. In his person he was slender and prim,
in his manner extremely artificial, in his temper
somewhat susceptible about trifles. His conversation, though much enlivened by fancy and epigram,
had great marks of preparation and study, and even
effort. These circumstances made Lord Ossory

z

observe in some MS. notes that " Walpole fell far short of his friend, George Selwyn ", who, let me add, was a friend somewhat unmerciful on the taste and appearance of Horace Walpole, describing Strawberry Hill to me as a catacomb, or at best, a museum, rather than a habitation, and the master of it as one of the most carefully finished miniatures and best preserved mummies in the whole collection.

' But whatever were his peculiarites, Walpole's published and unpublished works are mines which abound in brilliant, and do not fail in solid materials for history and biography. . . . The scandalous chronicle reported him to be a son of a Lord Hervey.   In affected humour, laborious application to trifles, occasional and unprovoked malignity, and whimsical ingenuity of understanding, he certainly bore some resemblance to that family. He felt, or pretended to feel, great disgust at the practice adopted by the bookmaking admirers of Johnson, who scrupled not to commit to print whatever they heard in private conversation. Hence he would suddenly purse up his mouth in a pointed but ludicrous manner whenever Boswell came into the room, and sit as mute as a fish till that angler for anecdotes and repartee had left it.   It is more than probable that he dreaded and disliked Dr. Johnson himself. Whig principles, Republican affectations, and loose notions of religion, were all likely to write an attack. . . . '

(*Further Memoirs of the Whig Party*, edited by Lord Stavordale, pp. 308 ff.)]

*APPENDIX*

# APPENDIX

## BOOKS PRINTED AT THE STRAWBERRY HILL PRESS

The following list [1] contains all the books mentioned in the *Description of the Villa of Mr. Horace Walpole*, etc., 1784, together with those issued between that date and Walpole's death. It does *not* include the several title-pages and labels which he printed from time to time, nor the quatrains and verses purporting to be addressed by the Press to Lady Rochford, Lady Townshend, Madame de Boufflers, the Miss Berrys, and others. Nor does it comprise the pieces struck off by Mr. Kirgate, the printer, for the benefit of himself and his friends. On the other hand, all the works enumerated here are, with one or two exceptions, described from copies either in the possession of the present writer or to be found in the British Museum, in the Dyce and Forster Libraries at South Kensington, or in private collections.

[1] [Many of the details given in this list as originally printed in the *Memoir* have been corrected in the light of the information supplied by the *Journal of the Printing-Office at Strawberry Hill* (see above, p. 163, n. 2).]

## 1757

## [Aug. 8] [1]

Odes By Mr Gray. ΦΩΝΑΝΤΑ ΣΥΝΕΤΟΙΣΙ—Pindar, Olymp. II. [Strawberry Hill Vignette.[2]] *Printed at Strawberry-Hill, for R. and J. Dodsley in Pall-Mall, MDCCLVII.*

Half-title, ' Odes by Mr. Gray. [Price One Shilling.] ' ; Title as above ; Text, pp. 5–21. 4to. 2,000 copies [3] printed. ' June 25th [1757], I erected a printing-press at my house at Strawberry Hill.' ' Aug. 8th, I published two Odes by Mr. Gray, the first production of my press ' (*Short Notes*). ' And with what do you think we open ? *Cedite, Romani Impressores* —with nothing under *Graii Carmina.* I found him [Gray] in town last week : he had brought his two Odes to be printed. I snatched them out of Dodsley's hands ' . . . (*Walpole to Chute*, 12 July 1757). ' I send you two copies (one for Dr. Cocchi) of a very honourable opening of my press—two amazing Odes of Mr. Gray ; they are Greek, they are Pindaric, they are sublime ! consequently I fear a little obscure ' (*Walpole to Mann*, 4 Aug. 1757). ' You are very particular, I can tell you, in liking Gray's Odes—but you must remember that the age likes Akenside, and did like Thomson ! can the same people like both? ' (*Walpole to Montagu*, 25 Aug. 1757).

[1] [The date given, unless otherwise stated, is that on which the printing was finished.]

[2] [There were two vignettes (or, as Walpole himself called them, ' fleurons '), one rather larger than the other, both designed by Bentley and engraved by Charles Grignion (see *Journal of the Printing-Office at Strawberry Hill*, pp. 23–4).]

[3] [All the printed lists, including Walpole's own, say 1,000 copies only were printed, except that of Pinkerton, which says 1,100. Walpole's entry in his *Journal* is : ' Aug. 8th, 2,000 copies published by Dodsley ' ; see also *Gray to Brown*, 25 July 1757.]

[Sept. 29]

Epitaph on King Theodore.

Single leaf. 4to. Two dozen copies only. An Italian translation (formerly in the Waller collection) is printed in *Supplement* (vol. ii, p. 103) to *Letters of Walpole* (ed. Toynbee).

[Oct. 17]

A Journey Into England. By Paul Hentzner, In the Year M.D.XC.VIII. [Strawberry Hill Vignette.] *Printed at Strawberry-Hill, MDCCLVII.*

Title, Dedication (2 leaves); 'Advertisement,' i–x; half-title; Latin and English Text on opposite pages, 1 to 103 (double numbers). Sm. 8vo. 220 copies printed. 'In Oct. 1757, was finished at my press an edition of Hentznerus, translated by Mr. Bentley, to which I wrote an advertisement. I dedicated it to the Society of Antiquaries, of which I am a member' (*Short Notes*). 'An edition of Hentznerus, with a version by Mr. Bentley, and a little preface of mine, were prepared [i.e. as the first issue of the press], but are to wait [for Gray's *Odes*]' (*Walpole to Chute*, 12 July 1757.]

[Oct. 26]

To Mr Gray On His Odes.

Single leaf containing six quatrains (24 lines by David Garrick). 4to. Sixty copies printed.[1] There is a copy in the Dyce Collection at South Kensington.

1758

[April 15]

A Catalogue Of the Royal And Noble Authors Of England, With Lists of their Works. *Dove, diavolo! Messer Ludovico, avete pigliato tante coglionerie?* Card. d'Este

---

[1] [It is usually stated that only six copies were printed.]

to Ariosto. Vol. i. [Strawberry Hill Vignette.] *Printed at Strawberry-Hill. MDCCLVIII.*

—— Vol. ii. [Strawberry Hill Vignette.] *Printed at Strawberry-Hill. MDCCLVIII.*

Vol. i—Title ; Dedication [1] of 2 leaves to Lord Hertford ; Advertisement, pp. i–viii ; half-title ; Text, pp. 1–219, and unpaged Index. There is also a frontispiece engraved by Grignion. Vol. ii—Half-title ; Title ; Text, pp. 1–215, and unpaged Index. 8vo. 300 copies issued. A second edition, ' corrected and enlarged ', was printed in 1758 (but dated 1759) in two vols. 8vo, ' for R. and J. Dodsley in Pallmall ; and J. Graham in the Strand '. In 1786 forty copies of a supplement or Postscript to the *Royal and Noble Authors* were printed by Kirgate.[2] ' In April 1758, was finished the first impression of my " Catalogue of Royal and Noble Authors ", which I had written the preceding year in less than five months ' (*Short Notes*). ' My book is marvellously in fashion, to my great astonishment. I did not expect so much truth and such notions of liberty would have made their fortune in this our day ' (*Walpole to Montagu*, 4 May 1758). ' Dec. 5th [1758] was published the second edition of my " Catalogue of Royal and Noble Authors ". Two thousand were printed, but *not* at Strawberry Hill ' (*Short Notes*).

## [July 13]

Fugitive Pieces In Verse and Prose. *Pereunt et imputantur.* [Strawberry Hill Vignette.] *Printed at Strawberry-Hill, MDCCLVIII.*

Title ; Dedication and ' Table of Contents ', iii–vi ; Text

1 [Walpole notes in his *Journal* : ' Half of the whole number of copies have a variation in the second page of the Dedication, which was corrected after part were printed off.' The ' variation ' consists in the substitution in the later copies of *to have a bias* for *to be partial.* Copies of both issues are in the British Museum and Bodleian.]    2 [See below, under 1786.]

1–219. Sm. 8vo. 200 copies printed.[1] 'In the summer of
1758, I printed some of my own Fugitive Pieces, and dedicated
them to my cousin, General Conway' (*Short Notes*). 'March
17 [1759]. I began to distribute some copies of my Fugitive
Pieces, collected and printed together at Strawberry Hill, and
dedicated to General Conway' (*ibid.*). One of these, which is
in the Forster Collection at South Kensington, went to Gray.
'This Book [says a MS. inscription] once belonged to Gray the
Poet, and has his autograph on the Title-page. I [i.e., George
Daniel, of Canonbury] bought it at Messrs. Sotheby and
Wilkinson's Sale Rooms for £1 19 on Thursday, 28 Augt.
1851, from the valuable collection of Mr. Penn of Stoke.'

## [Sept. 29]

An Account Of Russia As It Was in the Year 1710. By
Charles Lord Whitworth. [Strawberry Hill Vignette.]
*Printed at Strawberry-Hill. MDCCLVIII.*

Title, 'Advertisement', pp. i–xxiv; Text, pp. 1–158;
Errata, one page. Sm. 8vo. 700 copies printed. 'The be-
ginning of October [1758] I published Lord Whitworth's ac-
count of Russia, to which I wrote the advertisement' (*Short
Notes*). 'A book has been left at your ladyship's house; it is
Lord Whitworth's Account of Russia' (*Walpole to Lady Her-
vey*, 17 Oct. 1758). Mr. (afterwards Lord) Whitworth was
Ambassador to St. Petersburg in the reign of Peter the Great.

The Mistakes; or, the Happy Resentment. A Comedy.
By the late Lord * * * * [Henry Hyde, Lord Hyde and

[1] [There were two issues of this book, both dated 1758. In
the second issue an unpaged leaf is inserted after p. 216 (or in
some copies after the last page), on the recto of which is printed
a Note relating to an alleged portrait of the Countess of Desmond
(see *Journal of the Printing-Office at Strawberry Hill*, ed. Toynbee, p. 31). Copies of both issues are in the British Museum,
and in Lord Waldegrave's collection at Chewton Priory.]

Cornbury.]   *London : Printed by S. Richardson, in the Year* 1758.

Title ;   List of Subscribers, pp. xvi ;   Advertisement, Prologue, and *Dramatis Personæ*, 2 leaves ;   Text, 1–83 ;   Epilogue
unpaged.   Baker gives the following particulars from the *Biographia Dramatica* as to this book :—' The Author of this
Piece was the learned, ingenious, and witty LORD CORNBURY,
but it was never acted.   He made a present of it to that great
Actress, Mrs. PORTER, to make what Emolument she could
by it.   And that Lady, after his Death, published it by Subscription, at Five Shillings, each Book, which was so much
patronized by the Nobility and Gentry that Three Thousand
Copies were disposed of.   Prefixed to it is a Preface, by Mr.
HORACE WALPOLE, at whose Press at Strawberry-Hill it was
printed.'   Baker adds, ' Mr. Yardley, who when living, kept a
Bookseller's Shop in New-Inn-Passage, confirmed this account,
by asserting, that he assisted in printing it at that Press '.[1]
But Baker nevertheless prefixes an asterisk to the title which
implies that it was ' not printed for Mr. Walpole ', and this
probably accounts for Richardson's name on the title-page.
By the subscription list, the Hon. Horace Walpole took 21
copies, David Garrick 38, and Mr. Samuel Richardson of
Salisbury Court, 4.   All Walpole says is, ' About the same time
[1758] Mrs. Porter published [for her benefit] Lord Hyde's
play, to which I had written the advertisement '[2] (*Short Notes*).

## [Nov. 11]

A Parallel ;  In the Manner of Plutarch :  Between a most
celebrated Man of Florence ;  and One, scarce ever heard

[1] [This assertion is very doubtful.  Walpole makes no mention
of the book in his *Journal*.]

[2] [Walpole reprinted this ' advertisement ' in the (unfinished)
Strawberry Hill edition of his *Works* ;  it is also printed in *Works
of Lord Orford*, i. 228–9.]

of, in England.  By the Reverend Mr. Spence.—*Parvis componere magna*—Virgil. [Portrait in circle of Magliabechi.] *Printed at Strawberry-Hill, By William Robinson ; And Sold by Messieurs Dodsley, at Tully's-Head, Pall-Mall ; for the Benefit of Mr Hill.  M.DCC.LVIII.*

Title ; Text, pp. 4–104.  Sm. 8vo.  700 copies printed. '1759.  Feb. 2nd.  I published Mr. Spence's Parallel of Magliabechi and Mr. Hill, a tailor of Buckingham ; calculated to raise a little sum of money for the latter poor man.  Six hundred copies were sold in a fortnight, and it was reprinted in London' (*Short Notes*).  'Mr. Spence's Magliabechi is published to-day from Strawberry ; I believe you saw it, and shall have it ; but 'tis not worth sending you on purpose' (*Walpole to Chute*, 2 Feb. 1759).

# 1760
# [Oct. 4]

M. Annæi Lucani Pharsalia Cum Notis Hugonis Grotii, Et Richardi Bentleii.  *Multa sunt condonanda in opere postumo.*  In Librum iv, Nota 641. [Emblematical plate.] *Strawberry-Hill, MDCCLX.*

Title, Dedication (by Richard Cumberland to Halifax) and Advertisement (*Ad Lectorem*), 3 leaves ; Text, pp. 1–525. 4to.  500 copies printed.  Cumberland took up the editing when Bentley the younger resigned it.  'I am just undertaking an edition of Lucan, my friend Mr. Bentley having in his possession his father's notes and emendations on the first seven books' (*Walpole to Zouch*, 9 Dec. 1758).  'I would not *alone* undertake to correct the press ; but I am so lucky as to live in the strictest friendship with Dr. Bentley's only son, who, to all the ornament of learning, has the amiable turn of mind, disposition, and easy wit' (*Walpole to Zouch*, 12 Jan. 1759). 'Lucan is in poor forwardness.  I have been plagued with a

succession of bad printers, and am not got beyond the fourth
book. It will scarce appear before next winter' (*Walpole to
Zouch*, 23 Dec. 1759). ' My Lucan is finished, but will not
be published till after Christmas ' [1] (*Walpole to Zouch*, 27 Nov.
1760). ' I have delivered to your brother . . . a Lucan, printed
at Strawberry, which, I trust, you will think a handsome
edition ' (*Walpole to Mann*, 27 Jan. 1761).

## [Oct. 20]

Catalogue of Pictures and Drawings in the Holbein-Cham-
ber, at Strawberry-Hill. *Strawberry-Hill, MDCCLX.*

Pp. 8. 8vo. Copy in British Museum.

## [Nov. 1]

Catalogues of the Collections of Pictures of The Duke of
Devonshire, General GUISE, and the late Sir Paul
Methuen. *Strawberry-Hill, MDCCLX.*

Pp. 44. 8vo. 12 copies, printed on one side only. Copy
in British Museum.

## 1761

## [June 20] [2]

Anecdotes Of Painting in England ; With some Account
of the principal Artists ; And incidental Notes on other
Arts ; Collected by the late M[r] George Vertue ; And
now digested and published from his original MSS. By
M[r] Horace Walpole. *Multa renascentur quæ jam ceci-
dere.* Vol. I. [Device with Walpole's crest.] *Printed
by Thomas Farmer at Strawberry-Hill, MDCCLXII.*

[1] [It was published on 9 Jan. 1761.]
[2] [Not published till 15 Feb. 1762.]

[Nov. 28] [1]

—— *Le Sachant Anglois, je crus qu'il m'alloit parler d'edifices et de peintures.* Nouvelle Eloise, vol. i, p. 245. Vol. II. [Device with Walpole's crest.] *Printed by Thomas Farmer at Strawberry-Hill, MDCCLXII.*

## 1762
### [Oct. 8] [2]

—— Vol. III. (Motto of six lines from Prior's *Protogenes and Apelles*.) *Strawberry-Hill: Printed in the Year MDCCLXIII.*

## 1771
### [April 13] [3]

—— To which is added The History of The Modern Taste in Gardening. *The Glory of* Lebanon *shall come unto thee, the Fir-tree, the Pine-tree, and the Box together, to beautify the Place of my Sanctuary, and I will make the Place of my Feet glorious.* Isaiah, lx. 13. Volume the Fourth and last. *Strawberry-Hill: Printed by Thomas Kirgate, MDCCLXXI.*

Vol. i—Title, Dedication, Preface, pp. i–xiii ; Contents ; Text, pp. 1–168, with Appendix and Index unpaged. Vol. ii— Title ; Text, pp. 1–158, with Appendix, Index and ' Errata ' unpaged ; and ' Additional Lives to the First Edition of Anecdotes of Painting in England ', pp. 1–12. Vol. iii—Title ; pp. 1–155, with Appendix and Index unpaged ; and ' Additional Lives to the First Edition of Anecdotes of Painting in England ', pp. 1–4. Vol. iv—Title, Dedication, Advertise-

[1] [Not published till 15 Feb. 1762.]
[2] [Not published till 6 Feb. 1764.]
[3] [Not published till 9 Oct. 1780.]

ment (dated October 1, 1780, pp. i–x ; Contents ; Text, pp. 1–151 (dated August 2, 1770) ; ' Errata '. Then come pp. x–52 ; Appendix of one leaf (' Prints by or after Hogarth, discovered since the Catalogue was finished '), and Index unpaged. The volumes are 4to, with many portraits and plates. 600 copies were printed. The fourth volume was in type in 1771, but not issued until Oct. 1780. It was dedicated to the Duke of Richmond—Lady Hervey, to whom the three earlier volumes had been inscribed, having died in 1768. A second edition of the first three volumes was printed by Thomas Kirgate at Strawberry Hill in 1763 and 1765, but was not published till June 1767. ' Sept. 1st [1759]. I began to look over Mr. Vertue's MSS., which I bought last year for one hundred pounds, in order to compose the Lives of English Painters ' (*Short Notes*). ' 1760, Jan. 1st. I began the Lives of English Artists, from Vertue's MSS. (that is, " Anecdotes of Painting ", &c.) ' (*ibid.*). ' Aug. 14th. Finished the first volume of my " Anecdotes of Painting in England ". Sept. 5th, began the second volume. Oct. 23rd, finished the second volume ' (*ibid.*). ' 1761. Jan. 4th, began the third volume ' (*ibid.*). ' June 29th, resumed the third volume of my " Anecdotes of Painting ", which I had laid aside after the first day ' (*ibid.*). ' Aug. 22nd, finished the third volume of my " Anecdotes of Painting " ' (*ibid.*). ' The " Anecdotes of Painting " have succeeded to the press : I have finished two volumes ; but as there will at least be a third, I am not determined whether I shall not wait to publish the whole together. You will be surprised, I think, to see what a quantity of materials the industry of one man [Vertue] could amass ! ' (*Walpole to Zouch*, 27 Nov. 1760). ' You drive your expectations much too fast, in thinking my " Anecdotes of Painting " are ready to appear, and in demanding three volumes. You will see but *two*, and it will be February first ' (*Walpole to Montagu*, 30 Dec. 1761). ' I am now publishing the third volume, and another of Engravers ' (*Walpole to Dalrymple*, 31 Jan. 1764). ' I have advertised my long-delayed last volume of " Painters " to come out, and must be in town to distribute it' (*Walpole to Lady Ossory*, 23 Sept. 1780). 'I have left with Lord Harcourt for you my new old last volume of "Painters"' (*Walpole to Mason*, 13 Oct. 1780).

## 1763
## [May 9] [1]

A Catalogue Of Engravers, Who have been born, or resided in *England* ; Digested by M^r Horace Walpole From the MSS. of M^r George Vertue ; To which is added An Account of the Life and Works Of the latter. *And Art reflected Images to Art. . . . Pope. Strawberry-Hill : Printed in the Year MDCCLXIII.*

Title ; pp. 1–128, last page dated 'Oct. 10th, 1762' ; 'Life of Mr. George Vertue', pp. 1–14 ; 'List of Vertue's Works', pp. 1–20, last page dated 'Oct. 22d, 1762' ; Index of Names of Engravers, unpaged. 4to. There are several portraits, including one of Vertue after Richardson. 'Aug. 2nd [1762], began the "Catalogue of Engravers". October 10th, finished it' (*Short Notes*). 'The volume of Engravers is printed off, and has been some time ; I only wait for some of the plates' (*Walpole to Cole*, 8 Oct. 1763). 'I am now publishing the third volume [of the "Anecdotes of Painting"], and another of Engravers' (*Walpole to Dalrymple*, 31 Jan. 1764). A second edition was printed in 1765, but was not published till June 1767.

## 1764
## [Jan. 27]

The Life Of Edward Lord Herbert Of Cherbury, Written by Himself. [Plate of Strawberry Hill.] *Strawberry-Hill : Printed in the Year MDCCLXIV.*

Title, Dedication, and Advertisement, 5 leaves ; Text,

[1] [Not published till 6 Feb. 1764.]

A a

pp. 1–171. Folding plate portrait, and genealogical table (on folded sheet, between advertisement and text, or in some copies between title and dedication).[1] 4to. 200 copies printed by Pratt. ' 1763. Beginning of September wrote the Dedication and Preface to Lord Herbert's Life ' (*Short Notes*). ' I have got a most delectable work to print, which I had great difficulty to obtain and which I must use while I can have it. It is the life of the famous Lord Herbert of Cherbury ' (*Walpole to Lyttelton*, 10 July 1763). ' It will not be long before I have the pleasure of sending you by far the most curious and entertaining book that my press has produced. . . . It is the life of the famous Lord Herbert of Cherbury, and written by himself— of the contents I will not anticipate one word ' (*Walpole to Mason*, 29 Dec. 1763). ' The thing most in fashion is my edition of Lord Herbert's Life ; people are mad after it, I believe because only two hundred were printed ' (*Walpole to Montagu*, 16 Dec. 1764). ' This singular work was printed from the original MS. in 1764, at Strawberry-hill, and is perhaps the most extraordinary account that ever was given seriously by a wise man of himself ' (Walpole, *Works of Lord Orford*, i. 363).

## [April 23]

Poems By Anna Chamber Countess Temple. [Plate of Strawberry Hill.] *Strawberry-Hill : Printed in the Year MDCCLXIV:*

The *Poems* end with *Finis* on p. 34 ; but in some copies an additional poem of 12 lines by Lady Temple (' Verses sent to Lady Charles Spencer with a painted Taffety, occasioned by saying she was low in Pocket and could not buy a new Gown ') is printed on the blank page [35] of the same sheet. A copy of

[1] [This table is often missing, it having been subsequently suppressed by Walpole (see *Journal of the Printing-Office at Strawberry Hill*, p. 43).]

this issue is in the collection of Mr. Percival Merritt, of Boston, Mass. The verses were also printed on a separate leaf, for insertion in copies of the *Poems*, two copies of which, accompanied by the separate leaf, are in Lord Waldegrave's collection at Chewton Priory. The addressee of this poem was Maria, only daughter of Vera Beauclerk, Lord Vere of Hanworth, and wife of Lord Charles Spencer, second son of the second Duke of Marlborough, and brother of Lady Di Beauclerk.

Title, Verses signed ' Horace Walpole January 26th, 1764 ', Text, 1–34 in all. 4to. 100 copies printed by Pratt. ' I shall send you, too, Lady Temple's Poems ' (*Walpole to Montagu*, 16 July 1764).

## [Oct. 17]

The Magpie and her Brood, A Fable, *From the Tales of* Bonaventure des Periers, *Valet de Chambre to the* Queen of Navarre ; Addressed to Miss Hotham.

4pp., containing 72 lines,—initialed ' H. W.' 4to. ' Oct. 15th, [1764] wrote the fable of The Magpie and her Brood for Miss [Henrietta] Hotham, then near eleven years old, great-niece of Henrietta Hobart, Countess Dowager of Suffolk. It was taken from *Les Nouvelles Récréations de Bonaventure des Periers*, Valet de Chambre to the Queen of Navarre ' (*Short Notes*).

## 1768

## [June 11]

Cornélie, Vestale. Tragedie. *Imprimée à Strawberry-Hill, MDCCLXVIII.*

Title ; Dedication ' *à Mons. Horace Walpole* ', dated ' *Paris ce 27 Novembre, 1767* ', pp. iii–iv ; ' Acteurs ' ; Text, 1–91. 8vo. 200 copies printed ; 150 went to Paris. Kirgate

printed it. ' My press is revived, and is printing a French play
written by the old President Hénault. It was damned many
years ago at Paris, and yet I think is better than some that
have succeeded, and much better than any of *our* modern
tragedies. I print it to please the old man, as he was exceedingly
kind to me at Paris ; but I doubt whether he will live till it
is finished. He is to have a hundred copies, and there are to
be but an hundred more, of which you shall have one ' (*Letter
to Montagu*, 15 Apr. 1768). President Hénault died Nov.
1770, aged eighty-five.

## [Aug. 6]

The Mysterious Mother. A Tragedy. By M^r Horace
Walpole. *Sit mihi fas audita loqui !* Virgil. *Printed at
Strawberry-Hill : MDCCLXVIII.*

Title, ' Erratum ', ' Persons ' (2 leaves) ; Text, pp. 1–120,
with Postscript, pp. 1–10 (which see for origin of play). Sm.
8vo. 50 copies issued. *The Mysterious Mother* is reprinted
in *Works of Lord Orford*, i. 37–129. ' March 15 [1768].
I finished a tragedy called " The Mysterious Mother ", which
I had begun Dec. 25, 1766 ' (*Short Notes*). ' I thank you for
myself, not for my Play. . . . I accept with great thankfulness
what you have voluntarily been so good as to do for me ; and
should the Mysterious Mother ever be performed when I am
dead, it will owe to you its presentation ' ¹ (*Walpole to Mason*,
11 May 1769).

## 1769
## [April 24]

Poems By The Reverend M^r Hoyland. *Printed at Strawberry-Hill : MDCCLXIX.*

Title, Advertisement [by Walpole], pp. i–iv ; Text, 1–19.
8vo. 300 copies printed. In the British Museum is a copy

¹ [See above, p. 217 n.]

which simply has ' Printed in the Year 1769 '. ' I enclose a
short Advertisement for Mr. Hoyland's poems. I mean by it
to tempt people to a little more charity, and to soften to him,
as much as I can, the humiliation of its being asked for him ;
if you approve it, it shall be prefixed to the edition ' (*Walpole
to Mason*, 5 Apr. 1769).

## 1770

Reply to the Observations of the Rev. Dr. Milles, Dean of
Exeter, and President of the Society of Antiquaries, on
the Ward Robe Account.[1]

Pp. 24. Six copies printed, dated 28 August, 1770 [Baker].
' In the summer of this year [1770] wrote an answer to Dr.
Milles' remarks on my " Richard the Third " ' (*Short Notes*).

## 1771
## [April 13] [2]

Anecdotes Of Painting in England. . . . Volume the Fourth
and last. *Strawberry-Hill : Printed by Thomas Kirgate,
MDCCLXXI.*

For collation see above, p. 351.

## [Oct. 8]

Vers Presentés à Sa Majesté Le Roi de Suede, A Ruel le
Samedy 9 Mai 1771, par Madame la Duchesse d'Aiguillon douairiere, en lui montrant le Portrait du Cardinal
de Richelieu.

Pp. 2. Single leaf. 4to. 40 copies printed, of which 24
were sent to the Duchess.

[1] [Not mentioned by Walpole in his *Journal*.]
[2] [Not published till 9 Oct. 1780.]

1772

[May]

Memoires Du Comte De Grammont, Par Monsieur le
Comte Antoine Hamilton. Nouvelle Edition, Aug-
mentée de Notes & d'Eclaircissemens necessaires, Par
M. Horace Walpole. *Des gens qui écrivent pour le Comte
de Grammont, peuvent compter sur quelque indulgence.*
V. l'Epitre prelim. p. xviii. *Imprimée à Strawberry-
Hill. M.DCC.LXXII.*

Title, Dedication, ' Avis de L'Editeur ', ' Avertissement ',
' Epitre à Monsieur le Comte de Grammont ', ' Table des
Chapitres ', ' Errata ', pp. xxiv ; Text, pp. 1–290 : ' Table des
Personnes ', 3 pp. Portraits of Hamilton, Mdlle. d'Hamilton,
and Philibert Comte de Grammont. 4to. 100 copies printed ;
25 went to Paris. It was dedicated to Madame du Deffand,
as follows :—' *L'Editeur vous consacre cette Edition, comme un
monument de son Amitié, de son Admiration, & de son Respect ; à
Vous, dont les Grâces, l'Esprit, & le Gout retracent au siecle
présent le siecle de Louis quatorze & les agremens de l'Auteur
de ces Mémoires.*' ' I want to send you . . . a Grammont of
which I have printed only an hundred copies, and which will
be extremely scarce, for twenty-five copies are gone to France '
(*Walpole to Cole*, 8 Jan. 1773).

[June 13]

Copies Of Seven Original Letters From King Edward VI.
To Barnaby Fitz-patrick. *Strawberry-Hill : Printed in
the Year M.DCC.LXXII.*

Pp. viii–14. 4to. 200 copies printed. ' 1771. End of
September, wrote the Advertisement to the Letters of King
Edward the Sixth ' (*Short Notes*). ' I have printed King

Edward's Letters, and will bring you a copy ' (*Walpole to Mason*, 6 July 1772).

## [June 28]

Miscellaneous Antiquities ; Or, A Collection of Curious Papers : Either republished from *scarce Tracts*, or now first printed from *original* MSS. Number 1. To be continued occasionally. *Invenies illic et festa domestica vobis. Sæpe tibi Pater est, sæpe legendus Avus.* Ovid. Fast. lib. i. *Strawberry-Hill : Printed by Thomas Kirgate*, M.DCC.LXXII.

Title, 'Advertisement', pp. i–iv ; Text, 1–48. 4to. 500 copies printed for sale, and 25 copies on writing paper for presents. 'I have since begun a kind of Desiderata Curiosa, and intend to publish it in numbers, as I get materials ; it is to be an Hospital of Foundlings ; and though I shall not take in all that offer, there will be no enquiry into the nobility of the parents ; nor shall I care how heterogeneous the brats are ' (*Walpole to Mason*, 6 July 1772). 'The first number of my " Miscellaneous Antiquities " . . . is only a republication of some tilts and tournaments ' (*Walpole to Mason*, 21 July 1772).

## [Dec. 10]

Miscellaneous Antiquities ; Or, A Collection of Curious Papers : Either republished from *scarce Tracts*, or now first printed from *original* MSS. Number II. To be continued occasionally. *Invenies illic et festa domestica vobis. Sæpe tibi Pater est, sæpe legendus Avus.* Ovid. Fast. lib. I. *Strawberry-Hill : Printed by Thomas Kirgate*, M.DCC.LXXII.

Title and Text, pp. 1–62. 500 copies printed. 'In July [1772] wrote the life of Sir Thomas Wyat [the Elder], No. II of my edition of Miscellaneous Antiquities ' (*Short Notes*).

## 1774

A Description Of The Villa Of Horace Walpole. [Plate of Strawberry Hill.] A Description Of The Villa Of Horace Walpole, Youngest Son of Sir Robert Walpole Earl of Orford, At Strawberry-Hill, near Twickenham. With an Inventory of the Furniture, Pictures, Curiosities, &c. *Strawberry-Hill : Printed by Thomas Kirgate,* M.DCC.LXXIV.

Half-title (with plate) and title ; Text, pp. 1–119. 4to. 100 copies printed, 6 on large paper. Many copies have the following,—'Appendix. Pictures and Curiosities added since the Catalogue was printed,' pp. 121–45 ; 'List of the Books printed at Strawberry-Hill', unpaged ; 'Additions since the Appendix ', pp. 149–52 ; 'More Additions ', pp. 153–8. A few copies were also printed of a shortened *Description* (65 pp.) —see above, p. 235, n. 4.

## 1775
### [June]

Dorinda, A Town Eclogue. [Plate of Strawberry Hill.] *Strawberry-Hill : Printed by Thomas Kirgate,* *M.DCC.LXXV.*

Title ; Text, 3–8. 4to. 300 copies printed. ' I shall send you soon Fitzpatrick's Town Eclogue, from my own furnace. The verses are charmingly smooth and easy . . . P.S. Here is the Eclogue ' (*Walpole to Mason,* 12 June 1775). The author was Hon. Richard Fitzpatrick, brother of the Earl of Ossory.

### [June]

To Mrs Crewe.

Thirty-eight lines, by Charles James Fox. Pp. 2. Single leaf. 4to. This was printed a week after Fitzpatrick's *Dorinda,* to which it was added. 300 copies printed. Walpole sent these

in a letter to Mason dated 27 May 1775. Mrs. Crewe, the
' Amoret ' addressed, was the daughter of Fulke Greville, and
the wife of J. Crewe. She was painted by Sir Joshua Reynolds
in the character of an Alpine shepherdess.

## 1778
## [Aug. 30]

The Sleep-Walker, A Comedy : In Two Acts. Translated
from the French, in March. M.DCC.LXXVIII. *Strawberry-Hill : Printed by T. Kirgate, M.DCC.LXXVIII.*

Title, Quatrain, Prologue, Epilogue, Persons, pp. i–viii ;
Text, 1–56. 8vo. 75 copies printed. The quatrain is by
Walpole to Lady Craven (afterwards Margravine of Anspach)
' On her Translation of the Somnambule '. The original was
by Antoine de Ferriol, Comte de Pont-de-Veyle, an old friend
of Madame du Deffand. ' I will send . . . for yourself a translation of a French play. . . . It is not for your reading, but as one
of the Strawberry editions, and one of the rarest, for I have
printed but seventy-five copies. It was to oblige Lady Craven,
the translatress . . .' (*Walpole to Cole*, 22 Aug. 1778).

## 1779
## [Jan.]

A Letter To The Editor of the Miscellanies Of Thomas
Chatterton. *Strawberry-Hill : Printed by T. Kirgate.*
M.DCC.LXXIX.

Half-title ; Title ; Text, pp. 1–55. The letter is dated at
end—' May 23, 1778 '. 8vo. 200 copies printed. ' 1779.
In the preceding autumn had written a defence of myself against
the unjust aspersions in the Preface to the Miscellanies of
Chatterton. Printed 200 copies at Strawberry Hill this
January, and gave them away. It was much enlarged from
what I had written in July ' (*Short Notes*). Also in *Gent.
Mag.*, 1782, vol. lii.

## 1780
### [Jan.]

To Lady Horatia Waldegrave, On The Death of the Duke of Ancaster.

Forty-four lines, by Charles Miller. Pp. 3, dated at end 'A.D. 1779'. 4to. 150 copies printed. 'I enclose a copy of verses, which I have just printed at Strawberry, only a few copies, and which I hope you will think pretty. They were written three months ago by Mr. Charles Miller, brother of Sir John, on seeing Lady Horatia at Nuneham. The poor girl is better' (*Walpole to Lady Ossory*, 29 Jan. 1780). Lady Horatia Waldegrave was to have been married to the Duke of Ancaster, who died in 1779.

## 1781
### [Aug. 11]

The Muse Recalled, An Ode, Occasioned by The Nuptials of Lord Viscount Althorp And Miss Lavinia Bingham, Eldest Daughter of Charles Lord Lucan, March vi, M.DCC.LXXXI. By William Jones, Esq. *Strawberry-Hill: Printed by Thomas Kirgate, M.DCC.LXXXI.*

Title; pp. 1–8. 4to. 250 copies printed. The author, afterwards Sir William Jones, the Orientalist, had been tutor to Lord Althorp. There is a well-known portrait of Lavinia Bingham by Reynolds, in which she wears a straw hat with a blue ribbon.

A Letter from the Honourable Thomas Walpole, to the Governor and Committee of the Treasury of the Bank of England. *Strawberry-Hill: Printed by Thomas Kirgate, M.DCC.LXXXI.*[1]

Title, and pp. 16 (last blank). 4to. 120 copies printed.

[1] [This piece is not mentioned by Walpole in his *Journal*.]

## 1784

A Description Of the Villa of M^r Horace Walpole, Youngest son of Sir Robert Walpole Earl of Orford, At Strawberry-Hill near Twickenham, Middlesex. With an Inventory of the Furniture, Pictures, Curiosities, &c. *Strawberry-Hill: Printed by Thomas Kirgate, M.DCC.LXXXIV.*

Title ; ' Preface ', i–iv ; Text, pp. 1–88, ' Errata, etc. ', ' Appendix ', pp. 89–92 ; ' Curiosities added ', etc., 93–4 ; ' More Additions ', 95–6. 27 plates.¹ 4to. 200 copies printed, 12 on large paper. ' The next time he [Sir Horace Mann's nephew] visits you, I may be able to send you a description of my *Galleria*,—I have long been preparing it, and it is almost finished,—with some prints, which, however, I doubt, will convey no very adequate idea of it ' (*Walpole to Mann*, 30 Sept. 1784). ' In the list for which Lord Ossory asks, is the Description of this place ; now, though printed, I have entirely kept it up [i.e., *held it back*], and mean to do so while I live ' (*Walpole to Lady Ossory*, 15 Sept. 1787).

## 1785

### [Aug.]

Essay On Modern Gardening, By M^r Horace Walpole. [Strawberry Hill Vignette.] Essai sur l'Art Des Jardins Modernes, Par M. Horace Walpole, Traduit en François Par M. le Duc de Nivernois, En

---

¹ [According to a MS. note by Earl Harcourt, dated 1801, in his copy (now in possession of Mr. S. A. Courtauld), twelve sets of the plates were struck off on French paper, one of the sets being in this copy.]

MDCCLXXXIV. *Imprimé à Strawberry-Hill, par T. Kirgate, MDCCLXXXV.*

Two titles ; English and French Text on opposite pages, 1–94. 4to. 400 copies printed, of which 200 were sent to the Duc in Paris. 'I ask how I may send you a new book printed here . . . It is the translation of my Essay on Modern Gardens by the Duc de Nivernois. . . . You will find it a most beautiful piece of French, of the genuine French spoken by the Duc de la Rochefoucauld and Madame de Sévigné, and not the metaphysical galimatias of La Harpe and Thomas, &c., which Madame du Deffand protested she did not understand. The versions of Milton and Pope are wonderfully exact and poetic and elegant, and the fidelity of the whole translation, extraordinary' (*Walpole to Lady Ossory*, 17 Sept. 1785). The original MS. of the Duc de Nivernois—'a most exquisite specimen of penmanship'—was among the papers at Strawberry Hill, and at the Sale in 1842 fetched £4. 14s. 6d.

## [Nov. 5]

Hieroglyphic Tales. *Schah Baham ne comprenoit jamais bien que les choses absurdes & hors de toute vraisemblance. Le Sopha, p. 5. Strawberry-Hill : Printed by T. Kirgate, MDCCLXXXV.*

Title ; ' Preface ', iii–ix ; Text, pp. 50 ; ' Postscript '. 8vo. Walpole's own MS. note in the Dyce example [1] says, ' Only six copies of this were printed, besides the revised copy '. ' 1772. This year, the last, and sometime before, wrote some Hieroglyphic Tales. There are only five ' (*Short Notes*). ' I have some strange things in my drawer, even wilder than the Castle of Otranto, and called Hieroglyphic Tales ; but they were not

[1] Another copy is in the Library of Princeton University. In the British Museum is a copy made up of proof sheets, with MS. notes by Walpole. (See *Journal of the Printing-Office at Strawberry Hill*, pp. 70–1.)

written lately, nor in the gout, nor, whatever they may seem, written when I was out of my senses ' (*Walpole to Cole*, 28 Jan. 1779). ' This [he is speaking of Darwin's *Botanic Garden*] is only the Second Part; for, like my King's eldest daughter in the Hieroglyphic Tales, the First Part is not born yet:—no matter' (*Walpole to the Miss Berrys*, 28 Apr. 1789). The *Hieroglyphic Tales* were reprinted in *Works of Lord Orford*, iv. 319–52; and again at Newcastle, for Emerson Charnley, in 1822.[1]

## 1786
### [Nov.]

Postscript To The Royal and Noble Authors. *Printed at Strawberry-Hill, MDCCLXXXVI.*[2]

Title; pp. 18. 8vo. 40 copies printed. ' I have but two motives for offering you the accompanying trifle : the first, to prove that the moment I have finished anything, *you* are of the earliest in my thoughts : the second, that coming from my press, I wish it may be added to your Strawberry Editions. It is so far from being designed for the public, that I have printed but forty copies ' (*Walpole to Hannah More*, 1 Jan. 1787).

## 1789
### [July]

Bishop Bonner's Ghost. [Plate of Strawberry Hill.] *Strawberry-Hill : Printed by Thomas Kirgate, MDCCLXXXIX.*

Title and argument, 2 leaves; Text, pp. 1–4. 4to. 96 copies printed ; 2 on brown paper, one of which was at Strawberry. It was written when Hannah More (' my *imprimée* ', as Walpole calls her) was on a visit to Dr. Beilby Porteus, Bishop

[1] [A third reprint (which claims to be the first separate reprint) was issued in London by the Bodoni Press in the present year (1926).]      [2] [See above, pp. 345–6.]

of London, at his palace at Fulham, June 1789. ' I will forgive
all your enormities if you will let me print your poem. I like
to filch a little immortality out of others, and the Strawberry
press could never have a better opportunity ' (*Walpole to Hannah
More*, 23 June 1789). ' The enclosed copy of verses pleased me
so much, that, though not intended for publication, I prevailed
on the authoress, Miss Hannah More, to allow me to take off a
small number. . . . I have been disappointed of the completion of
Bonner's Ghost, by my rolling press being out of order, and was
forced to send the whole impression to town to have the copper-
plate taken off. . . . Kirgate has brought the whole impression,
and I shall have the pleasure of sending your Ladyship this with
a Bonner's Ghost to-morrow morning ' (*Walpole to Lady Ossory*,
16–18 July 1789).

[The History of Alcidalis and Zelida. A Tale of the
Fourteenth Century. *Printed at Strawberry-Hill.*
*MDCCLXXXIX.*

Title ; Text, pp. 3–96. 8vo. This is a translation of Voiture's unfinished *Histoire d'Alcidalis et de Zelide.* (See *Nouvelles
Œuvres de Monsieur de Voiture. Nouvelle Edition. A Paris,
Chez Louis Bilaine, au Palais, au second Pilier de la grand' Salle,
à la Palme & au grand Cesar*, MDCLXXII.) There are copies
in the Dyce Collection, and in Lord Waldegrave's Collection at
Chewton Priory. Another was sold in 1823 with the books of
John Trotter Brockett, in whose catalogue it was said to be
' surreptitiously printed '.[1] Kirgate had a copy, although Baker
does not mention it.]

Besides the above, Walpole printed at his press Vol. i and
part of Vol. ii of a 4to edition of his works ; this was
begun on 24 Aug. 1768 ; resumed on 24 Apr. 1769 ;
resumed again on 6 July 1787, and finally abandoned.[2]

[There is no mention of this alleged Strawberry Hill edition
in Walpole's *Journal.*]    [2] [See above, pp. 277–8, 306, n. 1.]

# INDEX

N.B. *Alphabetical lists will be found under* Strawberry Hill (*of the rooms, buildings, &c.*), Strawberry Hill Press (*of its productions*), *and* Walpole, Horace (*of his works*).
(H.W. = Horace Walpole ; S.H. = Strawberry Hill.)

Addison, Joseph, 66, 111.

Aiguillon, Anne Charlotte de Crussol de Florensac, Duchesse d', 197 ; her verses to King of Sweden, 357.

Ailesbury, Caroline Campbell, Countess of, one of H.W.'s ' Beauties ', 116–17 ; portrait of, at S.H., 244.

*Alcidalis and Zelida, History of*, alleged S.H. ed. of, 366.

' Almanzor '. *See* Ashton, Thomas.

Althorp, George John Spencer, Viscount (aft. Earl Spencer), Jones's ode on his marriage, 277, 362.

Amelia Sophia Eleanora, Princess, 137, 193, 246, 259, 267.

Amorevoli, Italian singer, 70, 93, 94.

Argyll, Archibald Campbell, third Duke of, prefers Garrick to Betterton, 94.

Ashe, Elizabeth, commiserates Maclean, 142 ; at Vauxhall party, 143–4, 146 ; ' Pollard Ashe ', 143, 146.

Ashton, Thomas, member of ' quadruple alliance ' at Eton, 18 ; ' Almanzor ', 18 ; Fellow of Eton, 19 *n.* ; at King's College, Cambridge, 20 ; H.W.'s *Epistle* to, from Florence, 66.

Aylesbury. *See* Ailesbury.

Balmerino, Arthur Elphinstone, sixth Baron, trial, 105–6 ; Gray's account of, 108 *n.* ; execution, 106–9.

Barry, Mrs., actress, 94.

Bath, Earl of. *See* Pulteney.